AF522550

Chasing a Conjecture

Inside the Mind of a Mathematician

Chandrashekhar B. Khare

JUGGERNAUT BOOKS
C-I-128, First Floor, Sangam Vihar, Near Holi Chowk,
New Delhi 110080, India

First published by Juggernaut Books 2025

10 9 8 7 6 5 4 3 2 1

P-ISBN: 9789353452537
E-ISBN: 9789353458201

Typeset in Adobe Caslon Pro by R. Ajith Kumar, Noida

Printed at Nutech Print Services - India

To Aai and Baba

तुका तुकासी तुकला । तुका तुकाहुनि निराळा ॥
तुकीं तुकला तुका । विश्व भरोनि उरला लोकां ॥

– TUKARAM
seventeenth-century poet–saint

Let us grant that the pursuit of mathematics is a divine madness of the human spirit, a refuge from the goading urgency of contingent happenings.

– ALFRED NORTH WHITEHEAD
1861–1947, mathematician and philosopher

Contents

Introduction

Symmetry, Symmetry, Symmetry

I am a number theorist, which means I think about questions related to what seem like the simplest of all things: the natural numbers 1, 2, 3, ... To say that something is straightforward, one says that it is as easy as one, two, three. And yet, the emergence of numbers is considered a major breakthrough in human civilization. Numbers allowed us to understand the world in powerful new ways. Numbers abstract and make precise and quantify our notions of size and numerousness. The number two is an abstraction and captures what is common between all pairs of things: two apples, two chairs, two horses.

Number theorists look at 1, 2, 3, ... for their own sake, and are tantalized by simple-sounding questions about them, whose answers often lie very deep. Some of the hardest questions in mathematics are about the natural numbers. A mathematician can obsess over these questions for years. Collectively, they have driven mathematical work over hundreds of years. Once lured into thinking about an innocent-looking question, one is hooked and can't let go of it – the more one understands its difficulty, the less one is able to move away from it. A wonderful example of such a question is one posed by Pierre de Fermat in the seventeenth century.

According to the famous Pythagoras theorem, in a right-angled triangle, the square of the length of the hypotenuse (the side opposite the right angle), is equal to the sum of the squares of the lengths of the other two sides. Mathematically, this is expressed as $a^2 + b^2 = c^2$. There are many solutions to the equation $a^2 + b^2 = c^2$ where *a, b, c* are natural numbers; $3^2 + 4^2 = 5^2$ or $5^2 + 12^2 = 13^2$ are just two of the infinite number of examples.

In 1637, Fermat mused if this could happen for powers of numbers higher than just their squares. Can a cube be the sum of two cubes, that is can $a^3 + b^3 = c^3$? Can a fourth power be the sum of two fourth powers? He made the assertion that this could never happen for powers bigger than 2, and further said that he could prove his assertion. He jotted this in a margin of the book that he was reading – Diophantus's *Arithmetica* – and noted that the margin was too small to contain his marvellous demonstration.

The assertion became notorious, as no one could prove it for the next three hundred and fifty years. It came to be known as Fermat's Last Theorem (FLT). In the 1960s, a ten-year-old boy stumbled upon the problem in a book called *The Last Problem* in a public library of his home town of Cambridge in England, and became fascinated by it. The boy was Andrew Wiles who went on to become a celebrated number theorist. FLT became an actual theorem only in 1994 when Wiles proved it after a herculean effort of seven years.

A theorem is like a statement of fact: the Pythagoras theorem, which states a relation between the side lengths of a right-angled triangle, is an example. In mathematics, the statement of a theorem has to be followed by a proof. Once proved, a theorem might become the foundation of a theory, or be able to solve problems by simply being invoked. To quote a theorem is almost like casting a spell. The tremendous effort and ingenuity expended in proving a theorem is compacted into its great power that can be activated by simply quoting it.

Fermat's problem is a mere riddle, by itself of no larger significance.[1] Yet, amazingly enough, Fermat's problem acted as a muse, leading to the discovery of important mathematical theories through the ensuing centuries. Many mathematicians engaged with it, developing methods that could prove it for powers that went up to several million. This was not the same, however, as proving it conclusively.[2]

Wiles's monumental proof of FLT is more than a hundred pages long. In his proof, Wiles is engaged in a much bigger enterprise than proving FLT. He states it as a theorem in the introduction of the paper. The rest of the paper is devoted to proving something called the 'elliptic symmetry conjecture'. If a theorem is a proven fact, a conjecture is like an unfulfilled fantasy in the world of mathematics in which the most fantastic things happen routinely. The best conjectures are more than just guesses, often having passed many plausibility tests. A conjecture reflects the sunny yet cautious optimism of the mathematicians who propose it: the conjecture would have to be true if we were living in the best of all possible worlds. A conjecture becoming a theorem is like a fantasy coming true, and takes the hard work and brilliant ideas of mathematicians who are consumed by their efforts to find its proof.

Mathematical developments in the 1980s showed that Fermat's problem is a wholly unexpected and fortuitous consequence of the powerful elliptic symmetry conjecture, made in the 1950s, that is at the heart of modern number theory. For the first time, there was a compelling mathematical reason to demonstrate that Fermat was right: the elliptic symmetry conjecture was too important for it to fail. Wiles was stimulated to work on his childhood dream of solving Fermat's question once it was found to be a quick corollary of the elliptic symmetry conjecture.

Wiles's proof illustrates an important mathematical idea: the power of abstraction. The development of mathematical ideas starts with a very concrete problem, such as FLT, as a provocation. However, if the problem is deep, it cannot be resolved simply by brute force computation. Its elusiveness can lead mathematicians on a long journey of developing ideas that seemingly take them further and further away from the problem. Mathematicians become increasingly interested in the ideas for themselves. In the case of FLT, the abstract theories it set in motion solved it almost as an afterthought.

∞

Wiles's marvellous proof of Fermat is very indirect. He uses ideas related to studying the 'symmetries' of solutions of equations. The use of symmetry in such questions goes back to the work of the extraordinary nineteenth-century French mathematician Évariste Galois, who died in a duel when he was just twenty but still managed to produce work that would revolutionize mathematics. Galois used abstract ideas of symmetry to answer a question about solutions of polynomial equations that had been around for hundreds of years.

In school, we learn the formula used since antiquity for solving one kind of polynomial equation: the quadratic, or second degree, equation. The formula involves taking square roots.[3] Mathematicians sought similar formulas for solutions of polynomial equations of higher degrees. In the sixteenth and seventeenth centuries, similar formulas using only radicals (extracting square roots, cube roots, and so on) were found for solutions of polynomial equations of third and fourth degree, but these solutions were more complicated than the one formulated for the quadratic equations.[4]

Despite strenuous efforts, no such formulas, using only radicals, could be found for solutions of polynomial equations of fifth degree and higher. Galois hit upon the idea of studying the symmetries of solutions of polynomial equations rather than the solutions themselves.[5] Before his tragic death, Galois wrote letters and manuscripts from a prison, summarizing his breakthrough ideas. One of them has the recurring sentence *Je n'ai pas le temps* (I do not have time) as an anguished refrain. Galois' work shows that there is a compelling reason that no one for centuries had been able to find clean-cut formulas for roots of polynomials of degree higher than 4: it was proven to be an impossible task.[6]

As a simple illustration of the idea of Galois symmetries, consider the quadratic equation $X^2 - 5 = 0$ with its solutions $\sqrt{5}$ and $-\sqrt{5}$: their Galois symmetry swaps them by changing the signs. This symmetry is analogous to the famous bilateral symmetry of the Taj Mahal. If we imagine a huge vertical mirror going through the middle of the Taj Mahal, the reflection of either side in the mirror looks the same as the part on the other side of the mirror. The Galois symmetry of the equation $X^2 - 5 = 0$ and the bilateral symmetry of the Taj Mahal both have the property that if you repeat them twice, you are back to square one.

I am writing this introduction sitting in a cafe, and I can see in its windows the reflection of a lovely vase with vivid red blossoms. Part of its beauty for me lies in the fact that it is balanced and symmetrical. Just as numbers abstract the intuitive ideas we have about quantity, mathematical ideas about symmetry abstract our intuitions about beauty and balance. Galois' ideas show that the symmetries of the solutions of a polynomial equation, whether or not they capture the equation's beauty, have a functional bearing on its solutions, revealing something vitally important about their nature.

∞

Mathematical ideas can be likened to viruses that infect mathematicians who end up becoming their carriers and transmitters. Once the idea that would go on to be known as 'Galois symmetry' infected its creator, its highly contagious nature ensured its spread across the mathematical community.

Wiles's proof is in the lineage of Galois' work on the impossibility of solving a general polynomial equation of a degree higher than 4 using only radicals. His proof is by contradiction: Wiles shows (via his work on the elliptic symmetry conjecture) that a counterexample to Fermat's assertion gives rise to a forbidden Galois symmetry. To give the tiniest hint about what this involves, Wiles rules out the Galois symmetry arising from a solution to Fermat's equation by relating it to a completely different kind of symmetry, namely a Ramanujan symmetry.[7] The latter type of symmetry was used to understand the genius mathematician Srinivasa Ramanujan's deep and subtle observations about patterns in a sequence of numbers that he described in a paper he wrote in 1916.

The only known way to rule out the Galois symmetry arising from a solution of the Fermat equation is by relating it to the far more tangible world of Ramanujan symmetries. Galois' work ended the age-old quest to find formulas using only simple-minded operations (like taking radicals) for solutions of polynomial equations but it started the still-ongoing quest to understand the complexity of their solutions, and their Galois symmetries, using various other types of symmetries. This is typical in mathematics: answering a compelling question gives rise to further fascinating questions, and so on ad infinitum. No answer is the last word on a subject.

When we talk about Wiles's work on symmetry, we are inevitably led to talking about a conjecture of Jean-Pierre Serre. Serre is a celebrated French mathematician, who made a powerful conjecture in the 1970s and 1980s about the connection between Galois and Ramanujan symmetries. It is like a beautiful metaphor which brings together two very different ideas. To make an analogy with physics, one could think of the two symmetries as similar in a way to electricity and magnetism. In the nineteenth century, Maxwell proposed his equations that tied electricity and magnetism together, making them two aspects of the electromagnetic field. This gave rise to new physics that emphasized fields rather than mechanical forces and led to the uncovering of the electromagnetic spectrum, with many applications (such as radio, TV, wireless internet) that make our modern way of living possible. In an analogous way, Serre's conjecture unifies the Galois and Ramanujan symmetries and has powerful applications within mathematics: a proof of the elliptic symmetry conjecture and FLT is part of its potent force field.

In mathematics, analogies between concepts that are very different play a vital role. André Weil, one of the giants of mathematics in the twentieth century, wrote about the importance of such analogies in a letter he sent to his philosopher sister Simone Weil from a prison in 1940. He had landed in prison because of dodging the draft to fight as a French soldier in World War II. In his letter, Weil compared the role of analogies in mathematics to the Rosetta Stone[8] which had the same text inscribed on it in Demotic, Ancient Greek and Egyptian hieroglyphics. The stone's discovery led to the deciphering of the Egyptian hieroglyphics. Serre's conjecture is like a Rosetta Stone that allows one to translate back and forth between Galois symmetries and Ramanujan symmetries. Before the conjecture was proved, mathematicians had not been able to invoke it unconditionally.

Wiles's work in 1994 showed that very particular types of Galois symmetries are the same as Ramanujan symmetries: this was enough to prove FLT but left most of Serre's conjecture untouched.[9] Despite this, there was hope that as his work gave a new method to relate Galois and Ramanujan symmetries, it might help with attacking Serre's conjecture.

My enduring love of symmetry, since the time I first encountered Galois theory as an undergraduate at Cambridge in the late 1980s, made the challenge of proving Serre's conjecture irresistible for me. Mathematical research is like a relay race and I wanted to pick up the baton after Wiles's astonishing work and run as much of the stretch as I could to the solution of Serre's conjecture. When I began, I had no idea how long this could take, or how far I or anyone could get. Many mathematicians all over the world had also picked up the baton and wanted to sprint their way to the proof of Serre's conjecture. The quest for its proof was that of a whole community of mathematicians spread all across the globe.

Pure mathematics might appear esoteric, but it can get intensely competitive. When the stakes are high and people are converging towards a breakthrough, many emotions are at play: envy, ambition, one-upmanship. After all, one is playing for a smidgen of immortality! Politics and gamesmanship can abound belying the 'pure' in pure mathematics. But it is these impurities that create the compelling alloy of the subject as practised at the frontiers of research.

Proving Serre's conjecture became my moonshot soon after I finished my PhD thesis in 1995. It took me more than a decade of work before my French collaborator Jean-Pierre Wintenberger and I could settle the conjecture in 2008. The mathematical plot of this book is about mathematicians who got infected by the 'virus' of Galois and Ramanujan symmetries, and as a result became obsessed, or afflicted, with them. Magnificent work throughout the twentieth century linked these two very different types of symmetries, bringing them closer and closer together. The proof of Serre's conjecture is a milestone in showing that these symmetries, in spite of their totally different morphology, astonishingly enough have essentially the same DNA. This book is mainly about the human story of this mathematical achievement.

∞

The interaction between mathematics and the person thinking about it unfolds almost like a dance. The subject enchants by its elegant questions and its powerful ideas. Even as it invites one in, it resists by its difficulty, its particular ways of argumentation that need to be learned. One cannot absorb the subject passively. There is little instant gratification on offer. We see in this book a researcher tussling with his limitations and inadequacy. I often thought of giving up during my struggles as a graduate student, or even later when I was making little progress in my research, when I felt overwhelmed by the difficulties of the subject.

The subject initially resists understanding, as if demanding that the student put in the necessary effort to grasp its core ideas and vital essence. A student experiences frustration and joy in battling and overcoming this resistance, and wants to learn further, go deeper, be all in, because there is always more to contend with, understand and then delight in. The work done in overcoming the resistance tests resilience and builds reserves of strength and experience to a point where a student can begin to add to the subject in modest ways, ask questions of it that lead to new insights and new connections. If you are lucky, the dance may also be able to draw out strengths within that you were unaware of at the beginning. Almost everything that I learnt or had engaged with seriously in mathematics got used in our proof of Serre's conjecture. My thesis work on manipulating Ramanujan symmetries gave me key intuitions that led to breakthroughs in the work years later on Serre's conjecture. (Many mathematicians can attest to this experience of feeling that mathematics cannibalizes all of yourself that you offer to it!)

This dance is not unique to mathematics, and probably occurs across all creative pursuits in challenging fields that require significant apprenticeship before one can begin original work. Indeed, mathematical research is regarded in this book as a particular kind of creative activity, cognate to composing music, designing a piece of public architecture or writing a novel. Similar, but with its own marked differences and rugged individuality. I hope this narrative-based account of creativity in mathematics will resonate with the readers interested, more generally, in the mysterious ways by which ideas arise in the mind, solving problems that seem impenetrable when one first thinks about them.

Thinking about mathematics is an important part of a mathematician's life, but it is far from all of it. Mathematical work is done in the midst of all that happens in one's life: what a person does when not thinking about mathematics affects decisively the mathematics they do. In a related vein, the nineteenth-century French mathematician Charles Hermite said it is the person and not the method that solves a mathematical problem. The open-ended nature of mathematical research leads to a freedom that provides scope for the expression of personal qualities, which can result in one seeing a problem in a way that is new. Contrary to the general perception that mathematics is a highly technical and hermetic subject that only certain types of people can study, in practice people from different backgrounds, and a breadth of sensibilities and talents, can make a great impact on the subject. But perhaps because of the way mathematics is viewed and its reputation as a Procrustean subject, there is a notable lack of diversity, across many aspects, in the mathematical community. Hermite's actual quote, 'It is the man, and not the method, who solves a problem' reflects the historic male dominance in the field at his time, one that sadly continues to this day. There is typically just a scattering of women mathematicians present at the conferences I attend. This is to the great detriment of the subject. A greater diversity in its practitioners would not only enrich the social context within which it is practised but also enhance and transform the theoretical core of the subject.

∞

One's mathematical creativity can draw sustenance from family and social ties. In my journey to the proof of Serre's conjecture, the support of my family was crucial. One also draws from one's other interests – poetry, music, art, or sports, to name a few. What this book also tries to bring alive is that mathematics is increasingly taking the form of a social endeavour in a world community of mathematicians. With the improved communications of the later part of the twentieth century, mathematics has become a far more collaborative enterprise than in the past; however, it goes without saying that it still requires a lot of individual effort. The popular conception of a mathematical scholar working in splendid isolation in a garret and discovering mathematical truths – while it might apply to a very few select celebrated figures, like Sir Isaac Newton or Carl Friedrich Gauss, or to the great Indian mathematicians Srinivasa Ramanujan or Harish-Chandra – is simply not the common experience of most mathematicians today.

I benefited from learning from the work of many mathematicians. I was inspired by direct contact with, and the personalities of, some of them. I was often lucky to be in the right place at the right time. Wiles's methods becoming available right around the time I finished my PhD was great timing for me. Furthermore, the proof of Serre's conjecture would not have been possible without the extensive work of many people that led to crucial developments all through the 1980s and 1990s.

The book may sometimes give the impression that mathematicians frequently sojourn in exotic locations in the cause of doing research; visits to places like Sapporo and Paris and Strasbourg feature prominently in my mathematical journey. While such trips are undeniably enjoyable as a way to experience different parts of the world, they can sometimes catalyse a breakthrough just by the alchemy of being in the same place as a colleague and asking a question or sharing an idea that would have never made it into an email, or just by the neurons being jostled by travel and the stimulation and novelty of new surroundings.

∞

The book does not try to teach its readers mathematics, at least not in any formal sense, but it does aim to make it vividly present to them. I have tried to explain, in plain English, the development of ideas from Gauss's eighteenth-century quadratic reciprocity law to Ramanujan's prophetic 1916 paper to the formulation of Serre's conjecture in the 1970s and 1980s, culminating in my proof of it with Wintenberger in the first decade of the twenty-first century.

In my initial drafts of this book, there was little mathematics. My intention was to focus on the creative endeavour, immerse the reader in the atmosphere of mathematical research, give a sense of the marathon aspect of research – thinking on walks, learning from mentors and collaborators, discussing mathematics at blackboards on several continents, or at restaurants with ideas scribbled on paper napkins, evoke in visceral detail periods of obsession with an idea or problem, talk of months or even years when I was lost, wandering in the wilderness of failing attempts to make headway with a problem. The focus on my personal journey to the proof of Serre's conjecture interested my colleagues – they already knew the mathematics, after all. But I was told that if the book is to have a broader readership beyond those already interested in Serre's conjecture, I had to level the playing field and give a sense to the general reader of what is being thought about, the nature of the mathematics being investigated. I knew the mathematics was glorious and had caught me in the sweep of its ideas, but I thought at first that it would be impossible to convey the spirit of the mathematics without it taking over and becoming overwhelming. However, I think – at least hope! – that I have found a way to talk about the maths without drowning the book in technicalities.

The book, as it stands now, can best be described as a mathematical memoir. The biographical story is in service of the mathematical plot, which is a tale of two symmetries labelled by the names of two brilliant mathematicians, Galois and Ramanujan. The maths of the book is like a central but enigmatic character in a play. This character has fewer lines than the others, but the other characters' actions and words seem mainly to revolve around this one. The enigma is deepened by the character speaking, when they do speak, in a strange, foreign-sounding tongue that seems to have the most unexpected diphthongs and triphthongs and guttural sounds. Nevertheless, everyone else on stage carries on as if this is totally normal: they can glean enough from the comportment of the mathematical character to get a sense of what they might be articulating. There are plenty of blissful periods when everyone just ignores what this character is saying; they fade into the background, adding to the atmosphere subliminally, while most of the reader's attention is directed towards the other characters and elements of the story.

One of the qualities that a mathematician needs is the ability to read a mathematical work without insisting on understanding everything, skipping parts that seem impenetrable at first reading, moving past these thickets, and yet getting a sense of the work without having understood all of it. Skipping strategically is an art and a very useful skill to develop for a mathematician. I ask that the reader of this book also be willing to skip parts that seem too abstruse, and press on.

Readers will engage with the mathematics at different levels of depth depending on their prior exposure to mathematical ideas: yet I believe that all readers, those who read the mathematical parts breezily as well as those who venture deeper into it, will get a sense of a life spent thinking about the mathematics, both the drama and the pathos of it. There are no mathematical prerequisites needed to read the book besides curiosity about the mathematical enterprise and the capacity to fast-forward through parts that have too much explicit maths for your taste. Much of the book has no mathematics in it, and my hope is that it won't be given a 'for mathematicians only' rating by even the most exacting of readers allergic to explicit mathematical content. (Readers who want to know more about the mathematical ideas that are touched upon in the book can look at the endnotes, which are optional reading.)

Finally, the way mathematics is sometimes taught in schools may give students the notion that there is nothing new left to discover in it. I hope this tale of a mathematical adventure will dispel such notions and convince the reader that mathematics is full of unsolved problems, which are in many ways its lifeblood. There are many exciting and important mathematical conjectures waiting to take a person, willing to invest time and effort, along on a personal journey of discovery.

1

Growing Up in Bombay

My early encounters with numbers were not happy ones. When I was six, so circa 1973, I interviewed for admission to St. Mary's, an all-boys school in the Byculla area of Bombay. I sat across a big desk from a Jesuit priest. He asked me to count the paper clips he had laid out on the desk. After I was done, he picked them up and scattered them, and asked how many were there now. In my confusion, I started counting again and almost failed the test. Perhaps because of my early struggles with numbers, they never stopped haunting me.

One of my early memories of pleasure in manipulating numbers comes from a little later at St. Mary's. A teacher in middle school, Mr. Derek, taught us Krypto. The game could be played with the seven-digit number on a ticket bought on one of Bombay's distinctive red BEST buses. The objective of Krypto was to punctuate the first six digits with operations of elementary arithmetic – addition, subtraction, multiplication and division – to produce the last digit.

The bus ticket was flimsy but printed densely with numbers. The digits of the ticket number my friends and I played with were printed in black near the top right corner of the ticket, which bled black and red in the rain. We tried to make the first six numerals interact to produce the seventh. There was a whoop of delight when someone got there first.

Imagine that the ticket number in black at the top right corner is 3852612. One has to compose the first 6 digits into an arithmetical sentence which means, or equals, 2 at the end. Here is a possible syncopation: $(((3 - 8) - 5) + (2 \times 6)) \times 1 = 2$. Voilà! Each time one is qualifying what has been done earlier by inserting arithmetic operations, the meaning changing as each operation qualifies what has preceded (when we subtract 5 from $3 - 8$ to get $(3 - 8) - 5$), or juxtaposes a new thought (when we add 2×6 to $(3 - 8) - 5$). The meaning becomes definitive only at the end, when we arrive at the sought for digit 2. This string of arithmetic is like a musical phrase, with each note altering the sounds already heard. The end result seems almost formal, like the title of a song, *A Summer's Night*. The delight is in treading the path that the notes or the arithmetical operations take us along. As we got better at the game, we could put the ticket away in a pocket, and work with the seven digits dancing in the mind's eye. Playing Krypto was my first experience of hearing the music of numbers.

∞

My sister Padmini and I grew up in a flat on Worli Sea Face with many dos and many more don'ts. I called my sister, only two years older than me, 'Tai' which was the formal way of addressing an older sister in a fairly traditional household. In the living room of our plainly furnished flat there hung a portrait of my grandfather wearing black-rimmed glasses, dressed in the traditional formal garb of sadra and pheta. I was very proud of my grandfather. Although he died when I was only five, I had heard many stories about him. His stern but concerned gaze followed me through my childhood. Originally from Ratnagiri in coastal Maharashtra, he had been a priest in a temple in Vile Parle, in suburban Bombay, living in genteel poverty. Being considered a learned holy man in the community, he was helped by the local elite. They took an interest in his children, especially in my father, whose ready wit and charm attracted attention. Widowed relatively early in his life, my grandfather had raised a family of seven on his salary as a priest which barely sufficed. His means and patience were almost stretched beyond their limits. He retired after his two eldest sons, my father and his older brother, started doing well. They led the entire family on a continuously upward path. But even when his children moved to grander neighbourhoods, he continued to live in his rooms at the temple.

My father, seduced by the beauty of Kalidasa's verses, had once wanted to be a Sanskrit scholar. My grandfather dissuaded him: the vocation of a Sanskrit scholar would not ameliorate the poverty that had been the family's lot for generations. 'To live without means gracefully requires a lot of character,' my grandfather said. My grandfather took my father to Sydenham College of Commerce and Arts in South Bombay after the deadline for admission to the bachelor's commerce degree had passed. My grandfather knew the registrar of the college. Dressed in traditional Indian clothes, he walked unselfconsciously into the formal Western setting of the college. He had enough force of personality to get my father enrolled.

My father vindicated my grandfather's hunch that he had it in him to succeed in the commercial world: he rose to the top of his chosen profession, accountancy, in an environment that provided few opportunities for upward mobility. Independent India was less than ten years old, the government controlled the commanding heights of the economy, private enterprise was looked down upon, and a government job was prized for its job security. Taxation at its peak rate was at 97.5 per cent of income. In this environment, my father managed to start and run his own highly successful accounting firm. He said, after he had won an unlikely judgement in his client's favour in a case before the Income Tax Tribunal, 'I do only the impossible!' It was a grand thing to say, and a potential slogan to live by, especially as he backed his words with action.

∞

My mother came from a very different background. Her own father's career had begun by carrying trunks full of textiles and going door to door to make his sales. He later became the proprietor of a textile factory called Swastik Mills. Her family lived in the Walkeshwar area of Bombay in a mansion on a road that went along the coast and climbed up Malabar Hill. They had moved there from the more modest neighbourhood of Girgaon, less than half a mile away but worlds apart.

She had become interested, while still in her teens, in a religious movement called the Warkaris. The movement had arisen centuries ago as part of a revival and reform movement within Hinduism to counter its growing domination by a ritualistic orthodoxy. Saints of the movement wrote commentaries on canonical Sanskrit texts like the Bhagvad Gita in vernacular languages to make them accessible to the layperson. The Warkari sect was primarily proletarian, many of its adherents working in mills like the one my maternal grandfather owned.

My mother married my father when he was still someone with just a promising career. She travelled from the riches of her childhood home to the small flat my father had bought in Vile Parle and brought with her an openness to life that could almost seem reckless.

There were many stories about my mother's unconventionality that we heard about and experienced as children. One day she hitched a ride on a truck to a location a hundred miles away to attend a religious conference. Another time, a taxi driver could not navigate the steep slope that led to my maternal uncle's house. My mother asked him to move aside, took over the wheel and drove the vehicle to the windy porch of the building. She made transitions easily. She would travel third class on a train and then go from there to the fanciest hotel in town. Once she shocked an older family friend when she gave up her first class train seats for him after discovering he had seats in a lower class.

The Gita delineates three paths to realization: knowledge, action and devotion. My mother's favourite verses of the Gita are in its twelfth canto, which speak of the path to enlightenment through devotion or bhakti. My father's path was one of work and knowledge. He was superstitious: in his commute to work he bowed as his car passed a temple or a Ganesh idol in a shop window.

My mother was almost my entire world as a child. She was avant-garde in seeking out specialists who were a rare breed in Bombay at that time to address my many shortcomings. I was diagnosed with flat feet and had special shoes made for me from a shop in Girgaon. She also took me to a speech therapist, and I remember shouting at the sea with marbles in my mouth as part of the therapy. She was very protective of me, and tried to shield me from my father's disappointment that as a very young child I did not seem particularly bright. Her influence on me was implicit as opposed to the more explicit influence of my father. While my father's example made me want to shine, she gave me the confidence to find my own interests, being the invisible catalyst in shaping my life.

∞

Both my parents were larger-than-life figures for their children, belonging to bigger worlds than that of the family. Their strong contrasting personalities gave my sister and me role models right at home. One day they came home with the entire collected works of Somerset Maugham and Charles Dickens bought from a ship docked in the Bombay harbour on its circumnavigation of the world. The Maugham works were bound in blue leather with titles in silver that faded with time. The Dickens volumes were a vomit green colour. My sister picked the Maugham books as her preserve, while I chose Dickens as my fiefdom. Some parts of certain Maugham's novels, like *Of Human Bondage* or *Ashenden*, were wildly inappropriate for young children. My parents did not know this as they had not read these books and had bought them thinking they would be good mental nourishment for their children. I read many of Dickens's novels – *Oliver Twist, David Copperfield* and *The Pickwick Papers*, among others. While I liked quite a lot of what I read, I did sometimes force my way to the end, reluctant to stop reading because I knew they were considered classic, canonical texts of English literature. When I went along with my mother to religious discourses I took these books along as talismans to protect me from boredom.

∞

One evening, my father returned from work with a mathematician in tow who was visiting from the United States where he taught at Purdue University. I fell under the spell of this man. He talked with such deliberation and drama about mathematics that one felt that he was revealing mysterious fundamental truths about numbers, and the world of mathematics they belonged to, of which he was the sole custodian! He asked me a question: find a number that when divided by 17 leaves a remainder of 5 and when divided by 37 leaves the remainder 3. I had learnt in school the division algorithm – you can divide any number by a positive number N, leaving a remainder (like an error term) between 0 and $N-1$. But here I was being asked to do something with the division algorithm that I had never been asked to do before. I realized through this meeting that there was much more to mathematics than we were exposed to at school, that even simple things like the division algorithm might have depths that I had not suspected. After I struggled with the question for a while (the smallest such number is 447), he told me there was nothing special about the numbers 17 and 37: if you are given any numbers A and B that have no common factor, then there are integers with arbitrarily prescribed remainders when divided by A and by B. This, he explained, was known as the Chinese Remainder Theorem.

The visiting mathematician, Professor Shreeram Shankar Abhyankar, seemed very outré to me. He had brilliant grey eyes and seemed to have a huge appetite for everything, including conversation and argument, although the overarching passion of his life was mathematics. He was proud of his Indian heritage and our common mother tongue, Marathi. His wife, an American, spoke grammatically perfect Marathi with a strong American accent. Bucking the worldwide trend of preferring to write mathematical research papers predominantly in English, he had tried to exposit his mathematical work in Marathi. He had set up a mathematical institute in India called the Bhaskaracharya Pratishthana and had come to see my father as part of his fundraising efforts for the institute. My father invited him home as he thought it would be inspiring for his children to meet this unusual man who was a renowned mathematician.

Abhyankar recounted stories that felt like broadcasts from an unknown world. During his PhD days in the 1950s at Harvard, his adviser Oscar Zariski, who I later learnt was one of the great algebraic geometers of the twentieth century, became worried after not seeing him for weeks. When Zariski sent a student to look for him, the latter found Abhyankar passed out at his desk with the solution of a problem he had been asked to solve written in an open notebook in front of him. He told us how he would study all night in the Harvard library, and often be there when the cleaning lady came in the early hours of the morning. She started bringing him breakfast. He even said that once after days of intense effort and concentration on a problem the blood vessels in his eyes burst. These felt like the stories I had heard of yogis doing years of penance in the Himalayas and finding enlightenment.

By this time I had migrated from St Mary's to another school. This was the Cathedral and John Connon School in South Bombay. While St. Mary's was a Jesuit institution, Cathedral was Anglican. A more salient difference was that Cathedral was a co-ed school. The admissions interview at St. Mary's was far behind me now, and I was doing well at school. However, it was only after meeting Abhyankar that I started focusing on mathematics in a different way, reading beyond what was taught in the classroom. I was perhaps in the ninth or tenth grade at the time.

It was hard to find all the books I wanted to read in the Bombay of the 1980s. My parents, eager to encourage my new passion for mathematics, helped me get some books from abroad.

I also went hunting for books locally, much like an addict wandering around the streets in Bombay. I once joined the crowd at a small bookshop in the Kalbadevi area called the Newhand and Secondhand Bookshop. Most of the other customers were there for coaching manuals to pass various competitive exams. I had heard that this bookshop had a second-hand copy of G.H. Hardy's book *A Course of Pure Mathematics*. Hardy had tried to reform the teaching of mathematics at Cambridge in the first few decades of the twentieth century, as it had fallen behind the times. The maths taught in Cambridge at the time did not have the breadth and depth of that taught on the continent, in France and Germany. Hardy's book, adopted for the Mathematical Tripos, the undergraduate mathematics course at Cambridge, had become a classic text. The bookshop had one used copy of Hardy's *Pure Mathematics*. It was in pristine condition and was carefully covered in plastic. It did not seem to have been read much. Not that I, after getting hold of a book, read it diligently either. Some of the joy is just the pleasure in the hunt for the book, like going in search of a rare bird that's been spotted in a woodland.

∞

I became fascinated by prime numbers. These are numbers bigger than 1 whose only factors are 1 and themselves. Prime numbers are like atoms. In fact, the etymology of the word 'atom' lies in the Greek word for 'indivisible' – the fundamental characteristic of a prime number. One of the oldest known theorems is Euclid's result that there are infinitely many primes. Every number can be factored as a product of primes just as molecules are made by atoms coming together. It is also true, and deeper, that factorization into primes is unique, which is to say there is only one way to write a number as a product of primes. The uniqueness of prime factorization goes by the name of the Fundamental Theorem of Arithmetic.[10]

Prime numbers occur in nature. There is a theory that cicadas have population cycles of 13 or 17 years, partly because these numbers are prime and this gives them a better chance of survival than if they had a cycle of, say, 12 years which has many factors: 1, 2, 3, 4, 6, 12. If there were predators with cycles of, say, 2, 3, 4 or 6 years, the cicadas would be in great jeopardy from multiple species of predators if they emerged every 12 years. In contrast, if they have a life cycle of 13 years, then they would be in jeopardy from a predator with a life cycle of, say, 3 years, only once every $3 \times 13 = 39$ years. Thus having a life cycle whose length is a prime number makes cicadas less vulnerable to predators. The processes of Darwinian evolution seem to lead to cicadas manifesting an unconscious predilection for prime numbers!

∞

I would try to talk about some of the maths I had read with my friends at school, showing off my newly acquired and half-digested mathematical wisdom. My excitement was greater than my understanding of it. Around this time, I also dabbled in chess. I went a few times to a chess club located in a warehouse in the compound of Zandu Pharmaceuticals, a company that made ayurvedic medicines. A big rectangular room had several tables set up with chessboards. Stepping inside was like stepping into the dense air of a greenhouse, heavy with the smell of ayurvedic medicines, an odd admixture of herbal, culinary and clinical smells. When in the room, one lost contact with the outside world. The club had a proletarian character, and I imagined a meeting of the local branch of the Communist Party of India (Marxist) would resemble this gathering, with young bearded men, mostly a little older than me, idealistic and uncompromising to a fault, arguing with restrained passion. Occasionally, the Thipsay brothers would come to the club. They were the leading chess players in India – one of the brothers was on the verge of becoming a grandmaster – but were treated at the chess club with a self-conscious heightened egalitarianism as just one of the in-crowd.

Chess has something of the quality of mathematics. The moves within both take place in a closed setting. In chess, the moves take place place within the confines of a board of 64 black and white squares, while in mathematics one reasons within the boundaries of an axiomatic system. There are elegant moves and surprising solutions to impasses in chess. In mathematics, elegance in arguments and the surprise element is prized as well. A fair number of people who like mathematics also like chess. Mathematics felt to me less hermetic than chess. It had surprising applications in science and the real world. This quality of mathematics is captured by the well-known phrase – 'the unreasonable effectiveness of mathematics' – which comes from Eugene Wigner's essay – 'The Unreasonable Effectiveness of Mathematics in the Natural Sciences' – and refers to the fact that mathematical ideas developed for their own sake sometimes serendipitously turn out to be exactly what a scientific theory needs.

∞

I read E.T. Bell's book *Men of Mathematics*, which gave gossipy, dramatic, and sometimes even lurid accounts of the lives of great mathematicians. Each chapter was devoted to a famous mathematician. Isaac Newton and Carl Friedrich Gauss were anointed as the greatest of them all. The chapter on Gauss was called 'Prince of Mathematicians'. It recounted the story of how Gauss as a schoolboy had astonished his teacher by solving almost instantly a problem which kept the rest of the class busy for an hour. It was about adding up the numbers from 1 to 100. Gauss wrote down the answer 5050 in a trice as he found a trick to do this. One could assemble the numbers in 50 pairs {100, 1}, {99, 2}, ... , {51, 50} in such a way that the sum of each pair would be 101 and so the answer was 101 × 50 = 5050. Others in the class must have tried to laboriously compute the sum 1 + 2 + ... + 100 which naturally took longer. Mathematics seemed to be about substituting calculation with ideas. Gauss came from peasant stock and rose to become the greatest mathematician of his era. I later found out that some parents give their eight-year-olds the Gauss test of asking them to sum up the numbers from 1 to 100 to detect mathematical precocity! Mathematical talent, it seemed to me, manifested early, and I was a little worried, but not unduly so, about not showing any exceptional talent so far.

Bell's book was almost exclusively about white, male and European mathematicians. I did not think about this aspect then, and only now does it seem amiss that not much mention is made of important contributions to the subject from all over the world. It is true that the West has dominated the modern era in the world of mathematics, but centuries before that the zero had been invented in India, which led to the place value system. Madhava and his school working on the banks of the river Nila in Kerala had formulated the basic ideas about calculus, especially related to trigonometric functions and their infinite series expansions, more than two hundred years before Newton.

I learnt from the biographies of mathematicians in Bell's book that the greatest of them often rated number theory very highly. Gauss proclaimed that number theory was the Queen of Mathematics. Mathematics was already the Queen of the Sciences, which gave number theory a very exalted station indeed. Mathematicians seemed to glory in the apparent uselessness of number theory as it seemed very distant from applications to the real world, unlike a subject such as calculus which Newton had invented to calculate the motion of bodies like planets in the solar system. Some mathematicians cast doubt on number theory being worthy of study because of its lack of applications in the real world. The German mathematician Carl Jacobi countered that mathematics is done for the honour of the human mind, and that such a lofty goal rendered irrelevant objections related to its practical relevance.

∞

I learnt about *modular arithmetic* when I was in high school: it is the arithmetic of remainders modulo a number N. This new type of arithmetic is modelled on a clock. We tell the time in periods of $N = 24$ hours. This is an instance of mod 24 arithmetic. If it's 8 a.m. and we want to know what time it will be after 1360 hours, we write $1360 = 56 \times 24 + 16$. Thus 1360 hours after 8 a.m. would be midnight as $8 + 16 = 24$. In practical life we also often work modulo 7 to determine the days of the week. If a meeting is scheduled every 10 days, and we just had one on Monday, then we know that the fifth meeting from now will be after 50 days, and as 50 leaves a remainder of 1 when divided by 7 ($50 = 7 \times 7 + 1$), it will take place on Tuesday, the day of the week after Monday.

Mathematicians are not constrained to think of only what is practically relevant. They study modular arithmetic for any natural number N. In modular arithmetic every number is reduced to its remainder when one divides it by N. Modular arithmetic had been considered for hundreds of years before Gauss formalized this notion in his classic book *Disquistiones Arithmeticae* (Arithmetical Investigations). He invented a suggestive notation and terminology for this. He defines two numbers a and b to be *congruent* modulo N, in notation $a \equiv b \pmod{N}$, if they leave the same remainder when divided by N. The equality $\equiv$ of numbers mod N is equality taken with pinches of salt that are multiples of the number N. We can do arithmetic on the numbers $0, 1, \ldots, N-1$ modulo (or mod) N taking into account the remainders modulo N when performing the usual operations.[11]

In the context of modular arithmetic I learnt about a theorem of Fermat that determines which numbers N occur as squares of distances between points in a square grid. Its proof uses modular arithmetic. By the Pythagorean theorem, these are the same as numbers N that are sums of two squares, namely of the form $a^2 + b^2$ for numbers a and b. Fermat proved that an odd prime number occurs as the square of a distance between points in a square grid precisely when it leaves a remainder of 1 when divided by 4. As an example of Fermat's result, consider 61 which is a prime that is 1 mod 4: it can be written as a sum of squares $61 = 5^2 + 6^2$. Fermat's theorem says that the same is true for every prime p that is 1 mod 4, it can be written as $p = a^2 + b^2$ although there is no simple formula for a and b. It felt like a surprising and beautiful result and used modular arithmetic.

Modular arithmetic was developed for internal needs in mathematics. Nevertheless, it has found applications in encryption algorithms, and is the basis of what keeps credit card transactions on the internet safe. The Rivest-Shamir-Adleman (RSA) method of encrypting uses modular arithmetic and relies on the fact that given large prime numbers p and q, it is computationally not expensive to form their product $N = pq$. On the other hand given such a number N there is no known efficient algorithm to perform the inverse operation of finding its prime factors p and q. This is an instance of the unreasonable effectiveness of mathematics: ideas developed for their own sake in maths find unexpected applications, in this case in the world of commerce.

For junior college (the eleventh and twelfth grades) I studied at Jai Hind College in the Churchgate area of Bombay from 1984 to 1986. Most of my brighter classmates used the two years of junior college to study for the board and competitive exams to enter medicine and engineering programmes. Having already pitched my tent as someone who wanted to study pure mathematics as an undergraduate, I had the luxury of mooching around, reading mathematics books and trying my luck at mathematical competitions with mixed fortunes. I remember securing the first position in the state of Maharashtra in a state-wide mathematical competition. In the national round I did not do well.

I wrote an essay for a mathematical essay competition held by IIT Bombay and got the prize. The essay, written on the concept of zero, ended with the witticism that zero 'denotes the presence of an absence' which my father liked very much. He made many copies of my essay and distributed it to friends and clients of his accounting firm. I was no longer a laggard child and he was proud of my interest in mathematics. From now on he routinely exaggerated my talents and achievements to his friends.

My father backed my decision to study pure mathematics. Perhaps there was a sense that I was reverting to another tradition in the family, my grandfather's, of scholarship and learning. My grandfather had studied the Vedas in a gurukul. There might have been some recollection here that he himself had once wanted to be a Sanskrit scholar. He now had the means, unlike his own father, for his son to be able to choose a scholarly vocation without worrying about the financial implications.

My father's backing of my interest in mathematics, and his willingness to pay for what turned out to be an expensive education abroad, was exceptional in the India of the time. Most students felt great pressure from their parents to do something in a practical field like medicine or engineering. If there was a business or professional firm in the family, the norm was that the children, and sons especially, would join the family firm.

My sister had also chosen to study mathematics for her undergraduate degree at St. Xavier's College in Bombay. She was three years ahead of me and through her I met a few young people who were passionate about mathematics. They were full of youthful, rebellious spirits and number theory fanatics. They knew far more maths than I did and I sometimes snuck past the security into St. Xavier's to meet them in the canteen. They were doing some small original research and I found their companionship stimulating. I also got my first real sense of being a mathematician and experiencing the culture of the subject: focused, passionate and irreverent.

∞

In the books that I read about elementary number theory, there was one result that was mentioned in hushed tones. It was the loftiest peak of classical number theory. This was Gauss's law of quadratic reciprocity. The law has a storied history. It was first discovered in the eighteenth century by Leonhard Euler, who was Swiss, and Adrien-Marie Legendre, a French mathematician. Euler was important enough to have a chapter of his own in Bell's book. In number theory, one can experiment with numbers in the laboratory of one's mind using the tools of pen and paper, and Euler and Legendre, through such experiments, found certain patterns arising from a question about modular arithmetic. Legendre boldly named this pattern the law of quadratic reciprocity, even though he was not able to prove it.

It took genius to look for and discover these patterns. It took even greater genius to prove the pattern discovered by Euler and Legendre. As a nineteen-year-old teenager, Gauss found a proof. Extremely indirect and ingenious, it is one of the crowning achievements in his masterpiece *Disquistiones Arithmeticae*. Gauss found several proofs (at least six) to understand this pattern from various points of view. The law of quadratic reciprocity and its generalizations run like a golden thread through much of number theory: in fact, Gauss called it his golden theorem. Legendre's quest to prove the law can be cast in tragic terms as it remained unfulfilled. But in mathematics one work leads to another; Legendre's insights led to Gauss's breakthrough.

∞

My sister had a friend in St. Xavier's whose father was a mathematician. He worked at the Tata Institute of Fundamental Research (TIFR), the hallowed institute at the edge of Bombay devoted to research in mathematics and the pure sciences. It would one day be my workplace, but right now, it had the same mystery and awe for me that Kafka's protagonist K. might have felt for the castle in his village, a seat of power and occult practices. It felt like a monastery in which the monks working and living in it had discovered recondite and fundamental truths that could only be learnt by being initiated and after years of intense study with the masters. I was full of diffidence when I went to meet Professor

Rangachari in his bare office, with the glimmer of the Arabian Sea visible from its windows. He inquired about my interests and perhaps I ventured to tell him about my keen interest in number theory. When he asked me to state the law of quadratic reciprocity, I fumbled.

How could I have fumbled, I wonder now, after having spent months reading about quadratic reciprocity? I think it was because I was yet to gain my ease with the ideas of modular arithmetic. Understanding something is like rising to an altitude at which one can see clearly, and it is hard to reconstruct how it felt to be lost in the clouds below, unable to see through their swarming thickness. This is perhaps the nature of ideas, but especially true of mathematical ideas as they are unambiguous and dusted with the sparkle and glitter of logic. Once one understands them, they stay lodged in the mind forever.

Quadratic reciprocity, which took me many years to grasp fully, is like black magic! It arises when one thinks of an innocent question about arithmetic in the numbers modulo a prime number p. The beauty and power of quadratic reciprocity can be illustrated in a particular but still illustrative case by the surprising answer it gives to the following question:

Question: *For which odd primes p is 5 mod p a square?*

In more explicit terms this is the same as asking for which primes p is there a number M for which $M^2 \equiv 5 \pmod{p}$. In other words, one is asking if there is a number whose square leaves the remainder 5 when divided by the prime number p. The primes p for which 5 is a square mod p has a beautifully simple and precise description! It turns out that 5 is a square mod p precisely when p leaves remainder either 1 or 4 on being divided by 5. This is a special case of the amazing law of quadratic reciprocity. It is called a reciprocity law because it can also be formulated as saying that 5 is a square modulo a prime p exactly when p is a square mod 5. One would have expected 5 being a square mod p to have little to do with p being a square mod 5: they seem like totally independent events.[12] Determining whether 5 is a square mod p might a priori take more and more laborious computation as the prime p becomes larger and larger. Quadratic reciprocity cuts out all the labour. For example, it seems hard to figure out if 5 is a square mod the millionth prime, 15485863, but here is how to do it. The prime 15485863 is congruent to 3 mod 5 (namely leaves remainder 3 when divided by 5) and 3 is not a square mod 5, so 5 is not a square mod 15485863 by quadratic reciprocity.

∞

While I was trying to learn number theory, I was also discovering Indian classical music. My mother had a melodious voice and when she sang *abhangas* and old Hindi film songs at home, it was very moving. When I began going to concerts with my sister, I heard sometimes the same compositions sung more elaborately, but losing little of their emotional intensity, by classical musicians like Pandit Bhimsen Joshi, Kishori Amonkar, Mallikarjun Mansur, Gangubai Hangal, Kumar Gandharva and many others. The concerts I attended of Kishoritai, an exponent of the Jaipur-Atrauli *gharana* founded by Ustad Alladiya Khan, made a deep impression on me. She lived just a mile away from us, in a small flat in Prabhadevi, and spoke Marathi at home. This gave me a sense that one could scale peaks of artistic achievement right in the here and now, and that these artists were not distant from our lives.

A common theme in the lives of musicians is their search for a guru. Pandit Bhimsen Joshi as a ten-year-old heard a recording of

Ustad Abdul Karim Khan of the Kirana *gharana*. He was bowled over by the sweetness of the music and wanted to learn to sing like the ustad. He left his home in Dharwad in the southern state of Karnataka and travelled ticketless on trains to the northern parts of the country, searching for a guru. He would sing a popular melody to placate the ticket collector if he was caught. He went as far as Punjab. In the end, he found a mentor close to his home, someone who had learnt from Abdul Karim Khan. Talking about his days of apprenticeship he emphasized the importance of *baithak*, the ability to sit for hours practising without squirming and growing restless. His guru had taught him ways to strengthen his voice and had advised him to exclusively sing notes in the lower octave in the early morning hours. He sang in the hours before dawn, drawing solace and encouragement from a black street dog who would come and sit under a tree, keeping him company as he practised. I slowly absorbed these stories. The search for a guru was something that was part of my legacy too. My grandfather had walked scores of miles over several days as a boy of ten to learn scriptures from a guru in a neighbouring town, seeking shelter at night by knocking on doors.

I became aware of, and was increasingly drawn to, a quality called *thehrav*, that is prized in Indian classical music. This is a quality of stillness, the ability to stay with a note, with a thought, without trying to force a conclusion, instead letting a mood unfold. As I listened more I found that this was the most important quality in a musical performance, requiring maturity and skill and confidence. When I became a mathematics researcher, the notion of *thehrav* resonated with me even more. The ability to stay with a thought and give it a chance to evolve, without interfering and blocking it with predetermined ideas, seemed essential. One could discover something new only if one was willing to sustain periods of uncertainty, and live with the suspense of not being in control. This was not the same as tenacity; *thehrav* was something that was present in the moment, a certain restraint in a mind that was eager and watchful, tense yet forbearing, while tenacity was more about not giving up on something you were pursuing.

∞

While in junior college I had to figure out where I would study mathematics as an undergraduate. One option was to go to a local college like St. Xavier's. I already had friends there. However, I was leaning towards going abroad, Cambridge in particular.

A day trip from London with my mother and sister to the university town, with its cobbled streets and bicycling students, had left a lasting impression on me. In Hardy's book *A Mathematician's Apology* he writes about being seduced by the idea of becoming a don (professor) at Cambridge after he read in a novel about the Fellows of a college in Cambridge drinking sherry and eating walnuts in the Combination Room. For me, there were other resonances.

I had read about Srinivasa Ramanujan, whom Hardy had brought to Cambridge in 1913 after being struck by letters Ramanujan sent him from Madras, full of exotic and beautiful formulas. Hardy could not fathom some of the formulas but said: 'They [formulae 1.10 – 1.12 of Ramanujan] must be true because, if they were not true, no one would have had the imagination to invent them.' They collaborated and in lectures on Ramanujan, years after he had died, Hardy said that 'my association with him is the one romantic incident in my life'. Indeed, he is one of the most romantic figures in all of mathematics.

They were a study in contrast. Hardy's talent had been meticulously groomed and encouraged right from his schooldays to his time as a university student and then as a don at Cambridge. Ramanujan was a self-taught genius, *swayambhu* or *sui generis*. His mathematics bloomed like a wildflower in a forest in a colonized India.

Ramanujan rediscovered many results in mathematics that had been proved by great masters like Euler and Jacobi, along with other results that turned out to be new and striking. Following his own instincts, he discovered mathematics in unlikely places. His mathematics has an intuitive and untamed quality, a touch of the uncanny. Ramanujan died when he was just 32 years old, but in his short life did work that made a great impact and has relevance to this day.

∞

Closer to home, there was Wrangler Paranjpye, a Maharashtrian who had a road named after him in Pune. About a decade older than Ramanujan, he had studied for the Mathematical Tripos in Cambridge towards the end of the nineteenth century and won acclaim for topping the exams, thus becoming the Senior Wrangler in his year. Since he had done it when India was a colony, his triumph had been viewed by Indians as repudiating the British view of them as an inferior race. To be the best in mathematics seemed like a redoubtable proof of the quality of the Indian mind. Perhaps I hoped to emulate him and cover myself in glory by topping the Mathematical Tripos.

Abhyankar poured scorn on Paranjpye's feat. Paranjpye did not go on to do any notable research, Abhyankar pointed out. Paranjpye had a distinguished career and went on to become Vice-Chancellor of Bombay University and India's High Commissioner to Australia. All this was mainly a result of the fame of Paranjpye's examination feat at the Tripos. Nevertheless it was true that Paranjpye did not do important research in mathematics, arguably the main distinction one looked for in a mathematician.

Around the time I was thinking about my future, I was also discussing mathematics with M.S. Huzurbazar who, at the time I met him, was almost going blind. There were echoes here of Euler, who had lost his eyesight towards the end of his life and yet kept on producing reams upon reams of mathematics. In his biographies, there was an endearing image of Euler mathematicizing even as his grandchildren played in his lap. Huzurbazar had a similarly endearing quality of being a loving family man. He had done some advanced mathematical training in the Soviet Union in a relatively obscure area of maths related to logic and the foundations of mathematics. He was very different from Abhyankar.

Abhyankar, famous for his work in algebraic geometry, was charismatic and had a combative personality. He managed to impose his formidable personality even on the milieu of a university town in the American Midwest: he taught in the traditional *gurukul* format in which students come to live with the teacher, learning not only what is taught directly by the guru, but also by osmosis from the atmosphere. He taught courses from his home in West Lafayette which was just a few blocks away from the Purdue maths department: students trekked from the university to listen to his lectures delivered there. He likened his lectures to *pravachans* or *kirtans*, religious sermons in the Hindu tradition, the difference being that he was discoursing on mathematical truths rather than divine ones, mathematics being his religion.

Huzurbazar was far more low-key, and also a sweeter man. I went to meet him once or twice a month in his modest flat in Haji Ali, and my parents also got to know him and became friends with him. He would give me mathematical problems to think about that he read out from a notebook, holding it close to his eyes. I would think about them before we met next, and then we would discuss my solutions to some of them; sometimes he would give me some more hints for the ones that had proved elusive.

Huzurbazar taught at the Institute of Science, which had both undergraduate and postgraduate programmes. It was a rather grand building in South Bombay that dated back to the colonial times. When I eventually applied to Cambridge, as part of the entrance requirements I had to do an exam called the Sixth Term Examination Papers, or STEP. The exam was sent to Huzurbazar and he administered it to me at the Institute of Science.

A few months later I got a letter from Cambridge saying I had been accepted, and it was probably the happiest day of my life until then. Abhyankar happened to be visiting my family. Ever the provocateur, he asked me why I would want to study in a country that had ruled and ruined India. Why not the United States, which was a bigger power and had overtaken England in science and maths? In spite of all he said, and despite having been offered a place at Yale University, it was Cambridge that I had set my heart on.

At the time there was strict control on remitting money abroad from India. A line item in the Foreign Exchange Act, a legacy of colonial times, turned out to be very useful. It allowed money to be remitted by a guardian for a child studying (in *statu pupillari*) in Cambridge or Oxford. I went to the Reserve Bank of India to apply for permission to remit money to the UK. I remember one of my father's most important clients saying that I would not only be taught mathematics there, but also learn about life and be taught how to think. Perhaps this was a variation of the trope of going up to Oxbridge to become a gentleman. All I wanted was to become a mathematician.

2

Cambridge Years

I would not say I was haunted by the figure of Ramanujan during my time at Cambridge. But as an Indian studying mathematics at this university, I did feel that I was walking on a path that he had made for others to tread on as best they could. Ramanujan had struggled to come to terms with life in England. The cold, and the lack of easy access to vegetarian food, had affected his health. He was not well equipped financially, socially or psychologically to take care of himself so far away from home. I had read of him 'cooking vegetables rather miserably in a frying pan in his own room', of him being cold in his rooms in college, and at first lying on top of blankets as he did not know that one could slip underneath them. He attempted suicide when Hardy's proposal to make him a Fellow of Trinity College was rejected by the college. He fell sick but, almost miraculously, through all this he discovered important mathematics. 'On Some Arithmetical Functions', a paper he wrote in 1916, has a big role to play in the story of Serre's conjecture and my work on it.

Ramanujan was able to achieve a lot despite all the handicaps that he faced and the almost complete lack of institutional support for him in an India that was still under the crushing yoke of British rule. More than Paranjpye's, it was Ramanujan's example that inspired Indians interested in the pure sciences, making them believe that they could make contributions at the highest level in spite of the odds stacked against them under colonial rule. The Nobel prize-winning physicist (and my almost namesake) S. Chandrasekhar was one of those inspired to take up science in the 1930s because of Ramanujan's example.

Seven decades later, there were some parallels between Ramanujan's travails and my life at Trinity College, Cambridge, which was also his college. Our backgrounds were very different. I was from an affluent family in independent India, had gone to fancy schools in Bombay, and generally had far more social capital available to negotiate life as a foreign student in Cambridge. Yet, there were similarities. Some of Ramanujan's Brahminical scruples and the resulting inhibitions and internal pressures were also ingrained in me from childhood. Like him I was vegetarian. There was certainly more vegetarian food to be had in 1986 than seven decades earlier, but the highlight was Welsh rarebit, an unexciting bread and cheese dish. In the three years I spent there, I never drank a drop of alcohol, missing out on all the excellent port and sherry and claret that Trinity famously had in its cellars.

India had long ceased to be a British colony by the time I arrived as a student in Cambridge, but there was still a certain complexity to the ties that bound Indians and the English. A memory that stands out from my early days in Cambridge is of being approached by a homeless man when walking down King's Parade with my parents. My father grandly took out a crisp 20-pound note and gave it to him. Although it was done on the spur of the moment, it was almost a political act declaring that India was no longer a colony.

And there were the travails of the cold and fickle English weather. When I arrived in October with my parents, a week ahead of term, our Bombay-bred bodies felt like they were shrivelling up underneath our multiple layers of clothing. Someone who had studied here had warned us that the land between Cambridge and Siberia was mostly flat, and its cold winds blew all the way here. It seemed to be true. I have a vivid memory of a Christmas break I spent at Cambridge. With most students away, I felt like the resident ghost of the college. Days were short. There was just the company of the indigent homeless to be found at the public library – slouched outside its doors with their dogs, slumped on sofas inside smelling of alcohol – a Noah's Ark for lost souls. Walking against a cold, cutting wind that tunnelled through the deserted narrow Trinity Street at night, one felt reduced to one's shivering body.

Ramanujan fell ill in England partly because of his struggles with the diet and weather there. A well-known anecdote about the friendship between Hardy and Ramanujan relates to a time when the latter was convalescing from an illness at a sanatorium in England. To cheer Ramanujan up, or maybe to provoke him, Hardy said that the licence number, 1729, of the cab he had taken did not seem special in any way. Ramanujan remarked that on the contrary it was very interesting, because it was the smallest number that can be written as the sum of two cubes in two different ways: $1729 = 10^3 + 9^3 = 12^3 + 1^3$.

∞

Our first-year lectures were held in a massive lecture hall with more than two hundred students squeezing into one room. The lectures were university-wide, bringing together students from different colleges, and all the maths students entering Cambridge had to attend mandatory courses. The air would become fetid, and there were bouts of sneezing and coughing. Once a girl even fainted in the lecture hall and the students had to be evacuated. We had to take both pure and applied mathematics courses, and I did not enjoy being made to study fluid mechanics and mathematical physics. In fact, the applied mathematics courses made me almost regret not going to Yale or another US university in which one did not specialize right away, and where I could have done pure maths courses and supplemented them with other courses in literature and philosophy and languages, subjects much more to my taste.

Some of our lecturers were charismatic, like Dr J.M.E. Hyland, who taught linear algebra, and was a logician. He imbued some of the material with a philosophical and mysterious air, and even now these concepts carry for me the charge he endowed them with. He riffed on the notion of 'dual of a vector space V' and the fact that 'the dual of the dual of a vector space V is canonically isomorphic to V'. Isomorphism between two objects means that they can be identified with each other. Confusion and controversy raged amongst students about what 'canonical' meant. It had a religious charge to it and stood for the mathematical ideal of being independent of all choices.

Many of the students were befuddled by Hyland's lectures on duality. He was probably guilty of playing up and exaggerating greatly the depth of things on which he discoursed. But the lectures took on the mad comic air of an episode of the 1980s political sitcom *Yes Minister* with Hyland tying the students up in knots of confusing, tongue-twisting statements reminiscent of Cabinet Secretary Sir Humphrey Appleby confusing his boss, Minister Jim Hacker, with his excessively complicated formulations. Like Appleby, Hyland invariably came out on the right side of debates.

He managed to point out something an objecting student had not considered in a putative counterexample to his assertion. I enjoyed the drama of Hyland's lectures, the back and forth between him and his students and the confusion he sowed in our minds that led to animated discussions. His polar opposite was Professor Alan Baker, who did not engage with students at all, and took to his heels after every lecture, almost fleeing in fear from any student who might want to ask him a question. He was a very distinguished mathematician, someone who had won a Fields Medal (as exalted as the Nobel prize for mathematicians) for his work in an area that, believe it or not, is called transcendental number theory.

The university-level lectures were complemented by college 'supervisions' in which pairs of students went to meet with a supervisor to discuss homework assignments and have their work checked. There were varying levels of sincerity among the supervisors. Some barely engaged with their students while others went above and beyond, and enthused students with their infectious love of the subject. The supervisions took us into the untidy homes of young couples with children bawling in the bedroom, at other times to basements with the footfalls of passing pedestrians falling like summary judgements.

∞

In my second year, I got to do more pure maths and my most memorable experience was learning group theory. The course was taught by Professor John Thompson, an American and an éminence grise in group theory. One of the most prominent mathematicians in Cambridge, he had won a Fields Medal for his work in group theory in the 1970s. It was an introductory course in group theory, and so the material was totally trivial for him. Yet he mumbled at the board and copied on to the blackboard from a textbook that he held open before his eyes. Students grumbled and complained about him.

In spite of his lecturing style, I found Professor Thompson very inspiring. He had a heavy beard and a fierce intensity in his eyes and persona. I would see him sometimes cycling down King's Parade with his head full of groups, I imagined. Though most of his audience probably found him excruciatingly boring, I found myself listening to him carefully. In the mumble of the lecture, he would sometimes drop a phrase that blazed in its evocativeness. 'You have to be really careful of this. It seems innocuous, but at times it can bite!' This was apropos a definition that was easy to misunderstand, and could lead one into making a grievous error. Something that seemed rather trivial in the text would become portentous: 'This simple thing can really build on itself, and the whole shebang could impose itself on you.' I imagined him in the American prairies, looking at distant horizons across limitless acres of cornfields, his thoughts resonating in those vast empty plains.

A good definition brings together many examples under one roof, identifying key structural elements which are common across them. The mathematical definition of 'group' is economical, and yet it allows for a rich array of examples.[13] Long before groups had been defined formally in the first half of the nineteenth century, they had already been an implicit, unnamed presence in many mathematical developments. Fermat, Euler, Legendre and Gauss had used what one now recognizes to be group theoretic ideas, related to multiplication of numbers in mod N arithmetic. Groups had arisen informally in Galois' study of symmetries of roots of polynomials and became one of the master topics of modern mathematics. Group theory studies symmetries for their own sake and is a vital area of pure mathematics.

After groups were formally defined, there arose the taxonomical task of classifying them. This turned out to be too hard a problem to solve completely, but by the 1980s, after decades of strenuous efforts by mathematicians working all over the world, the classification of all finite groups that further have a special property called *simple* (which does not mean 'easy'!) was completed. Without defining 'simple group' formally, we can just say that they are to groups what prime numbers are to numbers. Simple groups are the atomic elements in group theory, and all groups are made by 'combining' simple groups in a certain way. Around the time I studied there as an undergraduate, the massive programme of 'classifying finite simple groups' had been completed, with significant contributions by Cambridge mathematicians. One of Professor Thompson's landmark theorems is the Feit-Thompson theorem, a cornerstone in the classification of finite simple groups. It says: 'A finite group G whose size is an odd composite number is never simple.'

The proof of this one-sentence theorem takes up more than two hundred pages. The Feit-Thompson theorem reflects a surprising interaction between the size of a finite group G and a property like it being simple which is internal to the group G. The axioms defining a group are spare but, as illustrated by this theorem, lead to an unexpectedly rich structure.

I thought of a basic question in group theory and wrote a note to Professor Thompson about it. I went and dropped it off in his pigeonhole near the main office of the Department of Pure Mathematics and Mathematical Statistics (DPMMS) on Mill Lane. I must have given him my address as, to my delight, there was a note for me a few days later in my pigeonhole at Trinity College. Professor Thompson suggested that I go meet him in the common room of the DPMMS.

When I went to the common room, I felt like an impostor. There were models of the five regular polyhedra discovered by the Greeks in antiquity – cubes, tetrahedrons, octahedrons, dodecahedrons and icosahedrons – dangling from the ceiling.[14]

On worn sofas and low tables people sat drinking tea or coffee and playing games like chess and Go. The best minds in the country were locked in bloodless combat. Knots of people formed around an ongoing game, watching and commenting. This scene before me seemed like the Kingdom of Symmetry with citizens sipping cups of tea, consuming orange-flavoured Pims biscuits and absorbed in board games.

Professor Thompson retained his mystique at close quarters. So many decades later I remember neither the question nor his answer, although at that time it must have been burned into my mind. The atmosphere in the common room of the mathematics department on Mill Lane reminded me of the chess club in the compound of Zandu Pharmaceuticals that I had frequented in Bombay. In both places one felt a narrowing down of the world to something hard, intricate and specific, which needed and consumed all of one's attention.

∞

I discovered Western classical music in Cambridge by listening to BBC Radio 3. There was one particular programme, *Composer of the Week*, which got me hooked. Every week the programme intertwined the music of a composer with their biography. I remember in one episode hearing a stirring story about Johann Sebastian Bach, narrated in the soothing tones of the BBC presenter. Bach, as a twenty-year-old in 1705, had walked more than two hundred and fifty miles from Arnstadt to Lübeck to hear the renowned Dieterich

Buxtehude play the organ. Already a virtuosic organist known for his dazzling improvisations, Bach still wanted to expand his techniques and repertoire. He stopped at inns in the night, for a meal washed down by beer and to rest his legs, weary after having walked all day. By the next morning he had recovered and hit the road again with a spring in his step. His ears strained to hear the notes of Buxtehude, imagining the great master at the organ, almost like a worker at a loom, busy, pulling the stops, working the pedals. Bach walked with music filling his head, trying out ideas for the chorales and preludes he had to write for the congregation at Arnstadt. Bach stayed at Lübeck for four months, far exceeding the leave of one month he had obtained from his employers. Quick learner that he was, four months perhaps was long enough for him to learn from the older Buxtehude dazzling new tricks of the trade. Bach justified his prolonged absence to his employers in Arnstadt thus: he would be able to better serve them for having become a better musician. I found these stories of apprenticeship leading to mastery of a difficult art form compelling. Bach's prodigious journey to Lübeck had echoes for me of my grandfather as a boy of ten walking miles to find a teacher.

In the third and final year of the Mathematical Tripos, called Part II, students could at last focus on what they liked, and I took courses only in pure mathematics. One of the courses in the third year that made a lasting impact on my mathematical career was the one on Galois theory. I read and learned more about it on my own. The mathematical ideas were novel and beautiful, and there was also the romance of the remarkable story of Évariste Galois.

Here is a fuller account of how his work revolutionized the study of polynomial equations and the search to find formulas for the roots (or solutions) of polynomial equations. For equations of degree 2 the formula was known to the Babylonians and in ancient India. For degree 3 equations the formula was obtained in Italy in the sixteenth century. Degree 4 equations yielded to an extension of the method that had worked for cubic equations. Then progress stalled.

A surprising development at the beginning of the nineteenth century showed that there could be no formula in terms of 'radicals' for the roots of general equations of degree 5 and higher. Soon after, Galois, then a teenager living in Paris, got to the heart of the matter. Rather than finding formulas for the roots of the polynomial equation, he studied the symmetries of the roots taken as an ensemble. Galois focused on the 'symmetries' that preserved all the relations between the roots. The symmetries of the roots that Galois attached to a polynomial, now called its *Galois group*, measured the difficulty of finding its roots. We will call the symmetries of an equation its *Galois symmetries*. There is a dichotomy between the symmetries: if the roots have many symmetries, they corral the roots into such a tight formation that the roots cannot be captured by simple formulas. On the other hand, if the Galois group is *solvable* (a precisely defined property that can be checked easily), then there is a formula for the roots expressible in terms of radicals. Galois submitted his manuscript to the Académie Francaise. But senior mathematicians like Joseph Fourier and Augustin-Louis Cauchy lost his manuscript, and his ideas were neglected during his tragically short life.

The theory he developed, now called Galois theory, is central to mathematics. Understanding a mathematical object by the study of its symmetries is now one of the key guiding ideas in pure mathematics. Sometimes the equations might get too complicated, as Galois found for many polynomial equations of degree greater than four, to solve explicitly. Instead, thinking of the equations more abstractly, like considering symmetries of their solutions, might give insights which brute force computations are not able to.

Galois got into trouble with authorities all the time. At his school, the famous Lycée Louis-le-Grand, he put off his instructors by his impudence and in-your-face brilliance. He was twice refused admission to one of the most sought after institutions, École Polytechnique. Legend has it that he threw a duster at his examiners in frustration. Galois was subsequently admitted to the École Normale Supérieure, but was expelled from there as well for not obeying a curfew imposed by the director to keep the students out of trouble.

At the time, there were fights on the streets of Paris between the Republican guards and the Royalist forces of the monarch Louis Philippe. Galois was a Republican and was arrested for being at a meeting in which he raised a toast, with an open dagger, asking for the death of the monarch if he were to betray the people and not keep his promises. He was released on account of his youth. But he was soon back in prison for leading a rabble of armed Republicans across Pont Neuf, the famous bridge over the Seine. Like a moth dashing against the glass of a lamp, Galois could not help getting into trouble. He died in Paris in 1832, barely out of his teens, in a duel at dawn over a girl he probably did not care about that much, someone who had rejected him after a dalliance. He had predicted that he would die for a trivial reason, unable as he was to resist any provocation. Perhaps he could survive only in an idealized world of ideas, of groups and symmetries.

His ideas were granted posthumous legitimacy when the French mathematician Joseph Liouville studied them and declared them to be astonishing, profound and correct. As I have mentioned, the transformative ideas of Galois played a starring role in my own mathematical work and became its main protagonists.

Galois explained his mathematical philosophy in the preface of his final manuscript written from a prison in the days before his death:

> Go to the roots of these calculations! Group the operations. Classify them according to their complexities rather than their appearances! This, I believe, is the mission of future mathematicians. This is the road on which I am embarking in this work.[15]

In the Galois theory course I also learnt about Gauss's marvellous construction by straightedge (a ruler with no markings) and compass of the regular heptadecagon (a regular seventeen-sided polygon). Gauss's work used ideas of symmetry to study the roots of a particular polynomial of degree 16, which was germane to this construction. This was three decades before Galois' discovery of symmetry as a key tool in probing the nature of roots of general polynomials. Gauss's work was progress in this topic two thousand years after Euclid's straightedge and compass constructions of equilateral triangles and regular pentagons. Gauss gave a complete analysis of which regular polygons with N sides could be constructed using only straightedge and compass: for example, this was not possible for $N = 7, 9, 11$ and 13 but was possible for $N = 17, 257$ and 65537.[16] Gauss's work is a telling illustration of the power of abstraction, and in particular of the ideas of symmetry, to solve very concrete questions. Such was the pleasure Gauss found in this discovery that it made him decide to become a mathematician over his other love, studying languages.

The year 1796 was an *annus mirabilis* for Gauss – not only did he find his ruler and compass construction of the heptadecagon, but also proved the law of quadratic reciprocity. Discoveries coming thick and fast to a young brilliant mind is a recurring feature in mathematics. Isaac Newton had his year of wonders in 1666 when, as a 23-year-old, living in the village of Woolsthorpe-by-Colsterworth while London was in the grip of the plague and fires, he discovered the universal law of gravitation as well as calculus. There is a statue of him in the ante-chapel of the Trinity Chapel. Newton had lived in rooms on the Great Court of the college. His celebrated treatise *Principia Mathematica*, which changed the world fundamentally, was written here. An original copy of the book was in the college's Wren Library. I heard that the transcendental number theorist Alan Baker, who was my lecturer in the complex analysis course, occupied Newton's rooms in college. Strolling across Great Court, I would sometimes think of the great figures who had walked on its cobbled paths: not only Newton but also Byron who had kept a bear as a pet in his days at Trinity. The beauty of the centuries-old buildings of the college, the tree-lined path through The Backs of the college, the lovely Fellows' Garden (which I lived close to in my second year), gave Trinity a grandeur that smaller colleges did not have. It made up in some ways for the cosier sense of intimacy that studying at a smaller college might have offered.

Trinity College was a magnet for the best maths students, partly because of its storied reputation as the college of greats like Newton. While I was dazzled by the brilliance of some students I met, I still sensed that what I had as a relative advantage was often a stronger intuition and feel for the maths I cared about. This would be a strength throughout my career, not Ramanujan-level intuition, but strong intuition nevertheless which far surpassed my analytical powers.

∞

I had begun to cross the *cordon sanitaire* that separated undergraduates and graduates, and went to some advanced courses given in Part III of the Tripos. Part III (which students did in their fourth year) was a bridge year between undergraduate studies and entering a PhD programme. It had a good record of helping students make this transition. On the basis of having got a First in each of my first two years, I was offered a fully funded place to do Part III, conditional on my getting a First in my third year exams. In the Lent term of my final year I interviewed at Oxford for a place to do my graduate work. I took the bus from Cambridge to Oxford, a journey that took around three hours, and was interviewed by three number theorists of repute at the Mathematical Institute in Oxford.

The interview was anticlimactic: the panel, consisting of Bryan Birch, Roger Heath-Brown and Andrew Wiles, did not ask me a single mathematical question. I was too overawed by their reputations to engage them in conversation. The interview was over in less than half an hour. Wiles was slightly built and remained quiet but left a lasting impression on me. I had no idea when I met Wiles in Professor Birch's office that he was at that time spending the majority of his waking hours thinking about the elliptic symmetry conjecture and FLT. However, he had by then, even before his proof of FLT, proved landmark theorems, starting with his thesis written at Cambridge in the late 1970s.

After the rather perfunctory non-event of my interview, I was surprised to get a letter offering me a place to do my PhD at Oxford. Professor Birch advised me in his letter that it would be better for me to stay in Cambridge to do Part III and then come to Oxford, as that would give me time to mature as a mathematician and prepare me for research. But I also had the option of starting right after the Tripos. This offer, too, was conditional on my getting a First in my

Part II exams. Getting that First was my focus right now – I could take a call on whether to go straight to Oxford later.

∞

My mother came to be with me for moral support during the weeks of my final exams. The Tripos had been reformed since Senior Wrangler Paranjpye's time and was no longer regarded as one of the most gruelling intellectual challenges in the world. The exam was not the torturous and exacting test of endurance and mathematical skill it had once been. Problems that demanded devilish ingenuity and hard calculation to solve had been replaced by more conceptual ones which tested understanding rather than the ability to perform mathematical acrobatics. This had been part of Hardy's reform of the Mathematical Tripos. There was a disquieting development, though, more worrying than even the exams. My mother had an episode of excessive bleeding from the nose which scared us. We decided to skip my graduation ceremony and go home right after my exams.

Back in Bombay my mother went to see specialists and there was no clear diagnosis. She seemed to be doing okay, but we were anxious and unsettled as she was clearly not her former energetic self. When in Bombay I got a letter from my tutor, Dr P.M.H. Wilson, congratulating me on getting a First. Getting a First made me a Wrangler. As I did not top the exam, the fantasy of going back to India as a Senior Wrangler with crowds waiting on the tarmac as my plane landed, to be given a hero's welcome, remained unfulfilled. Not that there would have been crowds anyway as the feat had much less significance in an India that was not a British colony. However, my family was overjoyed with my success. It was something to celebrate in the gloom over my mother's health. Whenever my father spoke of me at this time, I always thought he was talking of someone very much like me, but far more successful.

∞

By the end of my visit home, I had decided to go to Oxford straight away, hoping to become Wiles's PhD student. I was going with a heavy heart as my mother's health was worrisome and I would have liked to be with her. But she would not hear of it. As luck would have it, by the time I arrived in Oxford in the autumn of 1989, Wiles had left to go back to Princeton. I would be Birch's PhD student instead. Yet the tenuous connection with Wiles would influence my path in mathematics. He would indirectly influence my choice of adviser when I moved later to California. I would browse his papers, not understanding much for several years.

Wiles came to occupy in my mind the place of an imaginary guru. I knew some precedents for co-opting as a teacher someone who existed in the real world, but whose relation to the student was founded principally in the student's imagination. I knew the story of Eklavya from the Mahabharata, a young boy from a low-born family who could not learn from the master archer Dronacharya, the famed guru of the royal families of the Kauravas and the Pandavas. As the next best thing, the boy made a statue of him and practised archery for hours in the gaze of the statue, and became an expert archer. The imaginary guru would not exist without the flesh-and-blood person from whom he was abstracted. The role he played in one's mind was almost symbolic, but still powerful. His role as a personification of a subject, as an ideal, as a guide and compass one found within oneself, made the relationship in its own way intimate and vital.

My time in Oxford was a disaster. There was no structure to cling to that year. Birch suggested a problem to me and gave me some papers to read. I did not know where to even begin. If I had stayed for Part III in Cambridge, as Birch had suggested, I would have had courses to do that might have prepared me better for the experience of trying to do research. I tried asking my old tutor Wilson if I could go back the following year to Cambridge to do Part III, but it was too late. I had made a wrong decision, one that could not be undone. I felt I had fallen vertiginously down a dark and bottomless shaft.

Meanwhile, my mother had seen a gastroenterologist in Bombay who diagnosed cirrhosis of the liver. This was almost a death sentence – cirrhosis was a chronic, wasting illness and her body would degrade over the years. My family had the means to take her to the United States for a liver transplant, but my mother did not want to undergo this massive, risky operation. Through many years of her illness, I was mostly away, fighting my own inner demons and battling with mathematics, and tended to be difficult and withdrawn with my family. Looking back on it now, I lament my behaviour with them during this period.

In Oxford I befriended Antonio, an older Brazilian student of Birch who was finishing up his thesis that year. Antonio had come on a scholarship from the Brazilian government to study at Oxford. I felt a certain affinity with him, probably owing to us both being from the developing world; we were darker than the English around us. His unshaven gruff look and small eyes made him look intense. He was friendly but also a bit detached, his smile almost a frown; the crinkling of his eyes when he smiled and the wry way he spoke made him seem wise and a little bemused, not cynical but perhaps a little disillusioned.

Antonio was at the end of his PhD, I was at the beginning. He did not seem very satisfied with what he had done in his thesis but Birch declared that it was enough to get a PhD. Antonio was at the end of his funding from the Brazilian government, and was living frugally to stretch his funds as far as they could go. He was going to return to his coastal home town of Recife to teach at a local university. But he feared that after going back there his mathematical research career would grind to a halt, and he would spend his weekdays teaching calculus, weekends grading homework and midterms, and his Oxford days would recede more and more into a remote past and eventually might seem like a distant dream.

Despite our respective disappointments, Antonio and I were able to do something together that would help shape the direction of my later work: we read the article 'Sur les représentations modulaires de degré 2 de Gal ($\overline{\mathbb{Q}}/\mathbb{Q}$)' in which Jean-Pierre Serre formulated his conjecture.

Serre's influential article published in the *Duke Mathematical Journal* in 1987 formulated in a precise form conjectures he had first made in a rougher form in 1973. It was rare to publish a paper in a prestigious research journal that formulated a conjecture. The norm was that papers had to state and prove theorems. Antonio and I decided to try and read Serre's paper and discuss it once a week. Serre's paper was in French and was written as a series of small sections with his conjectures printed as numbered statements or equations. The numbers were embellished with the symbol '?' to indicate that these were hoped for, conjectured, rather than proven statements or equalities.

We soon gave up on trying to understand the paper. Serre had arrived at these conjectures after the subject had reached a certain maturity. A research paper like this was not self-contained, it only had to be self-contained enough so that an informed reader could dive into it. Typically, such a reader would look through the few pages that set up the stage, recall notations and notions that were assumed to be part of the reader's mathematical background and arrive quickly at the parts of the paper that were new, in which the arguments, conjectures in this case, were original.

While I could see that Serre's conjecture was powerful as it implied FLT, I was a novice and lacked the maturity to get much out of Serre's paper. However, crossing paths with the conjecture early in my career was still fortuitous. I may not have followed the path I did had I not done so. There are many things in number theory one can pursue, and what you choose to study involves an element of happenstance.

Adrift as I was at Oxford, my family began to worry about my career and mental state. Abhyankar made things worse by playing mischief. He visited Oxford for a conference at which Serre and Thompson were speakers. I went for dinner with him, his wife, and a friend of mine. A few weeks later, he visited my parents in Bombay and told them that I was depressed and wandering unshaven, unkempt and penniless in Oxford. The part about my being penniless was especially galling since I had paid for the dinner! But there was a happy ending: My family got alarmed and my father, with his resourcefulness and faith in his ability to move mountains using his contacts, came to my rescue. Someone he knew put me in touch with Professor Dinakar Ramakrishnan, a number theorist at the California Institute of Technology (Caltech). He was surprisingly responsive and offered me admission in the PhD programme right away. He may have been well disposed towards a student from Oxbridge, and my performance in the Tripos may also have helped. I was happy with my new beginning.

∞

Back home from Oxford for a few weeks before going on to Caltech, I immersed myself in Serre's book *A Course in Arithmetic* when not worrying about my mother. She was in a relatively stable phase after a year full of crises and hospitalizations but her condition still needed close monitoring. I was prompted to study Serre's book by my difficulties in understanding his conjectures in Oxford. I felt I needed to know more about the context and background against which the conjectures had been made.

I had purchased *A Course in Arithmetic* when I was studying at Jai Hind College in Bombay, before I went to Cambridge. This was an advanced book, despite its elementary-sounding title. The Indian edition of the book was quite cheap. The binding of my copy had already started giving way, not because I wore the book out by my frequent study of it, but because of its poor quality. The stitches became visible, giving it the look of a well-worn garment that could be worn only at home. The paper it was printed on had a hue that was yellowish brown, like the colour of an old newspaper. The cover was a garish yellow. Curiously, the shoddiness deepened my appreciation of the contents.

Serre's book, translated from the original French, was based on lectures he had given to undergraduates at the École Normale Supérieure in Paris in the 1960s. The use of the word 'arithmetic' in this context went back to the Ancient Greeks, specifically Diophantus's *Arithmetica*. A more recent and relevant antecedent is Gauss's *Disquistiones Arithmeticae* written in Latin in the eighteenth century. Gauss's book encompassed all of the number theory of his time, a lot of it attributed to Gauss himself. Serre's book was in that lineage, although at a slender one hundred pages it did not cover all of modern number theory. It rather gave an introduction to some of its principal themes.

It did not feel like other textbooks prescribed for the undergraduate curriculum. The topics it dealt with had greater sophistication, the mathematics in it seemed alive. There were references to contemporary papers. Serre mentioned questions that had still not been resolved. One got the impression that one was seeing mere tips of icebergs of magnificent theories.

The last chapter of Serre's book is about *modular forms*. They are functions with many symmetries, and their symmetries are coarsely measured by two numbers, a level N and a weight k, attached to each modular form. (Serre focuses on the level $N = 1$ case for his book.) Modular forms are ubiquitous in mathematics; in this book I call them *modular symmetries*. Modular symmetries, or rather their proxies that we call *Ramanujan symmetries*, and *Galois symmetries*, are the two main characters in the mathematical tale of Serre's conjecture, and will loom large later in this book.

The number theorist Martin Eichler once said that modular forms are the fifth operation in arithmetic, besides addition, subtraction, multiplication and division. Not quite the classification of operations one encounters in *Alice's Adventures in Wonderland*. 'Reeling and Writhing of course, to begin with,' the Mock Turtle replied, 'and the different branches of arithmetic-ambition, distraction, uglification, and derision.'

Serre introduces the Ramanujan Δ-function ('delta-function') and talks about Ramanujan's prophetic work on it in the 1916 paper 'On Some Arithmetical Functions' written when he was in Cambridge. The Δ-function for our purposes is defined by the nice formula:

$$\Delta(T) = T(1 - T)^{24}(1 - T^2)^{24}(1 - T^3)^{24}(1 - T^4)^{24}(1 - T^5)^{24} \cdots$$

This when spelled out looks like:

$$\Delta(T) = \tau(1)T + \tau(2)T^2 + \tau(3)T^3 + \tau(4)T^4 + \tau(5)T^5 + \cdots$$
$$= T - 24T^2 + 252T^3 - 1472T^4 + 4830T^5 + \cdots$$

The Δ-function is a modular symmetry of weight $k = 12$ and level $N = 1$. Ramanujan studied the values $\tau(n)$ of what is now called Ramanujan's τ-function ('tau-function'). The Δ and τ-functions play a pivotal role in the story of Serre's conjecture, both in how Serre came to make his conjecture, and in its proof in my work with Jean-Pierre Wintenberger. This lay almost two decades in the future when I studied Serre's book.[17]

The problem that led Ramanujan to consider the numbers $\tau(n)$ has perhaps fallen by the wayside but in thinking about it he stumbled on his remarkable observations and conjectures about $\tau(n)$. In his 1916 paper, based on his computation of the first 30 values of $\tau(n)$, Ramanujan makes his subtle observations about $\tau(n)$ that led to magnificent theories that came to grips with them. These theoretical developments have become part of the essential infrastructure of modern number theory.

Some of his eminent and generally sympathetic contemporaries like G.H. Hardy thought that Ramanujan might have drifted into the backwaters of mathematics in this work about $\tau(n)$, especially when he conjectured the delicate estimate $|\tau(q)| \leq 2q^{5.5}$ (for all primes q) in the third and last of his conjectures about $\tau(n)$. It was not clear at the time what significance this had, if any. The slightly weaker statement $|\tau(q)| \leq 2q^6$ is easy to prove and the power savings of 0.5, reducing the exponent from 6 to 5.5, that Ramanujan predicted might have seemed like pointless finesse. Hardy qualified his doubts by saying that 'the problem might have some features which made it not unworthy of Ramanujan's attention'. The conjecture $|\tau(q)| \leq 2q^{5.5}$ was proved almost six decades after it was proposed in

Ramanujan's 1916 paper and its generalizations (collectively called the Ramanujan conjectures) are at the heart of modern number theory. The prime number 691 belongs even more integrally to Ramanujan's legacy than the taxicab number 1729. Ramanujan in his 1916 paper observed the striking congruence $\tau(q) \equiv 1 + q^{11}$ (mod 691) for primes q that influenced number theory profoundly. We call this the *Ramanujan congruence*: congruence means that the numbers $\tau(q)$ and $1 + q^{11}$ leave the same remainder when divided by 691. For instance when $q = 23$, $\tau(23) = 18643272$ and $1 + 23^{11}$ both leave remainder 92 when divided by 691. The charm of the prime 691 lies in it being neither too small, like 2 or 3, nor too big[18] which makes it a perfect Goldilocks-sized prime. There is a clean line that can be drawn from the Ramanujan congruence to Serre's conjecture and Andrew Wiles's solution of FLT. Ramanujan found interesting mathematics in the unlikeliest corners. No one before him had thought of looking at congruences for numbers like $\tau(n)$. It took someone whose mathematical intuition brooked no boundaries to look into numbers like $\tau(n)$ and see in them such depths!

Ramanujan credited the goddess of Namakkal for his mathematical discoveries, saying that she placed the beautiful and baroque formulas he discovered on the tip of his tongue. Serre later told me that the way he understood this was that some of Ramanujan's discoveries came to him when he was half asleep. When I had advanced more in my career, I too sometimes felt that my ideas came from a source outside myself. One could court inspiration with obsessive effort, but at the moment of breakthrough one almost stepped aside, or became just a conduit, to let inspiration flow through. This made you feel lucky to have proven something that you could not claim full ownership of. Kishori Amonkar said that when her music was at its best, there was no singer and the song, they became one, and she became an incarnation of the raga. To lose the sense of self when creating something, to feel the sense of being taken over at the moment of breakthrough, seems to be a common factor in many acts of discovery and creation.

A textbook like *A Course in Arithmetic* is distinguished by its selection of topics and their clean presentation. It has been a big influence on many budding number theorists. Jean-Pierre Wintenberger later told me, 'If you want to learn a topic, and Serre has written something about it, he is the first source you should consult.' Serre was like a reliable tourist guide who would show you what was interesting in an area. Given the limited amount of time one had to learn about a topic, if you followed him, he ensured that you saw the most important parts of a region. Like a skilled landscaper, he was able to tame the wilderness of a subject. He also made you aware throughout the text of the pitfalls to be wary of when learning the material. Mathematical ideas were nuanced, one realized, and one could easily make mistakes by extrapolating from the known. I was reminded of John Thompson's exclamation 'This can bite!', alluding to such perils of innocent and ultimately fatal misunderstandings.

3

A Flailing Graduate Student

In England, the light often had a moody, watery quality, leading the eye from one thing to the next. Things almost drowned in the associations they evoked in me from the novels set in England that I had devoured in Bombay. Brooks babbled, breezes whispered in the leaves. Upon moving to Caltech in Pasadena, near Los Angeles, everything at first seemed much starker, the sun shone more brightly, and there was an overwhelming sense of space that separated everything under the wide Californian sky. To describe the difference in mathematical terms one might say that in England the world was continuous, things connected up with each other, while here the world seemed discrete, and the light emphasized differences between things. It was also a journey from the Old World to the New World. In Cambridge, the colleges were hundreds of years old. Caltech had been around for just about a hundred years.

The feeling I remember from my first few months at Caltech is of being in what seemed like a semi-permanent state of jet lag. It began with the physical jet lag of coming all the way across the world, and the body struggling to adjust to the twelve-and-a-half-hour time difference between Bombay and Los Angeles. Night was turned into day, day into night. The brutal physical feeling of jet lag receded, as it eventually does, but jet lag continued to be relevant as a metaphor of sorts to describe my unsettled emotional state for my first few months there. I would even go so far as to say it could describe almost all of the four and a half years, between 1990 and 1994, that I was to spend in Pasadena.

I had opted to share a two-bedroom apartment in Caltech graduate housing on Catalina Avenue with another randomly selected student. He had literally turned the clock on its head. He slept through most of the daylight hours and worked through the night, making jet lag a way of life for him. I rarely saw him, and it led me to sometimes wonder if my brief glimpses of him had been hallucinations. I logically knew they were not. I had only to open the fridge to know that I was not alone in the flat. The first time I did this, I almost screamed in fright. It was full of strange fantastical creatures with tentacles and antennas and eyes popping out. I had never had a flatmate in England and this introduction to life in an apartment with a seafood-eating, nocturnal flatmate was more than I could handle. I am sure if I had stayed longer I could have gotten my revenge by filling the apartment with the strong smells of Indian masalas. But I decided instead to ask for a change of apartment. I tamely settled for the known and familiar, and found a graduate student, Dhiraj Thakkar, also from Bombay, who was also in housing limbo. Dhiraj came from a very different part of Bombay and a less privileged background than mine. He had made his way to Caltech to study astronomy, after doing his undergraduate degree at IIT, overcoming challenges and hardships. His path to Caltech made me feel that I took too much for granted all the advantages I had grown up with.

I was one of nine first-year maths graduate students, all dumped into a big room on the ground floor of the Sloan building of the maths department. It was divided into cubicles and lit by bright white lights that burned 24/7. Many students worked late into the evening, an hour at which janitors came with their carts, cleaning blackboards and emptying dustbins that in the maths department served in part as receptacles of discarded ideas. My cubicle was right in the centre of the room. There were blackboards on the walls. We were a motley crew from all over the world and one could count at least five nationalities in the warehouse-like office. My fellow students had come from as close by as Canada, and as far as China, Hong Kong, South Korea, India and Ireland. I am not sure if there was any American in the room.

∞

The graduate programme at Caltech provided funding for five years to write a thesis that could earn you a PhD. The first year consisted of basic courses in algebra, analysis and topology, and at the end of the year you had to pass 'qualifying exams' in two of the three subjects. You then moved on to more specialized reading courses with faculty who could potentially be PhD advisers. Once you had an adviser, typically sometime in the third year, you had a problem to work on. Ideally, you would have essentially solved the problem, or made significant enough progress, to have enough material to write a thesis by around the beginning of the fifth year. The point of the thesis was to solve a problem, in other words to find and prove a theorem, that had not been proved before. This was also the point at which you applied and went on the job market for postdoctoral positions. These postdoc positions typically lasted for three years and were a period in which you could build on your thesis and also do new work beyond it. One had a mentor in this phase as well, but the connection to the mentor was less tight than with an adviser and you were more on your own. Of course there were many variations of this schedule, but broadly this was the timeline the department envisaged for the typical student. Throughout, I would also be working as a teaching assistant to earn my stipend, grading homework and, once a week, leading a discussion.

Galois theory and group theory, topics that I had studied enthusiastically in Cambridge, were the mainstays of the algebra course. Analysis was mathematics of the continuous and a subject which had its origins in calculus. Topology was the mathematics of shapes, and sought to classify spaces using algebraic invariants. After plunging into research at Oxford, even if not successfully, I found it hard to buckle down to do coursework again at Caltech. I felt like someone who had failed a class and had been kept back for another year. I asked to test out of the first-year algebra course, and barely managed to pass the written and oral qualifying exam I was given. While my fellow students would be hard at work doing an assignment for a course late at night in our office, I would struggle to work at my desk and turn in shoddily written work. I made friends with Haseo Ki, the Korean student in my program. He thought I had the understanding and intuition to solve the trickiest problems, but lacked the discipline to write down rigorous solutions.

A traumatic day towards the latter part of my first year is still etched in my mind. I had not spent enough time studying for the oral exam in topology. I had stayed up all night to prepare for it. Trying to make up at the last minute for a year's worth of wasted time, Shakespeare's famous line floated into my head: 'I wasted time and now doth time waste me.' One of my examiners would be the professor who had taught the first-year topology course. He was vaunted for his visual intuition but could not communicate it to the students in his class. In class he often spent up to half a minute or more at the blackboard staring at his shoes as if struggling with bringing himself to say the next thing; he could have been struggling to convert into coherent exposition visualizations of mathematical objects crowding his mind. Unlike Thompson in Cambridge, whom I had found inspiring despite his poor lecturing style, I did not find my topology professor simpatico. I often skipped his lectures or when I did attend, stopped paying attention after the first few minutes. I was also negligent in turning in assignments and doing the work for the course. The only way I could deal with my hopeless state on the day of the topology exam was by representing it to myself as a burlesque.

∞

I set out from my apartment on Catalina Avenue early to go to the department. The morning light is the kind of light painters like to paint in. The palm trees on the way to the department seem joyful, exulting in the waxing light. I pass the library by a fountain-splashed pond. A bridge is arched in pleasure over the pond. The campus is a popular venue for wedding shoots which take place on weekends, and I have seen couples posing on the bridge. I am led into the room where the exam is going to be conducted. In my fevered state, it feels like a monk's cell with a window letting in gorgeous southern Californian light. I imagine a crucifix set on a wooden table, a candlestand beside it, and a bed which could double up as a wrack: a space of torture and repose. There is a long conference table taking up almost the whole room. Two professors are at the table gossiping about departmental politics. Before them is a dossier in which all my sins – grades in the first year courses – are chronicled. The two topologists offer a study in contrast. One is rubicund with a sunny disposition. The other lanky one is whose coursework I had dodged. Now the day of reckoning has arrived. I feel it in my bones that this is not going to end well.

Rubicund topologist:
Shall we get going? It should not take too long.
(*He looks expectantly at his colleague.*)
Gaunt topologist:
Ummm... (*Looking down at the sheaf of papers*)
I had you in my class.
Let's see how things have progressed.
(*Significant pause*)
Can we start with fundamental groups?
Van Kampen's theorem?
Me:
The Van Kampen theorem states...
Rubicund topologist:
I think you are forgetting some hypothesis.
Of connectedness?
Gaunt topologist: (growing agitated)
Please state the theorem precisely.
Me:
Oh sorry!
I meant to say that subspaces are path-connected.
Gaunt topologist:
That's not good enough.
Intentions are no good here.
I want you to know things well.

A Flailing Graduate Student

You can't try and wing this exam.
(*Goes up to the board, draws a skein of lines*
blurring pink and blue squiggly lines
like the nervous system of an exotic animal)
Can you use this theorem
After you state it precisely
To compute the fundamental group of this space?
Me:
I can try...
A disastrous end seems nigh to me.
Me:
Each of the spaces has π_1 that is cyclic of order 2.
Rubicund topologist:
That's a good start...
Gaunt topologist:
Why? Give us a precise explanation.
Me:
I hem and haw, try and wriggle my way out of a tight corner.
Gaunt topologist (getting riled up):
Let's see if you can do better
With covering spaces.
Homology and cohomology groups.
The universal coefficient theorem.
(*The viva voce hurtles to its ineluctable conclusion.*
My mind is addled,
My face burning with shame.)
Rubicund topologist: (putting an end to my misery)
Okay. You can leave the room.
Come back in 10 minutes.

I walk outside the building. The sun has risen in the sky. Then I go back and knock at the door of the room which is ajar. Light streams in, setting ablaze the unkempt hair of the gaunt topologist.

Gaunt topologist: (*gets up, exercised, starts pacing up and down*)
I think I know students like you.
Trying to get by, coast through a course
I want you to remember this humiliation
Learn a lesson here today right now
That will teach you not to get by with half-knowledge.
(Hands buried in his back pockets he walks to and fro
Speech halting as if impaired by a
barely controlled rage.
Hard to tell how angry he is as his speech always has the tortuous quality of toothpaste extruded from a tube in its death throes.)
I would have liked it better if you had told us
At the get go
I am not prepared.
If you had been honest about it.
I can't stand sham and pretence.
I want you to remember this failure
So that you get a pain in the pit of your stomach
Next time you try to get by with guesses
And half-truths.
Rubicund topologist:
(Wanting this done with, mildly embarrassed with colleague's fit of temper)
We seem all done then.
You have failed this attempt. Better luck next time.

I was ready to pack up and leave. I felt despondent about my future as a mathematician. Did I have the intellect and discipline, the work ethic, to keep going? I had been a competent exam-taker, managing firsts at Cambridge but the mathematics was harder now, and I wondered if my exam-taking talents had deserted me with age. I tried to shore myself up by telling myself that if I survived being a graduate student, it would not matter how hard or how little I had worked. What mattered was how good a thesis I was able to write, and the quality of the theorems I managed to prove. What saved me from abject despair is that sense I have always had, that I have strong intuition, be it in mathematics, reading someone's mood or sensing quality, be it in a piece of writing or a mathematical argument. But so far I had nothing to show for it. I joked rather self-pityingly to a friend that my entire life did not even amount to a line in a poem.

On coming back to the apartment on Catalina Avenue, Dhiraj persuaded me to wait till the end of the academic year before taking any drastic steps. Students were allowed more than one attempt at passing the qualifying exams so I had another stab. This time the faculty on the committee was different. I did a bit better, and felt reprieved. It was a great relief to have navigated past the shoals of the qualifying exams. Now, along with most of my fellow students I was sailing on the wide open seas, trying to read more deeply into an area which was close to the research interests of one of the Caltech faculty. I felt I should choose my adviser and area of specialization with care.

∞

It was Wiles who led me, in a manner of speaking, to Professor Haruzo Hida who worked at UCLA. Wiles's mathematical output had been influenced by Hida's work, and I came across references to

Hida in Wiles's papers. As UCLA was not far from Caltech (both being in the greater Los Angeles area), I decided to try and see if he would accept me as his student. Professor Hida, who was dressed, I recall, with striking formality for California, accepted me as a student without much fuss. What sealed the deal was that Dinakar Ramakrishnan allowed me to work with Professor Hida instead of himself, though he did remain my adviser as far as Caltech was concerned. It was a presumptuous thing to do, to look for an adviser outside Caltech, and a less generous person might have been offended. Ramakrishnan did warn me that the funding from Caltech would run out after five years, and so I had to finish in that period; even if I was switching advisers, my time had started when I joined Caltech. Thus I officially became the unofficial student of Professor Hida.

Hida was a self-made mathematician. In his undergraduate days, Kyoto University was shut down for months by student strikes. He was majoring then in chemistry but got interested in maths and studied on his own. He made rapid progress and soon was proving theorems that made the maths world sit up and take notice. He worked for a few years as a professor at the university in Sapporo, on the second largest island of Japan, Hokkaido, before coming to UCLA. It was in the department in Sapporo that he proved some of his famous theorems that had impacted Wiles's work amongst others.

Hida asked me to come to UCLA for a weekly meeting with him. He had an American student working with him at the time who lectured to him every week in his office from Hida's notes of a course he had given in Paris on his revolutionary theory of 'families of p-adic modular forms'. The notes were in French. In a graduate programme in a maths department in the US, there was typically a language requirement. One was asked to translate a short passage of a maths paper written either in French, German or Russian into English. Like most students I had chosen French, as that was the language easiest to wing for this exam if one had a fair command of English. The choice of French, German and Russian was steeped in history. These were the languages, along with English, most used in the mathematical literature of the nineteenth century, and even well into the twentieth century. I knew very little French – I would struggle reading a French newspaper – but the range of French words used in a maths paper is more limited in scope, and so it was actually easier to read.

In our weekly meetings in Hida's office, his other student and I took turns in lecturing to Hida from his French notes. Hida did not say much, except to correct us when, in transcribing from his notes on to the blackboard in his office, like novice drivers we drove straight into one of the potholes in the theory. He could perhaps easily anticipate the points at which we would stumble. Sometimes he would go to the board himself, and explain what the point of the argument was which I had been second-guessing. I struggled as I tried to understand his French notes. The difficulty was not the French, even if I did not know that language well, but rather the maths. I read Hida's notes without getting an intuitive sense of the mathematics in it, like staring at a score of music without getting any sense of the melody.

There seemed a difference in the way his other student and I related to the material we were lecturing on, and our obvious struggles with it. He thought it was the fault of the complicated material in Hida's notes, or its exposition, that it was so hard to understand. I ascribed the shortcomings to myself.

I found Hida a little intimidating, partly because of having heard about the powerful new theory, now called 'Hida theory', that he had invented. It was a rare feat to invent a theory. Mathematicians were roughly classified into theory builders and problem solvers and the former breed was rarer. When I got to know Hida better towards the end of my graduate student days and later, I realized that my initial, somewhat daunting, impressions of his formality and reticence were deceptive, and that he could be quite informal and garrulous.

∞

The setting of Hida's work is the world of 'p-adic numbers', a world that was to figure largely in my mathematical career. The proof of Serre's conjecture in my later work with Wintenberger would take place in this brave new world of p-adic numbers. Like most new concepts in mathematics, p-adic numbers arose organically, and were created to help solve basic questions about solving equations in numbers that number theorists have been preoccupied with for millennia.

The p-adic numbers evolved from the usual numbers …, –3, –2, –1, 0, 1, 2, 3, … The nineteenth-century German mathematician Leopold Kronecker said: 'God made the integers, the rest is the work of man.' Thus in the beginning were the whole numbers and their negative counterparts (collectively called integers), and their ratios (which are often called fractions). We will call them 'rational numbers'. These were regarded as perfect and wholesome. The Pythagorean sect of mathematics in Ancient Greece made rational numbers the basis of their worldview.

Pythagoreans were traumatized by the discovery that there are numbers that are not rational. The hypotenuse of a right-angled triangle with sides equal to 1, has length $\sqrt{2}$ (the square root of 2) which they proved is not rational. This shook their beliefs to the core and led to the collapse of the cult. Numbers like $\sqrt{2}$ are called irrational numbers. The name itself suggests that irrational numbers were regarded as sinister and dangerous.[19]

After the Pythagoreans, irrationals were accepted and the rationals were 'completed' by adding all the irrationals in to give us the real number line. The irrational numbers have decimal expansions that go on indefinitely and do not recur. Completion refers to the passage from the fractions to all the numbers on the number line, filling in the numerous 'holes' left by the missing irrational numbers; $\sqrt{2} = 1.4142 \ldots$ is an example.

In the nineteenth century, Georg Cantor showed that in a precise sense there are many more irrational numbers than there are rational ones, which accords with our intuition that there is more irrationality than rationality in the world!

At the end of the nineteenth century, Kurt Hensel realized that there were other ways to 'fill in the holes' of the rational numbers besides the real numbers. For each prime p, there is a 'p-adic completion' which gives rise to the totally new number system called the p-adic numbers. These arise from a novel notion of p-adic distance between fractions that depends on p.

In my later work the process of 'lifting' a 'mod p symmetry' to a 'p-adic symmetry', and conversely 'reducing' a 'p-adic symmetry' to a 'mod p symmetry' would figure in a big way. To illustrate the procedures of 'lifting' and 'reducing' in the simpler case of just p-adic numbers, rather than p-adic symmetries, let's take for concreteness $p = 5$. The integer 2 mod 5 can be 'lifted' to many integers mod 5^2, namely 2, 7, 12, 17, 22. We can continue the 'lifting' process mod higher and higher powers of 5. In the other direction, given an integer like 123 mod 53, we can 'reduce' it mod 5^2 to get 23, and mod 5 to get 3. Later in the book I will focus on congruences between

'p-adic Galois symmetries'. This generalizes the simpler concept of congruences between numbers: for instance the congruence $7 \equiv 12 \pmod 5$. In fact all of the lifts of the number 2 mod 5 to 2, 7, 12, 17, 22 mod 5^2 are *congruent* to 2 mod 5. The p-adic number system is built on such congruences: it expresses information modulo p^n simultaneously for all n in a visual way by using a new concept of distance.

We can think of p-adic numbers in analogy with the numbers we usually encounter which are in 'base 10'. For instance a number like 4783 is 3 mod 10 (its last digit), 83 mod $10^2 = 100$ (its last two digits), 783 mod 1000: the number 4783 is like a tower with its truncations 3, 83, 783 rising up to it. The p-adic numbers are analogous to the usual numbers which we write in base 10 – with digits being the remainders 0, 1, ... , 9 modulo 10 – except that the digits are the remainders 0, 1, ... , $p-1$ mod p, and we allow infinitely many digits like in a decimal expansion. This would make sense in a topsy-turvy world in which positive powers of 10 (like 10^{56}) are 'small' while negative powers of 10 (like 10^{-113}) are 'big': the prime p plays a role akin to ⅒.[20] A p-adic number is like a skyscraper except that it is allowed to have infinitely many floors (this is the ideal world of mathematics after all, the usual constraints of reality are relaxed), with its mod p^n truncations being like towers which rise up to it. The p-adic world is an exotic place to inhabit at first, with its new notion of distance that has unusual properties.

The p-adic numbers add to our repertoire of numbers. They are not mere curiosities: if we ignore them we lose many vital aspects of the world that number theorists seek to understand. Once one understands the p-adic version of a question for *all* primes p, one is in a better position to understand the question for ordinary numbers. A 'local-to-global principle' asserts that in some favourable situations, having solutions of a system of equations in the p-adic numbers for every prime p implies there is a solution in the rationals. When such a principle is true for equations, it is highly prized. This local-to-global strategy used in number theory is similar in spirit to the credo of environmentalists to 'think globally, act locally'. The urgent questions to tackle are of a global nature, but one can only hope to make incremental progress by actions that directly impact one's neighbourhood. This cemented my vague understanding during my senior school years in Bombay about the strategy number theorists use to understand questions in integers by first studying their easier analogues in mod p arithmetic.

∞

There are varying estimates about how many hours it takes to get good at something challenging: at something that needs technical smarts and creativity it could be 10,000 hours, could even be 20,000. I often thought during my days in Pasadena that the time I needed surpassed all these estimates. The pressing question that haunted me through my years as a graduate student was: how could one log in those hours, keep at something when one was not yet good at it, in order to ultimately get good at it? If one was good at something, I imagined it would be easier to work hard at it, the effort would be frictionless, or at least well-lubricated; it might be like floating in a regime of lower gravity, rather than being weighed down by feelings of inadequacy that further impeded efforts. Learning and acquiring expertise in an area of mathematics, grinding one's way through the basics and absorbing the abstract and initially unmotivated formalism, was sometimes psychologically very hard and grating on one's brain. One had to tell oneself that this was all worth it, that it would lead to the striking theorems for which this was preparatory material. One felt the unease and nervousness of an audience, looking on to a stage with all the props set out but the main characters missing, wondering if anything would ever happen.

For months after passing the exams I still struggled to work systematically. I kept oscillating between my room on Catalina Avenue and the Caltech maths department on California Boulevard just a few blocks away. I tried to go to the department at what felt like a propitious hour when the early morning light was still tentative. I would leave my apartment full of energy, bent on spending the hours before lunch reading a chapter of a book, or a paper that I had been asked to read. The first thing I did when I got to the department was check my mailbox, although there was little chance someone would have left a note overnight. The department office was still shut. I went to my office, and leafed through a book, put my head on the desk, and then got up and walked around the small room. The goal of proving a new theorem seemed a mammoth, almost impossible, task.

The campus began coming alive. I heard the beeping of a delivery vehicle. I rode the elevator to the eighth floor of the library building, the floor with the maths books. I frequented particular sections of the floor that had books I hoped to master with time. The book racks occupied the centre of the floor with reading desks at the periphery. Passing the tall, narrow windows by each reading desk, I caught glimpses in successive frames of the Spanish-style buildings of the campus, of the fountain next to the ornamental bridge, of the campus auditorium, like a birthday cake covered with white frosting, then of the San Gabriel range in the distance. The San Gabriel valley held the campus in its outspread palm. The institute was small, but had played a big role in the scientific developments of the twentieth century.

Now it was time for some coffee, at the Red Door Cafe, or sometimes at the lounge in the department which had inferior coffee, but was closer. Near the lounge there was a smaller departmental library that had issues of older journals. I could wander into it and easily while away half an hour, looking at old papers by famous mathematicians in my area. Windowless and lying between two corridors running along its sides, the departmental library was small, perhaps no more than a hundred square feet. Stepping into it felt like descending into a cool well. I knew with some accuracy the placement of the journals: *Annals of Mathematics*, *Inventiones mathematicae* and other prestigious journals. I could probably go and pick out a particular volume even in the dark.

I eventually made it back to my office which was just a few doors away from the windowless library. I sat at my desk. From my window I looked down on the no man's land between the maths and physics departments. It had rows of roses, a few benches, and a small tiled fountain. As graduate students in a rich and small institute, we were spoiled. After our first year, we had offices with windows, rather than being banished to a windowless netherworld which was often the fate of graduate students in bigger departments

By now the flame of my morning optimism was guttering. It was almost time for lunch. I decided that I needed to walk to clear my mind, to think things over. I walked the streets of Pasadena past the Middle Eastern shop that sold baklava, heavy with honey and almond paste. One piece of it would suffice for lunch. I walked towards the San Gabriel mountains, getting no closer to them. When I came back to my office after the walk, Haseo, who was now my office-mate, was working at his desk, staring at the wall in front of him. He often berated me for my malingering, and would say: 'You have read enough, you know a lot of things. Think of a problem, man, focus!' He was already ahead in the game. He had gotten through the coursework, and was making progress on his thesis problem. I was still lost, browsing endlessly through papers and books, trying to find my footing. Mathematicians in various specialities – number theorists, algebraic geometers, topologists, logicians – from all over the world visited the institute to give talks about their latest results. The speakers were like nomadic troubadours wandering the academic globe, giving seminar talks, at one maths department after another, on their latest theorems. I would catch a seminar in the afternoon. It felt sometimes like going to a cinema hall for a matinee show, yet another way of putting off doing one's own work. There was tea afterwards in the lounge on the third floor of the maths department. It was soon time to call it an evening.

The sun rose
Having nothing else to do
And set, having seen nothing new.

This was the way I misremembered these lines from Samuel Beckett. 'The sun shone, having no alternative, on the nothing new.'

The experience of being a graduate student, given five years to write a thesis, seemed oftentimes like being given enough rope to hang.

4

Reading the Masters

I had seen Serre before, at Oxford, but I only really felt his vigorous, engaged presence when I saw him at a conference in Seattle at the end of my first year in Pasadena. Serre, who was one of the conference organizers, gave a series of lectures on the 'yoga of motives', a guiding philosophy that had been formulated by the influential geometer Alexander Grothendieck in the 1960s. It was a form of inspired guesswork. You made arguments you could not justify logically in the hope they would lead you somewhere. Serre had played a crucial role in forming Grothendieck's ideas; they had both worked in Paris.

The motivic philosophy was almost metaphysical. According to it, the objects one encountered in number theory were realizations or 'avatars' of an elusive structure that Grothendieck called a 'motive'. Mathematicians, the argument went, often had access only to manifestations, or realizations, of these motives. Motives themselves remained elusive; still they were a powerful heuristic leading to the discovery of new mathematics. The existence of motives would explain why mathematical data that superficially looked disparate seemed to correlate uncannily. If the different sets of data were descriptions of the same object this would explain their mysterious concordance. It was as if one had access to observations made about a mountain from different trails to the top through the mist, even if the mountain itself lay shrouded.

Grothendieck had been inspired by Weil, who was interested in Indian philosophy and Sanskrit, and his influence had probably been responsible for introducing Sanskrit words (like 'yoga' and 'avatar') into this branch of mathematics. Although the philosophy of motives was largely conjectural, it made concrete predictions, and Serre's lectures focused on these. He talked about some of his very influential work in which he had proved some of these predictions. Such proofs could be seen as evidence for the existence of motives.

I understood very little during the conference in Seattle, but still got the sense that this was an exciting subject, mature and yet very much alive. Great strides had been made, yet many open questions – even the most important questions – remained unresolved. In fact Serre had raised a number of open questions in his lectures.

I was also very struck by Serre's personality. He was then in his 60s. He sat in the first couple of rows and often interrupted the speaker, wanting some clarification about the notation used or greater precision in the formulation of a statement that the speaker had made. Later I heard him say that it was okay for a speaker to be dry and technical, but they had to be precise, or to be hand-wavy, as long as they were inspiring; the worst speakers were those who gave dry, uninspiring technical lectures, and yet were imprecise! I could think of a few like that. Serre was short and energetic, and was often in animated conversation with colleagues and students. A keen and competitive ping-pong player, he played with the younger lot in the evenings and mostly won. He relied on his strong defence and wore his opponents out by absorbing their aggression and returning all their attacking shots. I did not talk to him; I felt like too much of a novice.

∞

I was quick, however, to snap up the three volumes of Serre's Collected Works. The German publication house Springer-Verlag, which had been a dominant force in mathematical publishing for decades, had an annual sale which was called the Yellow Sale referring to the the colour the publishing company most-used for its maths books. Bookshelves of mathematics books were often a haze of yellow, like a sunset in the abstract realm of mathematical ideas. For the price of a hundred-odd dollars (far more than I paid for *A Course in Arithmetic*), in my second year at Caltech, towards the end of 1991, I got three handsomely bound thick volumes of Serre's Collected Works in the mail, papers he had written over a period of thirty-five years. Many of them had represented breakthroughs when they were first written. At the end of each volume, Serre had added notes, pointing to future work done by him and others on the topic. The volumes came in a cardboard case, and for the rest of my graduate student years they were among my most treasured books. These volumes had blue covers rather than the usual yellow, each embossed with the name of the author in golden letters. All the books were beautifully produced, with thick creamy-white paper.

As you open each of the three volumes, there is a black-and-white photo of Serre. In the first, you see a young Serre with round glasses. He seems to have been caught in the frame just before racing away to create new theories solving old classical problems. Bursting on the mathematical scene in Paris in the 1950s, Serre had proved many fundamental results. In his doctoral thesis he had solved a long-standing problem in topology about computing 'homotopy groups of spheres'. Serre said later that some of the constructions he made in his thesis were so complicated that he could see them only lying down and staring at the ceiling. Otherwise, thinking of them gave him vertigo.

The first volume, covering Serre's work from 1949–1959, consists of papers mainly in algebraic topology, several complex variables and algebraic geometry. The papers Serre wrote on algebraic geometry led to Grothendieck's revolutionary work which recast the subject. Grothendieck reimagined the mathematical idea of space, much like Einstein had reimagined space–time in physics. These papers of Serre are widely used and quoted decades after they were written. And he had done all this work by the time he was thirty-two.

Just that volume would have ensured Serre a prominent place in the history of mathematics. I thought of a composer like Schubert who died when he was thirty-two. His music was a vital part of the canon. Volumes Two and Three of Serre's Collected Works made me think of all the beautiful and important music that Schubert never got to compose. Perhaps a closer comparison would be to Ramanujan whose life was also cut short at thirty-two. One could only marvel at the work ethic, besides the brilliance, needed to accomplish the work of these three volumes, easily running to over 1500 pages. To be gifted seemed wonderful, but the gift could also be like a tiger chasing one down a path, allowing very little repose. Talent would exert great pressure from within, as it pushed its way to realize itself, like seeds wanting to burst out of their pods. It also came with the responsibility to fulfil its promise; one was compelled to labour more than the average composer or journeyman mathematician.

The photo of Serre in his second volume, with papers from 1960–1971, shows a man of the world in his 40s, dressed in a jacket, with his adviser Henri Cartan. Serre credited his formation as a mathematician to the Cartan seminar in which new topics were presented every year, starting from scratch with all the details worked out. Serre gave many lectures in the Séminaire Cartan. Paris was a hive of mathematical activity. Just like designers, models, patrons and critics converge at Parisian fashion shows, mathematicians from all over the world came to participate in the important seminars taking place all over the city: Séminaire Cartan, Séminaire Chevalley, Séminaire Bourbaki. French mathematics had a distinctive tone and style: spare, elegant, formally innovative, modern. Serre was one of the key figures in the mathematical world of Paris, influencing mathematicians by his style, mathematical taste, exposition and research.

The third volume, covering the years 1972–1984, has a picture of Serre in his early 50s looking down, smiling: he was now a senior statesman of the subject. He had already achieved a lot, but had still more to accomplish. One of the papers in the volume is a paper written in 1975 which formulates his conjecture for the first time in print. The Duke paper in which he formulated the definitive form of his conjecture, and which I had struggled to fathom in my year at Oxford, was written after the period covered by the three volumes. Serre's oeuvre extended well beyond them. *A Course in Arithmetic* was one of several textbooks authored by him which were not in these volumes.

Serre was also part of a collective of mathematicians that used a *nom de plume*, Nicolas Bourbaki, for a series of books aiming to present all of pure mathematics from a clean modern viewpoint. They fell short of their objective, but still got very far. No individual got credit for the Bourbaki books. This was selfless work, done for the subject rather than oneself. The method of writing these books was that, first, someone made a draft which was ruthlessly criticized in meetings held in various locations in France. Someone else would then write another draft from scratch which received the same harsh treatment. The draft that finally prevailed was the one that emerged after many such iterations. The books had an idiosyncratic way of signalling to its reader the potential pitfalls: A road sign warning of a dangerous bend ahead would be placed beside paragraphs explaining why something that might seem plausible was actually wrong.

∞

Reading Serre's work made me feel I was making progress in learning mathematics that appealed to me, even if I was still adrift at Caltech. One of the pieces of mathematics that particularly resonated with me was the beautiful explanation found by Serre for Ramanujan's remarkable congruence for the values $\tau(n)$ of his 'tau-function'. The Ramanujan congruence $\tau(q) \equiv 1 + q^{11} \pmod{691}$ (for prime numbers q) dates from his 1916 paper. This congruence is striking as $\tau(q)$ itself is a complicated quantity, and there is this nice expression for it after looking at it modulo the Ramanujan prime 691. The prime 691 makes a surprising appearance here which begged explanation. Similar congruences were found by mathematicians working after Ramanujan modulo the primes 2, 3, 5, 7 and 23 in addition to the Ramanujan prime 691. The congruences were a puzzle: why congruences modulo these primes and no others?

Almost exactly 50 years later, Serre wrote about his structural explanation of Ramanujan's observations in a paper published in 1967 (the year I was born!); this paper can be found in the second volume of his Collected Works. It was the written account of a talk he gave in the Séminaire Delange-Pisot-Poitou. This was one of the many seminars that contributed to the hectic mathematical life of Paris. As I read this work of Serre, I felt for the first time the frisson that arises from understanding a piece of deep and beautiful mathematics; it felt almost like being shocked by touching a live wire!

In his seminar Serre conjectured that the Ramanujan Δ-function gave rise to 'Galois symmetries': the Ramanujan numbers $\tau(n)$ were thus given a higher meaning by their relation to such Galois symmetries. It seemed remarkable that modular symmetries like Δ should give rise to Galois symmetries as they a priori belong to different worlds. The Galois symmetries are denizens of the world of algebra, and thus beasts of a completely different sort than the Δ-function that at first sight belongs to the world of complex analysis (a subject that has its roots in the calculus of Newton and Leibniz).

Galois symmetries arise from the symmetries of solutions of systems of polynomial equations with coefficients that are rational numbers. The Galois symmetries attached to the Δ-function come in p-adic flavours for each prime p. Each of these Galois symmetries contain within them *local* Galois symmetries for each prime q. The local Galois symmetry for a prime q is given simply by knowing the number $\tau(q)$. For each prime p, the 'p-adic symmetry' has a shadow, the mod p Galois symmetry which arises from the p-adic one by reducing it mod p.[21]

Corralling the numbers $\tau(q)$ into Galois symmetries allows one to use many of the tools of modern mathematics to analyse them. Serre, collaborating with the British mathematician Peter Swinnerton-Dyer, used the hypothetical existence of the p-adic Galois symmetries arising from Δ to resolve the puzzle of why there were congruences for $\tau(n)$ modulo primes 2, 3, 5, 7, 23, 691, and no such congruences known for any of the other primes. Galois symmetries explained the congruences Ramanujan had discovered for the Δ-function, a little like how a detective might use a magnifying glass to find a vital clue that solves a case.

Pierre Deligne rapidly proved the existence of the p-adic Galois symmetries that Serre had conjectured should arise from Δ. Deligne's construction of these p-adic symmetries relies on powerful abstract machinery, in particular *étale cohomology*, developed by Grothendieck and his school in the 1960's at Institut des Hautes Études Scientifiques (IHES) located in the Bures-sur-Yvette suburb of Paris. Deligne was a student of Grothendieck.[22] The connection of $\tau(n)$ to Galois symmetries also led to Deligne's proof of the bound $|\tau(q)| \leq 2q^{5.5}$ almost six decades after Ramanujan conjectured it. Deligne won a Fields Medal for his proof. Ramanujan's work in 1916 had helped pave the way to this extravagance of mathematical riches!

The compatible systems of p-adic Galois symmetries attached to the Δ-function is an instance of the motivic philosophy which I had first heard about in the conference in Seattle. The Galois symmetries are manifestations of a motive attached to Δ; this motive was constructed many years after the work of Deligne which produced the manifestations.

Deligne attached Galois symmetries to all modular symmetries like the ones which were exposited in the last chapter of Serre's book *A Course in Arithmetic*. I am going to call the Galois symmetries arising from modular symmetries, like the ones arising from Δ-function, 'Ramanujan symmetries'. The conversion of modular symmetries to Ramanujan symmetries, which are in principle very particular kinds of Galois symmetries, makes modular symmetries part of the world of Galois symmetries. They come in various flavours: p-adic Ramanujan symmetries, mod p Ramanujan symmetries, and compatible systems of p-adic

Ramanujan symmetries, like the ones arising from the Δ-function. In this book, we are going to identify modular symmetries with the (p-adic) Ramanujan symmetries they give rise to. Serre's conjecture, which he made in a few passes starting in the early 1970's, says that, in fact, all Galois symmetries are of Ramanujan-type; this was to become the guiding light of my mathematical career.

∞

As I delved deeper into Serre's writings, I saw in them a mathematical ethic for which precision was almost a moral requirement. In the exposition the optimal route to a result was sought out. He had an allergy to imprecision; as an audience member he would not let the lecturer get away with sloppy formulations. He said he could not tolerate pollution in mathematics; pollution outside it was not in his control. Even when he autographed one of his books, he corrected with the same pen the misprints in it. This ethic led to the very helpful clarity of his writing. Serre had continued to do mathematics at a high level of quality and quantity even after he was world-famous (in the global yet relatively small community of mathematicians) and did not stand much to gain by continuing to work hard. This was unlike many other brilliant mathematicians whose output declined after getting big prizes. A friend later remarked that this showed that Serre loved mathematics more than some other famous mathematicians whose work dwindled or their intensity dropped after achieving great fame.

Of the great figures of twentieth-century mathematics, his work seemed most accessible. His mathematics combined a lightness of touch with depth that was very attractive to me. He had done deep theoretical work, but he had also written papers that delighted in examples and smaller problems. In interviews, he downplayed the labour and effort of will that his work might have needed. He said he pursued whatever amused him.

Like me, many were drawn to Serre's mathematics by the clarity of his exposition, which made difficult things as simple as they could possibly be. The relationship of Serre's textbooks to the research papers in his Collected Works was that of a music lesson to a concert. In the papers in the three volumes of his Collected Works, Serre was giving concerts, presenting new mathematics to an initiated audience. As a student of maths or music one had to learn the basics by reading textbooks, or taking music lessons, and read research papers, or attend concerts, to hear and experience live what the art was really about. By learning and listening and through one's own *riyaz*, one hoped eventually to be able to give solo concerts in small auditoriums. One's anxiety as a novice could make even these small spaces feel large, cold and empty. Serre's writings offered guidance to both the novice and the seasoned mathematician.

∞

Once Serre introduced in his 1967 seminar the p-adic Galois symmetries, and the mod p Galois symmetries that are their shadows, arising from the Δ-function, they acquired a life of their own that went beyond the purpose for which they were *invented*, or *constructed*, or *discovered*. The word you would like to use depends on whether you think mathematics is invented, discovered or even tangibly constructed by you. For a working mathematician all these words are good descriptions of the work they do: it feels like what one finds out or proves is already *out there*, and so doing new mathematics feels like discovering or uncovering something that already exists. One feels the joy of invention and creativity, of ideas popping up in one's head. And there is a tangibility to what one discovers or invents: it has been constructed out of you actively thinking about it over weeks and months, it has taken shape within you.

Serre formulated the first version of his conjecture in a letter to his friend John Tate in 1973. John Tate worked at Harvard, and along with Serre, his work shaped the course of number theory in the second half of the twentieth century. Serre's publication 'Valeurs propres des opérateurs de Hecke modulo *l*' in 1975 marks the official debut of his conjecture. The most definitive and comprehensive formulation is in his 1987 Duke paper. I had struggled in my Oxford days when reading Serre's 1987 paper, but when I studied it again in Pasadena I fared better in understanding it.

Serre's conjecture is a twentieth-century descendant of the eighteenth-century law of quadratic reciprocity that studies Galois symmetries arising from solutions of quadratic equations like $X^2 - 5 = 0$. Serre's conjecture studies the more complicated Galois symmetries arising from the Δ-function. This is a lovely example of mathematics being a long conversation in which older results, like quadratic reciprocity, are alive and, far from being mute witnesses to later developments, are in lively dialogue with contemporary mathematics, influencing it and also being influenced retrospectively. The earlier work is given new meaning and significance by being placed in broader contexts.

Serre's conjecture asserts in essence that all mod p Galois symmetries come from p-adic Ramanujan symmetries.[23] The power of the equality posited by Serre's conjecture

Mod p Galois symmetries = Mod p Ramanujan symmetries

is that modular symmetries, and hence Ramanujan symmetries that are their proxies, have a priori a completely different character to Galois symmetries.[24] Ramanujan symmetries are easier to calculate, and thus if we knew that all Galois symmetries are of Ramanujan type, it gives one much more control on Galois symmetries. Ramanujan symmetries can be manipulated in interesting ways. We will see examples of such manipulations, which we call 'congruences between Ramanujan symmetries'. They were vital for the proof of Serre's conjecture in my later work with Wintenberger.

In his 1987 paper, Serre makes the formulation of his conjecture from the 1970s much more quantitative and precise. For this purpose Serre attaches two numbers, the level N and the weight k, to a mod p Galois symmetry which are defined in terms of the corresponding local Galois symmetries. They are a measure of how complicated these symmetries are.[25]

As an analogy we may think of Galois symmetries and Ramanujan symmetries as particles of radically different types in particle physics, and Serre conjectures that they are miraculously identified. The weight and level of a symmetry are subtle properties of the symmetries, a little like the 'charge' and 'spin' of particles in physics.[26]

The version of Serre's conjecture in his 1987 paper asserts that a mod p Galois symmetry of weight k and level N arises from the reduction modulo p of a p-adic Ramanujan symmetry of weight k and level N. This quantitative form of Serre's conjecture, which embellishes its qualitative form by specifying weights and levels, can thus be equivalently formulated as:[27]

Mod p Galois symmetries of weight k and level N

are the same as

Mod p Ramanujan symmetries of weight k and level N

This is an amazing prediction, as the meaning of weight and level for a Galois symmetry and for a Ramanujan symmetry are a priori far removed. Serre's conjecture in its more precise form not only conflates these two very different types of symmetries, but further asserts that in passing between them the level N (analogue of charge) and weight k (analogue of spin), which have very different significance for the two types of symmetry, are both preserved. This is an instance of the deep connections that are rife in mathematics between concepts that seem far away.

The quantitative version of Serre's conjecture was related, and partly made in response, to an astonishing development related to FLT. In the 1980s the German number theorist Gerhard Frey made a connection between Ramanujan symmetries and FLT. Frey had the intuition that another important conjecture in number theory called the elliptic symmetry conjecture should imply FLT, but he struggled to make his intuition precise. The elliptic symmetry conjecture asserts that Galois symmetries arising from geometric objects called elliptic curves are Ramanujan symmetries.

Serre made Frey's idea precise and in his paper deduces (the elliptic symmetry conjecture as well as) FLT as a consequence of the quantitative form of his conjecture. The work of Frey and Serre shows that the falsity of FLT leads to the existence of a mod p Galois symmetry of weight 2 and level 2 which one suspects should not exist. But this seems impossible to show working only with Galois symmetries. Serre's conjecture says that this Galois symmetry is a Ramanujan symmetry of weight $k = 2$ and level $N = 2$.[28] But it is easy to show (by mere inspection!) that there is no Ramanujan symmetry of level and weight both 2, thus allowing one to deduce FLT. This is a telling illustration of the power of converting a Galois symmetry to a Ramanujan symmetry.

The last section of Serre's 1987 paper verifies his conjectures in a few specific cases. He checks the qualitative conjecture for mod *p* Galois symmetries that are 'solvable' in that they arise from solutions of equations which can be solved by radicals. Like in Galois' work, there is a dichotomy between the solvable and non-solvable cases, and the solvable cases are tractable. Serre's conjecture asserts that Ramanujan symmetries give a new and powerful way to analyse all Galois symmetries. The Ramanujan property of all Galois symmetries can be viewed as a development of Galois' ideas, adding the powerful weapon of Ramanujan symmetries to the arsenal of methods for solving polynomial equations.

In the introduction, I used an analogy comparing Galois and Ramanujan symmetries to electricity and magnetism. Orsted showed that electric currents can move a magnetic needle, and Faraday conversely showed that magnetic fields give rise to electric currents. Maxwell unified electricity and magnetism by making both of them aspects of the electromagnetic field. In an analogous way Deligne built Ramanujan symmetries that explained Ramanujan's congruences and conjectural bounds for $\tau(n)$. Serre then conjectured a path from mod *p* Galois symmetries to mod *p* Ramanujan symmetries. Serre's conjecture creates a powerful force field at the conjectural level that weaves together these very different symmetries. The elliptic symmetry conjecture and FLT are some of its striking consequences. It is a powerful metaphor that brings together algebra (Galois symmetries), analysis (modular symmetries) and geometry (elliptic curves).

I later read that Serre had struggled when making a quantitative form of his conjecture. He wanted to be as precise as possible in order to make the conjecture amenable to checking by computation, and thus falsifiable. He fought hard to get a formulation that would be exact and optimal. Serre wrote about a period of uncertainty he went through when formulating his conjecture:*

> At the time I made this conjecture (in its refined form), I had decided to write it in a setting with which I was familiar and which could be explained easily. But, on a higher level, I knew that it should be done a different way. The two ways were of course similar, but not a priori equivalent. There was a conflict between my conscious decision of making things 'easy' and my unconscious feeling that it was not 'the right way'. This conflict haunted me; it made me very unhappy. There was even one horrible night where I had the impression that there were two parts of my brain which were fighting each other and spinning endlessly. Then, a few months later, I found an example showing that the two points of view are not equivalent, and the correct one is not the one I had chosen. But I also saw that, in all the really interesting cases, they are equivalent. Curiously, finding this 'counterexample' made me incredibly happy: the two sides of my brain had reconciled. Happy End.

This shows the care and effort which Serre put into formulating his conjecture which I was not in a position to appreciate when I first encountered his conjectures at Oxford in 1989.

∞

Ken Ribet is a professor at the University of California in Berkeley. He is of a generation after Serre; he had spent many years in Paris, and his work was influenced by Serre. Ribet's work is one of the key

---

* Cook, Mariana. *Mathematicians: An Outer View of the Inner World.* Princeton University Press. 2009.

results that were proven in the late 1980s and early 1990s related to Serre's conjecture. This work showed that the qualitative form of Serre's conjecture implied its more precise form. Ribet's paper, published in the prestigious journal *Inventiones mathematicae*, implied that FLT was a consequence of the elliptic symmetry conjecture.

I started studying Ribet's work intensely around the end of my second year at Caltech. I was getting nowhere with the problem Hida had suggested. Often the weekly meeting with him would turn out to be a non-event. I would not even be able to summon up a few intelligent questions to ask him. My gut feeling was that my adviser knew how to solve this problem. A typical thesis problem, something to get started on in one's research career, is often a problem which the adviser could have solved, but has left unsolved for a student to work on, a bit like a lion leaving the cleaning up of the bones to the jackals.

There was a calculation I had to make. I kept postponing doing it. I was not sure I could do it, and I did not want to find out. I probably subconsciously prized this precious ambiguity and resisted squandering it in a self-defeating effort. We think we can do a certain task if we tried, but we tell ourselves we just couldn't be bothered. If you don't do something consistently, and you keep thinking you could if you tried, is it proof that deep down you think you can't do it? I had picked up this observation from the legendary Caltech theoretical physicist Richard Feynman's book *'Surely You're Joking, Mr. Feynman!'* and it seemed to ring true.

Sometimes I would bail out of the weekly meeting with Hida the night before. I once went to the windowless room that had terminals in it available for grad students to use. As I plunged my key into the lock I heard chairs being moved. I found a group of Russian students there who had recently migrated with their adviser. It was a time of such migrations, following the collapse of the Soviet Union in 1991. These students were more advanced in their mathematical preparation compared to the rest of us. One of the Russians, I had noticed, seemed to only play video games. He played at the boxy terminals then in vogue with green symbols traipsing across the black screen. He was there when I came back to the room later to write a message to my adviser, telling him I was feeling unwell and asking him if we could postpone our meeting to the next week.

Laconically, he replied, 'Okay. See you next Wednesday.' I felt reprieved. The victory was of course pyrrhic. I could not use the same excuse next week. At least part of my reluctance to think about the problem my adviser had suggested was my fascination with Ribet's paper. It was around 50 pages long. I kept reading the introduction that announced the result and gave the strategy of the proof. It was like reading a travel brochure that made one savour the exotic country that featured in its packages. The paper used the latest technology to prove a very important result. There were conferences all over the world on the paper starring Ribet. The maths seemed very elegant and sophisticated and quite beyond me. It was more demanding work to read Ribet's paper with its detailed, sophisticated arguments than Serre's paper about his conjecture. One could admire the statement of the conjecture, contemplating its beauty like a sunset on the distant horizon, while reading Ribet's proof was like journeying through difficult terrain.

∞

I tried different techniques to read the paper. I tried to understand it linearly, line by line, and found myself stuck in infinite regress.

If I looked up a reference in the bibliography, the reference would sometimes be to a tome full of the most arcane mathematics. Sometimes the reference was to a shorter paper, but then that itself would refer to other works.

Perhaps I could reconnoitre over the expanse of the paper to try and get a bird's-eye view? The problem was I didn't know enough about the basic structure of the type of number theory this paper was situated in. The blurs of greens and browns and blues I saw from hovering above the paper did not make me any wiser about the lay of the land.

There were periods of excitement, nevertheless. Sometimes when I read the paper, it felt like flying in a cockpit, low over the terrain, with the sun directly in my eyes almost blinding me. These solo flights gave me a secret thrill. Secret because initially I did not tell my adviser that I was spending more time reading this paper than working on the problem he had suggested.

The notation was befuddling. Even granted all the machinery, in those first few months struggling with the paper, I was still confused about the strategy of the proof. Yet I kept getting a kick out of the paper. I understood a couple of sections towards the end. The maths of the paper seemed fresh and contemporary. I admired the style of the author. The paper was my constant companion. On trains. On buses. Sometimes I carried it in my hands on my walks. Looked at it as I waited to cross a street at a light. Looking at the paper quietened my mind. The first and last pages were getting increasingly soiled. The binding was loosening as if the pages physically wanted to escape from me.

Sometimes I spotted a mistake, a hidden contradiction in the argument. This made me briefly happy. I had seen a flaw no one else had. I could at least gain a sort of negative fame as a debunker.

Alas, the contradiction resolved itself. But through these stumbles my understanding grew. I was still hazy about many parts of the paper. It was a little like skating on a river that was frozen over, but had hidden cracks in the ice. After having fallen frequently into icy-cold water at the beginning, the periods I stayed above water grew longer and longer. I could even attempt a few complicated manoeuvres to show off my understanding.

Finally, I wrote an email to Ken Ribet telling him that I had been studying his paper and asked him a question about a technical point in the paper. I had written to him earlier asking him for reprints. I had written previously to famous mathematicians all over the world asking them to send me reprints of their papers. They often obliged and it made my day to see bulky envelopes in my mailbox with addresses of famous mathematical centres in France, Germany and the United States. The papers were often beyond me. But reading from the official reprints gave me a sense of a closer relationship with the author than reading from the blackened photocopies of the same papers. It added to the aesthetic of reading, besides saving me hours in the photocopy room, photocopying noisily, which made me feel like a factory hand.

Professor Ribet responded. He said he was happy that I was reading his paper carefully. He sent me a working version of an expository paper explaining his theorem for a wider audience. He sent me, over the next few weeks, evolving versions of this survey paper. The survey paper helped me understand the original, more technical, paper. It also introduced some simplifications that shortened some of the arguments. In a key case some of the arguments became less baroque. I was content to understand that key case, the simplest non-trivial case. The simplifying assumptions pruned some of the details – the branches in the corner – leaving the essential picture intact.

I was getting more familiar with the ideas and methods of his paper, and sometimes would email Ribet to ask if certain technical variants were possible. Tentatively, I pushed and poked at the boundaries of what the ideas of the paper could do. Often I would realize after having hit 'Send' that I had made a stupid mistake. Then I had to write and retract what I had said earlier. Sometimes I even had to retract the retraction. I would check my email several times a day to see if he had replied. At times he would reply immediately, at others he would ignore the messages, or write back after a few days. His messages were sometimes written at 4 a.m.

One day, Ribet emailed me that he had been invited to give a talk at Caltech. He was going to drive down the coast and spend a few days in southern California. On the day he was scheduled to arrive, I came early to the department. I saw him on campus, having lunch with Ramakrishnan. Later I saw him in the library reading a newspaper and went and said hello. He was cordial and charismatic. The seminar room was full. Ribet was famous in the maths community, like a movie star with a hit in the recent past. Hearing him talk about the paper I had been studying for months was like hearing music live that I had heard repeatedly in recordings. It seemed more vivid. He was an engaging speaker, with a slightly disconcerting manner of looking above the heads of the audience, at a point somewhere high up on the wall opposite the blackboard. He built up to the climax of the argument, and turning back from the blackboard, addressed a focal point of the room that lay above the audience's heads. Ribet and Caltech's number theory group went to a Malaysian restaurant for dinner afterwards. At the table were Ribet and Ramakrishnan and a handful of graduate students at Caltech who were working with Ramakrishnan.

When I looked again at Ribet's paper after meeting him, some more of the fog hanging over patches of it lifted. Recalling things he had said in his talk and at dinner afterwards helped clear up points that had been obscure. Reading the paper now became a dialogue between its author and me. Such encounters with mathematicians – starting with meeting Thompson in Cambridge, Ribet in Pasadena, and later Serre in Paris – at different points of my mathematical career helped me come closer to the mathematics I was studying and thinking about obsessively at those times.

5

Escaping Pasadena

We were singing Fauré's Requiem. The ethereality of the music made the notes seem like light-reflecting clouds floating above humdrum life. The liturgical text was in Latin.

> *Requiem eternam dona eis domine* (Give them eternal rest, Lord)
> *Et lux perpetua* (and perpetual light)

These were beseeching words, suggesting immense loss and a desire for the peace of a departed soul. I had listened to Western classical music on the radio and on compact discs since my first introduction to it on BBC Radio 3 in my Cambridge days. But now in the well of singers the music sounded very different from the passive experience of listening to it on radio: it felt like I was crouching inside an organ and being swept by wave after wave of the sound. The music had a much rawer physicality, while at the same time being ethereal. I felt my lungs filling with the rising hush of the music from the thrush-like voices of the sopranos. Mouths shaped the sounds of the words. The mechanics of the vocal cords, the bellows of the lungs, produced a music that was imperfect yet moving. It would give one a bit of a jolt when the music trumped the banality of a singer. The singers in the choir were like puppets pulled around by their vocal cords. Bass singers scraped the bottom of their chest to produce gravelly sounds. Tenors sang more in their heads, the echoing chamber of chaotic thoughts. The high notes of the sopranos were like unguents for bleeding souls.

Almost three academic years with their succession of Fall, Winter, and Spring quarters, from late September to early June, had now bitten the dust. Around the end of my third year at Caltech I joined the Glee Club on campus. No great credentials were required besides being able to sing a little tunefully. Expectations were low and being unable to read music was fine. I approached the person in charge: he was down to earth, forthright, encouraging. He had no illusions that he was running a high-class choir. He gave me an audition to determine the range of my voice. It turned out that I was a baritone, somewhere in between bass and tenor. The first time I attended practice, I felt a frisson of non-belonging. I was entering a room full of people all of whom knew each other a little. But as I eased into the singing it became a welcome diversion from feeling stuck in my thesis work.

∞

My adviser and I cut a deal around this time that I would finish at the end of the first quarter of my fifth year, in December 1994, at least six months before the final year was up. At this point it seemed like a good idea to end my misery and move on. I did not have enough material to write a satisfactory thesis, but enough to cobble together a mediocre thesis. Most of my progress was fragmentary, effort scattered on the different problems that I had tried. I travelled across Los Angeles to see Hida every week for the hour-long meeting, but it was increasingly becoming pro forma as I was not making any progress. I kept changing my problem, and now I was on to the third problem he had suggested. I tried to understand the problem, and made feeble attempts to make progress by relating the problem to other known results in the field. But nothing was happening. I had learnt exciting new mathematics, some of it related to linking Galois and Ramanujan symmetries, even developing a feel for it. But this had not resulted in new results of my own, and I despaired whether this would ever happen.

Typically students who had been doing well would have completed most of their work by the end of the fourth year. They would have resolved their thesis problem, or made substantial progress in that direction. Over the summer they would write their theses, and begin applying for postdocs at the start of the fifth year. The market had become intensively competitive with the fall of the Berlin Wall, which had happened just around the time I finished my degree at Cambridge. In the five years since then, there was an exodus of talented academics to the United States and Western Europe from countries no longer behind the Iron Curtain. It was all for the best, I thought, that I would not even be at the starting line for the Fall races for postdoctoral math jobs in the States. I had decided to go back to India, to be with my mother, whose health was failing.

∞

Unexpectedly, a couple of green shoots surfaced. These promised escape, or at least temporary reprieves, from my failures in Pasadena. One was that an Indian number theorist, Dipendra Prasad, visited Pasadena for a few days in my third year at Caltech, and I discussed some maths with him. He was encouraging and for the first time I was able to talk in a freewheeling interactive way with a real mathematician. He was generous with his time and I expressed my enthusiasm for some of the ideas I had learnt in my obsessive readings. Mathematics was a huge field, and even within number theory, one could be an expert in one area and know little of adjoining areas beyond hearsay. Dipendra was a mathematician of broad culture and interested in a great many things and, encouragingly, found it interesting to talk to me about some of the things I had picked up in my studies. He seemed to feel that I understood some of the ideas I was talking about, which were still alive and kicking within me. Most importantly, he expressed some optimism that things would work out for me.

He was himself making a move to a small institute in the town of Allahabad in North India. He suggested that I visit for a few weeks to check out the new institute and the surroundings, and even offered very generously the possibility of a permanent position there right after I finished my thesis. Allahabad had been a centre of learning for a long time. Harish-Chandra had studied there as an undergraduate a few decades ago. But it had become a bit of an academic backwater. It was far better known as a pilgrimage place for Hindus, located as it was at the confluence of the Ganga and the Yamuna. It was not an obvious place for me to go to renew myself, but I was eager for the escape it offered.

The other green shoot was that my adviser Professor Hida was going to spend the spring and summer quarters in Japan and he offered me funding to spend three months in Sapporo whilst he was there. With some sense of relief, I arranged to be away from Pasadena for the spring and summer quarters of 1994, from April to August, and spend time in Allahabad and Sapporo. This would be a way of escaping the stasis of my US life at least temporarily, before I defended my thesis and severed my links with it for good.

∞

I arrived at the station in Allahabad after almost a twenty-four-hour journey from Bombay that took me across the breadth of the country. Physically, the institute in Allahabad was several continents away from the one in Pasadena. But in its academic quality and infrastructure, it was light years away. Its building used to be someone's home and had a makeshift quality to it. I arrived there when the winter was not even a memory and the days were hot. The loo gusted through the city, hot winds rising from deserts in the west, scorching the earth, shrivelling minds and bodies. Most of the city had a half-finished look to it. One stayed out of the sun during the day as heatstrokes were common.

Allahabad was the seat of the High Court of the state. On my walk from the guest house to the maths institute, I passed the whitewashed buildings of the sessions court. Outside the court compound there were flimsy stalls made of bamboo and covered with tarpaulin in which lawyers sat, killing flies, dressed in white shirts and trousers that shimmered in the harsh light of the sun. It was getting hotter by the minute, and it was not even eight in the morning. The lawyers wore black coats and ties that hung loosely from their necks. At most times they sat idle, incongruously drinking, in the blistering heat, hot tea from clay vessels. Petitioners from towns and villages nearby straggled towards the courts in search of justice. Their sight would briefly energize the lawyers as they helped the village folk fill forms, and perhaps also grease palms so that they could get a day in court. I would go to the institute every day, passing through this dystopia. The lawyers keeping vigil near the court looked at times like barbers waiting for clients to wander in for a close shave or haircut. I could have sworn seeing one of them swishing a lathered brush around a client's face, before the mirage quivered and melted away in the heat.

∞

I was given a desk in a windowless office. There was a noisy air cooler, which made one think one was in the middle of a factory. The atmosphere, though, was less formal than in the department at Caltech, and this was a refreshing change for me. I had two or three officemates. One was a postdoc from Chennai who was newly married and came with lunch from home, mostly rice and sambar. There was another student who was from Allahabad itself. We conversed in a mixture of English and Hindi. He had given up bright prospects, he told me, of a career in the administrative services, to do maths. It seemed like a gamble: making a career in mathematics was risky, less of a sure thing than as an administrator. This was particularly true given the nature of life in the city. Allahabad was a centre for students to train for the Indian Administrative Service exam; it was not a centre for academic research in the sciences and mathematics.

I talked for a couple of hours a day with Dipendra about mathematics related to Galois and Ramanujan symmetries. We discussed Ribet's paper, the one that I had read obsessively. Dipendra had been asked to write a survey article about the paper. He had just begun grappling with it while I had already spent months thinking about it.

Dipendra was already on his way to establishing himself in another difficult central area of number theory, the Langlands programme, a grand programme to unify number theory. Robert

Langlands had, over the 1960s and 1970s, laid out in detail his vision and fashioned tools that could be used to realize his vision. Even now, only fragments of this programme are known. Langlands wrote about the difficulties of his programme:

> We are in a forest whose trees will not fall with a few timid hatchet blows. We have to take up the double-bitted axe and the cross-cut saw, and hope that our muscles are equal to them.

The elliptic symmetry conjecture and Ken Ribet's work was related to this programme but was a different take on it. My somewhat fragile understanding of the mathematics we discussed was tested in Dipendra's mind. There were gaps in my understanding that he helped fill. I understood better the structure of the papers we discussed even though at times I was working with objects whose definition was not completely clear to me. Thus I seemed to be floating without foundations. I found out that I could work with these objects, understand them in action, in nature as it were, even when they had a shaky basis in my mind. In the mofussil surroundings of the institute we were discussing cutting-edge mathematics.

∞

I met a musician during my stay in Allahabad who had retired as director of the Gandharva Sangeet Mahavidyalaya, a pedagogical institute devoted to Hindustani classical music. He lived in a house that was full of old world charm. I went to him with a couple of friends I had made at the maths institute. He regaled us with stories of musicians. We talked about the celebrated musician Kumar Gandharva who had come to small-town India after he lost a lung – still in his early twenties and already one of the brightest stars of the musical world – battling tuberculosis. Our host had known him. Kumarji had been advised to leave Bombay and live in a place with a dry climate. His doctors warned that singing could kill him, he was forbidden to sing even a note. He exiled himself in the small town of Dewas, far away from the megapolis of Bombay, the great centre not only of commerce but also art and culture. In the enforced silence of his convalescence in Dewas, he listened intently to his surroundings, absorbed the moods of the different seasons expressed through the different sounds of birds.

In my time in Allahabad I was restless, falling short of my goals, but making unconscious progress, turned inwards by the scorching heat, finding riches in connecting with mathematicians and musicians, sensing that I could not do mathematics in isolation. I began to see mathematics as part of a spectrum stretching from music to literature, as part of a culture that weaved these together seamlessly, like in the traditional arts, philosophy and sciences of an older India. Mathematics to me seemed closer to the arts rather than the sciences. Or at least the parts of mathematics that appealed to me. The India around me in Allahabad seemed to be in disrepair, but my spirit was renewed here. Parts of me that had atrophied in Pasadena were revived, and I felt the stirrings of a new life.

In preparation for the trip to Sapporo, in the few weeks I had in my parents' home in Bombay between my stays in Allahabad and Japan, I tried to learn rudimentary Japanese. A young woman came home a few times to drill me in the basics. She had lived in Japan for a few years, and I got the impression she had been in a relationship with someone there. She had stayed in love with the country even after having fallen out of love with one of its people. Some of the sentences I learnt went beyond shop talk. One of them alluded to the beauty of Mount Fuji. The lessons added to my growing optimism that Japan would be a decisive trip for me. Make or break. Even if I did not make any progress with the problems my mind had circled around for months, the trip would set me free from my own expectations, and then I could move on, do something else. There was a very small chance that I might be granted a vision of my own Mount Fuji in my days in Sapporo – the breakthrough in my thesis work that had eluded me so far.

∞

I have memories of my bags being opened at the airport in Sapporo. I was carrying some masalas so that I could be more self-reliant and cook in my rooms which came with an attached kitchen. The Japanese customs or security officials inspected my bags for at least half an hour, puzzled by the various packets containing brown and yellow powders. This all happened fairly close to where Professor Hida and his friend were waiting to receive me. I could see them and was mildly embarrassed that they could see my bags being scrutinized.

Hida and his friend drove me to the International Guest House where I would stay for three months. They knew each other well. They tried to speak in English for my benefit. The English spoken by Hida's friend was rudimentary; he typically just repeated the last few words my adviser had said and laughed loudly. I was grateful to Hida for his efforts on my behalf when I saw the modern, brightly lit building of the guest house. The next day he came by and gave me a bicycle I could use to commute from the guest house to the university where I would be given a desk to work at.

One of the first things that happened in my stay was that I lost my bicycle at a nearby garden. I had spent some time walking around the garden, watching groups of schoolchildren who had stopped there on the way back home after school. There were older retired men too, sitting on benches, enjoying the ruckus the children made and yet impatient for them to continue their journey homewards, waiting for the garden to become quiet again. When I came back to where I had left the bicycle it was gone. I had not chained it to a post, naively, subconsciously assuming that Japan was very safe. I felt ashamed and anxious to have to tell my adviser that I had lost his bicycle. He shrugged it off, but he probably did not forget my carelessness.

Not having a bicycle meant that throughout my stay I most often walked to the university. It was a long walk, taking me close to two hours. I could have taken public transport, and I sometimes did, but I preferred to walk. The path was along a river. I would pass the occasional bicyclist or pedestrian, but for the most part I had the path to myself. The thing I most remember about my stay in Sapporo are those long walks. Rather than simply being a means of getting from the guest house to the university, they became the centrepiece of my day. The path passed through the city, and the wide open skies and the stillness made me feel I had the whole city to myself.

I mused over the maths problem Hida had suggested I think about as I walked. The one I had been stuck on for months. This was to be the final problem that my thesis ended up being focused on. The problem was related to the dictionary between Galois symmetries and Ramanujan symmetries. To compare them systematically Barry Mazur had developed the language and formalism of 'deformation theory'. Barry Mazur worked at Harvard and was one of the most prominent number theorists in the world.[29] My adviser's highly original 'Hida theory' was related to 'families of p-adic Ramanujan symmetries' and had inspired Mazur to introduce his new ideas.[30]

While it was conjectured that p-adic Galois and Ramanujan symmetries are the same for fixed weight and level, Hida's hunch was that if one allowed arbitrarily high powers of p to divide the levels then this should fail. Hida asked me to show that the 'space of p-adic Galois symmetries of fixed weight k and level Np^{∞}' is much larger than the 'space of p-adic Ramanujan symmetries of fixed weight k and level Np^{∞}'.

A couple of times a week I went to Hida's office and we talked at the blackboard, or rather he talked and I listened. He explained to me the strategy that he had in mind for solving my thesis problem. Often, it seemed to me that Hida's strategy for showing this could simply not work and had to be wrong. But then I would give it another chance, and become energized for a few days to pursue it from another perspective, before getting discouraged again. It was hard to quit thinking about it. It was hard to prove definitively that something did not work; it could just be that one had not tried hard enough, or that one had missed a trick. Much human effort would be saved if there was a *yaksha*, creatures neither of heaven nor of the earth, who specialized in telling people when they were on the wrong track, counselling them that what they were trying could simply never work.[31]

∞

There was a certain unboundedness in thinking as I walked. For those three months, I never stopped thinking about my thesis problem. Even if I was discouraged one day, I felt fresh the next morning, or if not the very next morning, within a few days my mind rebounded, ready to take stock of all the ways that I had tried and learnt did not work, that still taught me something about my problem. I felt I had found a way to do mathematics: it was just to walk and let the mind think, wandering in a state of suspended disbelief as I kept trying ideas that had not worked. I felt that maybe if I did not give up on the problem, the problem also would not give up on me.

I learnt later that this was common practice amongst mathematicians, to keep trying ideas that may not have worked but which one could not let go of. Wiles has compared mathematical research to evolution: one keeps trying something that does not work, but over time there are minute changes in the way one thinks about it. One keeps coming back to it periodically and failing, but never failing in the same way twice, as each time, one unconsciously introduces a new variant of the method. This is inevitable as one cannot remember exactly what one had tried before that had not worked. An idea that ultimately works might emerge from this process, a variant of the original idea arrived at by constantly fiddling around.

The fact that the walk had a start and an end was important to my being able to think effectively on it. The feet made progress even if in my mind I hit a brick wall, which relieved some of the tension of trying to make an idea work. The rhythms of walking set the mind free, perhaps generating the right theta waves that induced meditative states, making the mind more receptive to the new. My mind explored without restlessness one path after another. By the time I reached the university I was pleasantly tired, and I would waste my time there till it was time to walk back again. Sometimes I took the bus back, but the moment I got on the bus, I regretted not having chosen to walk back.

∞

Curiously, I had visited the two places that had played a significant role in my life so far – Cambridge and Pasadena – with my mother many years before I actually went there as a student. It was the same with Japan. I had been on a trip with her to Tokyo and Kyoto when I was in high school. Even though these famous cities were quite far away from where I was now, memories of that trip added to my excitement about being in Japan. I remembered taking off our footwear at the entrance of a home where my mother and I were invited for dinner – our host was a business acquaintance of my uncle – and slipping into home slippers. Tatami covered the floors, and we sat cross-legged. I remembered the generosity of the dinner. The food was astonishing in its variety of lightly cooked vegetables. Kyoto had been festooned with sakura. There were maps one could buy indicating the shifting locations where the blossoms were at their peak. The world seemed dressed and bejewelled like a bride. There was a street with a small, shallow brook running through it. Petals had fallen into it, covering the water completely. It looked like a brook with only petals flowing through it. One of the traditional tourist attractions was to sit in a boat pushed by a few men, shouting lustily as the boat slid along in the stream of petals.

There was a sweet shop next to the brook that had been around for centuries. We ordered some sweets at random, picking ones that were powdered like French ladies in the times of Louis XIV. Meticulous steps followed. The person behind the counter wrote down our order in pencil, then handed it to a person at the cash register who calculated the bill amount. The sweets were wrapped by yet another person with the confounding skills of an origamist. The paper seemed too good to be used merely as wrapping. When we tasted the sweets, they were made of red bean paste. Everything about the country seemed enticingly strange, in a sense familiar, comfortingly Asian, but still very foreign.

∞

There were other mathematicians who visited my adviser that summer. A younger French collaborator of his, Jacques Tilouine, was also visiting Sapporo for a few months at Hida's invitation. We would go as a group for lunch to the university cafeteria or a restaurant nearby. My being vegetarian always complicated matters as everything had some fish in it; if nothing else bonito flakes – fish shavings with a strong umami flavour – were almost unavoidable. At some point I decided to compromise and not look the gift horse in the mouth. If a bowl of noodles looked vegetarian, if it had no obvious pieces of fish or meat floating in it, I would just deem it was vegetarian. I typically had a bowl of soba noodles. It was probably flavoured with bonito flakes. The bowl of noodles had a satisfying plainness to it, with an egg floating sunny side up in the liquid broth. It looked like a painting; I felt I could keep staring at it, and it seemed a pity that it had to be eaten in the end.

After lunch we stopped by a store on campus to buy powdered, bean-filled sweets similar to the ones I had tasted in Kyoto on my vacation more than a decade ago. They felt like clay, or like the skin of an animal, when one touched them. We went to my adviser's large office and sat in a semicircle consuming the sweets. I listened to my adviser and his French visitor talk about politics and exchange rates of the yen and dollar, and occasionally exchange some maths gossip as well.

There were also on a few occasions short-term visitors who had come to give a talk. Sapporo was quite a remote place, even mathematically speaking, since Hokkaido University was not traditionally one of the centres of mathematical research in Japan, that place of honour being reserved for universities in Tokyo and Kyoto. Thus someone who visited here short term would have to be on a fairly eccentric orbit. A young mathematician from

Germany seemed to be on one such mission. He was hitchhiking in Hokkaido. I later learnt that he had a misadventure on his hike when he was deep in a forest. As he rested against a stone, he noticed that he was uncomfortably close to a bear! There was a stream flowing below and he jumped into the stream out of fright. In other situations he might not have chosen to jump, as he had to fall through several metres of air before he hit the water. The bear jumped in right after him! Fortunately it did not pursue the young German very far. After hearing this story, any difficulties with mathematics I had in Sapporo began to seem harmless.

∞

Japan has a strong tradition in mathematics. After the devastation of World War II, a young generation of mathematicians working in relative isolation had produced a stunning body of work in number theory. One of the famous people from that generation was Goro Shimura. The famed elliptic symmetry conjecture had arisen from the work of Shimura's friend Yutaka Taniyama in 1950's Tokyo, in the aftermath of the war. It was made more precise through the work of Shimura, and Weil made it more quantitative and falsifiable in a paper published in 1967. The elliptic symmetry conjecture in essence asserts that p-adic Galois symmetries arising from certain geometric objects called elliptic curves are Ramanujan symmetries. Weil's refinement of Taniyama's formulation of his conjecture is similar in spirit to Serre's refinement of his own conjecture when he pins down the weight and level of the mod p Galois symmetry to be the same as that of a p-adic Ramanujan symmetry it is conjectured to arise from.

Shimura wrote a tribute to Taniyama decades after Taniyama inexplicably died by suicide when he was in his thirties. Shimura's moving tribute to his friend starts with the following paragraph.

> To write about Taniyama's time, first I have to emphasize that it was the mid to late 1950s, and the situation was totally different from that of Japan today, to say nothing of the comparison with the United States or Europe, now or then. Pollution was not a household word in those days, and in fine weather one could see, from the center of Tokyo, Mt Fuji on the western horizon 70 miles away, with its snowed crown in the morning and silhouetted in the evening. The destruction and deprivation of wartime and the succeeding period were things of the past, but not forgotten. We were no longer hungry. The whole country was aspiring and hopeful, but still very poor. This was so in a collective sense and also on the individual level. Taniyama and his peers were no exception, though it may be said, in any country at any time, one is usually both ambitious and poor at the beginning of one's career.[32]

My adviser talked about Shimura's personality and work often, and his interactions with Shimura at Princeton where the latter worked for most of his later career. Professor Hida's French visitor in Sapporo spoke about a colleague of his, Henri Carayol, who devoted almost seven years to a problem with the resolve to either finish the problem or be finished by it. Tilouine reported that Carayol had said he would commit harakiri if he did not succeed in proving the theorem he had set out to prove. It was likely Carayol had spoken in jest, but his true intent could not be determined as he actually ended up proving the theorem before the end of seven years. Taniyama's suicide did give the story a dark complexion. The theorem Carayol succeeded in proving later proved useful in my thesis.[33]

On weekends I would spend time in the guest house. I ended up lying in my bed staring at the ceiling for hours. There was a TV in the room and I would watch the news and the advertisements. They were in Japanese and thus left my mind free to wander. I also followed a serial about a group of friends. They were attractive young people, and some parts of the story seemed universal. I could make sense of the flickering images even if I did not understand a word of what they said. The friends hung out together, fell in love, fought; some of the friends drifted away. For my part, I made friends with the receptionist who worked downstairs in the lobby of the guest house. She was amused that I had come here for three months to essentially spend most of my time walking back and forth to the University.

∞

The marginality of my existence in Allahabad and Sapporo, which themselves were rather marginal to the larger mathematical world, perhaps encouraged me to think about mathematics in a freer way than in Pasadena. Sapporo felt more like home. The narrow streets in parts of the city. The exposed low-lying electric cables. Small shops. It was also the fact that I was in Asia. I did not feel alienated from my surroundings. It also helped that I was here for a very well-defined period of time. Three months is long, but not so long as to make me feel at any point that I was marooned in the middle of a sea of time. The day of departure was known from the day I arrived.

I went with Tilouine and his family to a garden that had a Shinto shrine in the middle. There was a stall selling amulets. It was a nature-based religion with multiple gods or *kami*. The *kami* could be propitiated to head off bad times. For instance, the year one turned thirty-three was seen as being unlucky for women and the age forty-two for men, and thus people would ask the *kami* to neutralize misfortunes that being this age might make them vulnerable to.

Like in India there seemed a certain complexity to the way the Japanese thought of religion that did not baulk at apparent contradictions. One could be a follower of Shintoism and Buddhism at the same time. Apparently contradictory, these were found in practice to be compatible, satisfying different impulses and needs. This world and the other world. One could believe in very abstract principles, the fundamental oneness of the world, seek enlightenment through renunciation and conquering of the senses, and yet delight in rituals, perform annual ceremonies in which one fed one's ancestors symbolic balls of rice. These practices incorporated fantasy and rigour seamlessly.

Shimura wrote about the time he spent with Taniyama in the 1950s in his memorial article:

> … we would enjoy, together with some other friends, relaxed times in those coffee shops, and spend a Saturday afternoon at a botanical garden in the city, or at a park in the outskirts. In the evenings, we would eat at a restaurant specializing in whale meat, not a particular delicacy in those days but perhaps unthinkable nowadays. We would also take a long walk after a day of work at our school, visiting a Shinto shrine, where we would purchase 'oracles' printed on small pieces of papers to amuse ourselves; they were supposed to tell our fortunes.[34]

These words strike a chord with my own experience of life in Sapporo, struggling to figure out a way to write a decent thesis, sustained by the gentle novelty of a culture that was different from mine, but still continuous with it in many ways.

On weekends too I oftentimes walked to the university. Weekend walks had a more desultory feel to them: no one would be in their offices in the maths department, and there was no hurry to reach my destination. I still wanted to miss my walks as little as possible. I had a key with which I could let myself into the building. I think I could check my email only in the department, and so that was one reason to go in. But I would have gone anyway to think to the rhythm of the walk, going down the same path. The sameness of the days here helped me to work. There was little choice to be made each morning, and I liked that each day was already spoken for. In this context, I remembered a story of the famous French mathematician Henri Poincaré. His wardrobe had only white shirts and black trousers so he would not have to choose what clothes to wear every morning.

∞

While in Sapporo, I was also working on a small paper with Dipendra, my host in Allahabad. It arose from a question I raised, and which he liked. There was little one could do about the question, but it seemed nice to formulate it; if one assumed the elliptic symmetry conjecture, one could answer it in some interesting cases.

Just a few months earlier, in the summer of 1993, Andrew Wiles had made the startling announcement that the elliptic symmetry conjecture was proved and FLT thus followed as a corollary. The deduction relied on Frey's observation, that together with Ribet's work towards Serre's conjecture made FLT a consequence of the elliptic symmetry conjecture. This was astonishing news and fuelled some of the mathematical gossip in Hida's office after lunch. When others expressed their amazement that the hoary elliptic symmetry conjecture seemed to have fallen, Hida rightfully claimed credit for having predicted this. I remembered that around a year prior to Wiles's announcement Hida had suggested at a coffee shop in

UCLA, where number theorists had gathered after a seminar, that he felt it would be proved within the next five years. Wiles's work appeared to have fulfilled Hida's prophecy although the conjecture had seemed completely out of reach with not even a known plausible strategy to attack it.

Wiles had announced the proof in lectures in Cambridge in June 1993. The title of Wiles's Cambridge lectures 'Modular Forms, Elliptic Curves, and Galois Representations', did not give a strong clue to what he would be presenting. He might be just presenting interesting new methods in this hot area of number theory. But there was growing excitement in the audience members as the ideas Wiles sketched in the first two lectures seemed to follow a narrowing path that could only lead to a proof of FLT. By the time of the third lecture, the room was packed; reporters had been alerted that a once-in-a-generation event in mathematics was imminent with the solution of a notorious 350-year-old problem likely being announced. Champagne bottles were kept ready to be popped.

Of course FLT had attracted a lot of attention from amateur mathematicians. Mathematics departments routinely received manuscripts claiming proof of it. The methods were typically elementary, and seemed unlikely to be novel enough to overcome a problem of this magnitude, that had resisted the best effort of mathematicians of outstanding calibre for centuries. There was often someone on the faculty who was given the job of debunking these proofs. But Wiles's work was proving something much more than just FLT, drawing on highly sophisticated techniques of modern number theory. Wiles was a number theorist of great repute, and so the chances that his solution would withstand close scrutiny were quite high. For mathematics of such sophistication and depth, just listening to three lectures would not be enough to check that Wiles's proof worked. It would require being refereed by several experts working closely with its ideas and poring over the manuscript for several months. But the audience could see the *grand lignes* of the argument, and sense the beauty and power of Wiles's ideas.

Wiles heard of Ribet's work showing that the elliptic symmetry conjecture implied FLT in 1986 at a colleague's house in Princeton. Wiles was electrified by this work of Ribet. The elliptic symmetry conjecture was widely believed by the mid-1980s, but the part of Serre's conjecture proved by Ribet was a delicate refinement. Upon hearing about Ribet's work, which made FLT a corollary of the elliptic symmetry conjecture, Wiles started working with relentless focus on the latter. If he succeeded, as a corollary he would realize his childhood dream of proving Fermat. The elliptic symmetry conjecture was widely thought to be out of reach, but Wiles decided to work on it nevertheless, knowing that even if he fell short of proving it, the ideas he developed would be valuable. Wiles worked for seven years on FLT in secrecy, spending most of his working hours in the attic of his Princeton home. Wiles's main new breakthrough was to show a *modularity lifting* result. He could in many important cases prove that all p-adic Galois symmetries of fixed weight and level, that 'reduce' to a fixed mod p Ramanujan symmetry, were Ramanujan.[35]

Wiles concluded his third Cambridge lecture by writing down FLT as a corollary to his proof of many cases of the elliptic symmetry conjecture. The breakthrough was reported in newspapers all over the world the next day. In the *New York Times* the article about Wiles's proof made it to the front page, and that too above the fold.

But soon, there were rumours that the proof had a gap. The refereeing of Wiles's paper uncovered a subtle error in a crucial part of the argument. Perhaps the celebrations after his Cambridge lectures had been premature. There were some who thought that Wiles's proof has fallen to Fermat's curse which had damned previous attempts to solve the problem. Some like Abhyankar had been skeptical on general grounds about using such high-powered mathematics to solve a concrete classical problem. Abhyankar was a proponent of what he called 'high school algebra', and felt that too many mathematicians were seduced by the lure of fancy mathematical tools. The jury on whether FLT was proved or close to being proved seemed to be out, although even with the mistake Wiles's ideas seemed novel and powerful, and he was able to prove cases of the elliptic symmetry conjecture far beyond what was known. This all seemed very exciting but yet very distant from my struggles of trying to write a decent thesis.

Writing a small joint paper with Dipendra helped me get to grips with the mechanics of writing a maths paper. My thoughts when printed out seemed to have a greater validity and definiteness compared to their tentative status when just in my mind or jotted down by hand on a page. On the walk back to the guest house I would often realize that the proof I had written had a hole, sometimes a hole so big that there was no longer any proof at all, and I would have to think of another argument altogether. But eventually the process converged and we finished this small manuscript. Even as a novice I knew that this paper was mildly interesting and cute, but did not move the needle of my thesis by that much. It would be one of the chapters of my thesis. But the Buddha of the thesis, the central theorem which would make it interesting, was still missing.

∞

It was almost time to go back to Pasadena. I would spend only the Fall quarter there before going back to Bombay. Before leaving for Pasadena there was one important development in my thesis work. I started focusing on understanding a question about 'congruences between Ramanujan symmetries' that had not been studied in the literature. I thought it might be a useful step in implementing Hida's strategy for resolving the thesis problem I was obsessing about and unable to make any progress with. The goal of the theory of congruences between Ramanujan symmetries was to understand the levels N and weights k at which there were p-adic Ramanujan symmetries that gave rise to a *fixed* mod p Ramanujan symmetry.

Congruences between p-adic Ramanujan symmetries studied weights k and levels N of all the p-adic Ramanujan symmetries that 'collided' at, in other words 'reduced' to, a fixed mod p Ramanujan symmetry. The work of Ribet and subsequent work of Fred Diamond and Richard Taylor, both students of Andrew Wiles, had furnished a complete answer to the question of which levels N occur that did not have p as a factor. I am going to call this the *tame case*. I wanted to understand the wild case in which one allowed powers of p to divide the level.[36]

This was moving away from the problem of my thesis to show that the 'cone of p-adic Ramanujan symmetries of fixed weight k and levels Np^{∞}' (namely levels allowed to vary by allowing higher and higher powers of p to occur in their factorization) emerging from a fixed mod p Ramanujan symmetry was much smaller than the corresponding 'cone of p-adic Galois symmetries'. My question just focused on the Ramanujan cone.[37]

I felt very motivated to think about the question of analysing 'wild congruences' partly because I had come up with it on my own. This made me more invested in answering it, and psychologically I felt a greater right to think about it. I started devoting all my time to tilting at the windmill of this question. Richard Taylor is a leading expert in the theory of congruences between Ramanujan symmetries, and I posed via email my question about 'wild congruences' to him. I knew him a little as he had visited Caltech and given a course on Ribet's work which I had attended. Taylor wrote back saying that he had mused about the question and he thought the answer lay very deep. He thought developments in 'p-adic Hodge theory', a theory developed in Paris by Jean-Marc Fontaine, might be needed before my question could be properly addressed. This was a little discouraging for me as I did not know any p-adic Hodge theory, and if the route to the answer had to cross this technically daunting and unfamiliar area, it was unlikely I would be the one to find the answer. Taylor's reply was in another way quite reassuring as it made me more confident that the question I had posed was interesting and meaningful and needed to be answered by someone. In spite of Taylor's expressed opinion, I decided to think about the question more directly, without first getting some grounding in p-adic Hodge theory. The time now available to me to finish my thesis did not allow me the luxury of learning the basics of this complicated theory before I attacked my question. This would turn out to be a blessing in disguise.

I made no progress with my question in the last few weeks of my stay in Sapporo, but carried it in my mind as I flew out to Pasadena for one final time.

6

Taming Wild Congruences

When I had first arrived in Pasadena, the five years ahead of me as a graduate student had seemed limitless. I was in my early twenties then; now I was in my late twenties. What seemed like an eternity of time had been consumed and the few months I had left in Caltech had a posthumous feel to them. I was back again to the aroma of office spaces that were perennially air-conditioned as if for their own comfort, and where the lights in the hallways were always on.

The final problem of my thesis suggested by Hida was later shown to be wrong: after a few years it was shown that the cones of Galois and Ramanujan symmetries I was trying to show to be unequal were actually equal. (This was done using the techniques Wiles introduced in his proof of FLT.) At the time I did not know this of course. My adviser's intuition in this case turned out to be mistaken. He had given me this more speculative problem after I had not been able to work out the other problems that he had suggested which were of a more technical nature. But in spite of the problem turning out to be wrong, it led me, perhaps because of its open-ended nature, to ask an interesting related question, which was almost like a sub-question that one needed to answer first.

To find the answer to a good question, one can't typically land on the correct answer right away. One proceeds by trial and error, making mistakes and learning about the pitfalls; intuitions need to be sharpened, instincts honed, before an answer is found. One starts with a naive intuitive approach (how else can one begin?), which is bound to be off the mark. Finding the answer to my question would require a purge of my misconceptions, and after much hard struggle, the answer could become immanent, almost contained in the question itself. A little like a sculptor chiselling away the superfluous to arrive at the essential figure implicit in the stone. This is true of questions as well; it's hard to ask a good question right away.

At one of our meetings Hida remarked that I wanted to become famous by answering an open-ended question rather than working my way through hard calculations to resolve the narrower problems he had first suggested. Be that as it may, my engagement with this last problem had been more fruitful than with the earlier ones and had led me to formulate my Sapporo question about wild congruences.

The question had been little studied in the rich literature about congruences. In the wild case, there were a plethora of congruences as compared to the tame case. To think of the wild case, it seemed one did not have a reliable guide to figure out what might be true. I felt more energized than I had in the previous four years of my existence in Pasadena. It was the question about wild congruences that led to this vividness, an opening up of the imagination, an opening up to my surroundings.

The last five-month-long phase of my life in Pasadena was inaugurated by a loss that could not be recouped. I had placed an order for the proceedings of the Seattle conference I had attended at the end of my first year at Caltech just before I left on my six-month-long sojourn to Bombay, Allahabad and Sapporo. I had understood nothing then, and I had ordered these volumes partly to see if I would understand more now. The two volumes that should have been waiting for me on my desk had vanished. Rather than making a vigorous effort to find them, I accepted the loss as a fait accompli, conforming to the stereotype of the fatalistic Indian. The lesson I inferred from the loss was that I should spend the next few months trying to narrow down my interests and concentrate all my efforts on completing my thesis.

∞

I figured I had nothing to lose and would think about my Sapporo question regardless of being ill-prepared for it. I was guaranteed to get a PhD – mediocre, euthanistic as it might be – on the basis of the fragments I had done, in a few months time. If I got nowhere with the question that would just add another few months to the years already wasted. A famous quote of Carl Jacobi is 'always invert'. Figuring out necessary conditions for the wild congruences to exist seemed very hard. I decided to follow Jacobi's advice of 'inverting', and try to find the wild congruences where I could, seek out sufficient conditions using what I knew, by a direct and almost naive attack on the question. It would be valuable to make some inroads, even if I could not find a complete answer to my question.

After returning to Pasadena from Sapporo, I kept up the routine of travelling once a week to UCLA to see Professor Hida. I commuted from Pasadena to the UCLA campus in Westwood on RTD buses. The bus moved from wealthy precincts of Pasadena towards poorer neighbourhoods. I had to change buses at a transit point. There was a part of the route which was on the freeways of Los Angeles. The bus had tinted glasses that made its interior look like a movie theatre. Many of my fellow commuters on the bus were people living on the margins of society, lost in their soliloquies. I sat amidst them haunted by my Sapporo question. As the bus approached UCLA, the surroundings became pristine. Sprinklers watered manicured lawns with the care of a pastor tending to his parish. Palm, Maple, and Foothill Boulevards went by, then the Beverly Hills Hotel which rose up from the sidewalk like a pink confection. When I arrived at UCLA there were waves of students criss-crossing the campus in the break between classes.

The interactions with my adviser had changed in character as I now working on something of my own, on a topic that I had spent more time thinking about than he had. I had more thought equity in this topic than him. Upon returning to Pasadena I had asked him my Sapporo question. Hida's view was that as Diamond and Taylor had avoided looking at wild congruences in their work this suggested that it may not be possible to analyse them. I said to myself that by this line of reasoning, nothing new would ever be done. Although I felt discouraged by his response, in a way it motivated me further to try and make progress with the Sapporo question.

∞

Such discouragement from an adviser, or a guru, in creative pursuits was par for the course. I had even read in an interview of Serre that he believed that a student should be discouraged initially from pursuing mathematics as a vocation. There were enough mathematicians and it was a hard career to take up: the success rate was low. If the student was not dissuaded by the initial discouragement, this demonstrated tenacity, and they had passed a test.

After the meeting with my adviser, I had an hour or so before the next bus that would take me part of the way back to Pasadena.

I wandered to the northern part of the campus. It was much prettier. In the Sculpture Garden I read the names of the sculptors whose work was present in it: Jean Arp, Barbara Hepworth, Henry Moore. The abstract pieces were mostly ignored by the students walking past them on the way to their classes. For someone who stopped and looked at them, as I sometimes did, they might slow time down, allowing the mind to expand and move away from its preoccupations, lifting a needle from the groove of a record spinning endlessly inside one's head.

The days were shortening and it was already getting dark. I thought about the maths I was stuck on. Parts of it clarified in my mind, like pieces of a puzzle coming together to form a missing corner. I came to a sloping road lined by tall trees. There was now a nip in the darkened air. The fragrance of eucalyptus hung densely. Fog had started to creep in. I felt I had lost my way in a forest. The bus stop was just a few minutes away on Hilgard Avenue.

∞

The breakthrough in answering my Sapporo question came within three or four weeks of returning to Pasadena from Japan. To answer it I tried to use a technique that Ribet had developed in a paper he published about a decade earlier to analyse tame congruences. This twelve-page paper was written well before his work that made Fermat's Last Theorem a logical consequence of the elliptic symmetry conjecture. It enthralled me by its succinct elegance. It had taken me several readings spread over months in my third year as a graduate student to absorb the paper which was published in the Proceedings of the International Congress of Mathematicians held in Warsaw in 1983. The International Congress happens once every four years. To be invited as a speaker is a mark of having arrived in the subject. It is also the occasion at which the Fields Medals are awarded, up to four of them, to mathematicians under forty who have done important transformative work. The stipulation of being no more than forty in the year the prize is awarded, together with the prize being awarded every four years, makes some years better to be born in than others, to improve very marginally the chances of getting a Fields medal.

Ribet's article in the proceedings was written close to the time Lech Wałęsa was leading workers of the Lenin Shipyard in Gdansk to strike. I had read about these strikes, which ground Poland to a halt, when in high school in India and had become fascinated with the union leader Lech Wałęsa, the shipyard electrician who led the Solidarity movement. The grainy pictures of him in the *Times of India* showed a burly man with a walrus moustache. Towards the end of my days in Cambridge, the Berlin Wall fell, brought down partly by the reverberations of the strikes in the Lenin Shipyard.

The Warsaw paper had the epigrammatic brilliance of a short story. It broached the issue of analysing tame congruences, and determined 'necessary and sufficient' conditions for their existence in one fell swoop. The phrase 'necessary and sufficient', and the kindred phrase, 'if and only if', is mathematical jargon oft used in mathematical papers: to be in good standing with a lender it is 'necessary' to pay this month's instalment on the loan, but not by itself 'sufficient' as if you do not pay next month you will be in default. But it is 'sufficient' to pay your instalments each month, and it is also 'sufficient' but not 'necessary' to pay a lump sum that discharges all of your loan. The necessity of the condition was quickly taken care of using general principles, and most of the paper was taken up with proving the sufficiency.

Ribet's proof of the sufficiency took place in two steps. In the first step he reduced the problem, by means of an insightful construction, to an auxiliary statement that seemed superficially to have nothing to do with analysing congruences. In the second step he verified the auxiliary statement by arguments from a different branch of mathematics, namely group theory. In a footnote to the Warsaw paper, Ribet thanked Serre for helping him out with the group theory argument. The footnote bore witness to the continuity of the mathematical enterprise. Serre and Ribet belonged to different generations – Serre was born in the 1920s. Ribet was born just after World War II. Serre giving a helping hand to Ribet at a crucial juncture in Ribet's argument made me aware of lines of communication through which inspiration and expertise flowed between different generations, between mathematicians working in different parts of the world. Ribet worked at Berkeley, while Serre was a professor at the very prestigious Collège de France in Paris, an apex body of French academia, established in 1530 with the avowed objective of enabling the best French minds to offer free courses in their specialities to the French citizenry. I had heard that in these courses at the Collège, some of the auditors were the homeless, sheltering from the cold of a Parisian fall and winter.

∞

The proof in a research paper is like a recipe. Using it the reader has to cook the ingredients. In trying to apply Ribet's ideas to analyse wild congruences, I was forced to undertake that labour, and bring his ideas to a boil in my mind, till they enveloped me as fully realized flavours and smells, glutting my senses.

There were points I had taken for granted when reading Ribet's paper that now flummoxed me when I tried to see if I could argue analogously in my wild case. This was part of making the transition from a passive reader of a maths paper to a more active user of its ideas. I had to now go deeper and quarry Ribet's paper for ideas, inspiration, or at least a plausible starting point from where to begin my efforts to answer the Sapporo question. The few lines in Ribet's paper that handled the necessity in his tame case led to a *terra incognita* in my wild case. I jumped over that paragraph and into the part of the paper where Ribet dealt with sufficiency, as his arguments for that could plausibly be useful in my wild case as well. Taking a cue from Ribet's paper, I tried to break down finding sufficient conditions into two steps. I mused over the first step for several days, thinking about Ribet's construction, hoping it could be carried over to my setting. The prospects looked good for succeeding in this. I could at least start in the same manner as he did, but there were still telling differences between our situations. His construction solved the problem up to error terms that in the second step were shown to be negligible. When I did the thought experiment and made his construction in the context of wild congruences, the error terms were infinite, and at first this disheartened me. Perhaps the attempt to mimic Ribet's proof was a non-starter and, in my case, the first step would introduce error terms that would overwhelm the main term, derailing the entire enterprise.

I carried the problem in my mind as I went through my days in Pasadena. The problem of the error term was on my mind as I ate my lunch at Chandler, the campus cafeteria. It played on my nerves as I drank a cappuccino at the neighbouring Red Door Cafe. It was with me as I took my clothes to the laundry room and was enveloped by its steamy atmosphere, overcome by the floral blooms of detergents that almost made one hallucinate that one was in a lush tropical forest.

Slowly I came to terms with the differences between Ribet's case and mine. Like the muscles in the iris of the eye that contract and expand to deal with changes in the light regime, my mind was making adjustments to the first step of Ribet's argument so that it would work for me. The error terms that seemed overwhelming at first began to seem less hopeless the more I thought about them. I saw that the error terms could be stratified; the infinite part that seemed damning at first took on an increasingly benign aspect as it could be separated out so as not to interfere with the main term. Once one filtered the infinite part out, the finite filtrate that was left over was what I needed to show was negligible. After several missteps and misunderstandings, I saw that a variation of Ribet's first step did work in my situation and reduced the problem to an assertion in group theory.

I made many mistakes along the way, declared victory too quickly and tripped on a detail I had overlooked or an argument I had misunderstood. Fortunately in this kind of work, I could make as many mistakes as I needed to: it only mattered that I eventually got it right. It was not like being a performing artist – a vocalist in the Hindustani classical music tradition or a concert pianist – where perfection in the moment mattered.

∞

The group theory statement that I had to contend with in my second step seemed to have a very different flavour to what Ribet had needed to prove in his second step. This was the stage at which Ribet had been helped by Serre, who had pointed out to Ribet a lemma – a smaller result proved along the way to proving a theorem – in a paper by the Japanese mathematician Yasutaka Ihara that would help Ribet's analysis. Ihara's lemma turned out to be exactly what Ribet needed to complete the argument.

I read and reread the last few pages of Ribet's Warsaw paper to see if what he was doing could be adapted to my case. I could imitate parts of what he did, and this helped me sharpen and make clearer the group theory issue I had to overcome. It helped me formulate a general group theory statement that, if I were able to prove it, would see me home and dry. This clarified the picture, as by formulating a clean general statement that was not implicated in the particulars of the situation I was studying, I could move away from the messiness of the constructions in the first step and work in a cleaner environment. I hoped that this might help to find the right group-theoretic arguments to consummate the second step.

There was nothing in Ribet's paper that could be of use to me at this point. In the work till now – generalizing Ribet's first step as well as some of the preliminary analysis needed in the second step to reduce the problem to a clean group theory statement that needed proof – I had the comfort of the companionship of Ribet's methods. Now the paths forked and this last stretch I would have to walk alone.

The statement that I had to prove was striking, but I did not have a clue how to begin proving it. I had reached the edge of a precipice in my attempt to find sufficient conditions for wild congruences. I needed a leap of the imagination to get me to the result I needed.

I took to the streets of Pasadena, trying to get myself unstuck by walking and keeping the group theory statement in my mind. I just kept repeating the statement to myself, rephrasing it with minor variations, like telling the beads of a rosary. Spending time with something that one had difficulty with and trying to dissolve its difficulties in the solvent of the time one spent with it, seemed the only way to resolve it. It was not really a choice as one was unable to think about anything else.

Shimura writes about Taniyama's approach to doing mathematics:

> He took up first the case of the jacobian variety of a hyperelliptic curve, and eventually that of more general abelian varieties. Since not much had been known in this field, the task was a 'hard fighting' against difficulties and a 'bitter struggle' of trial and error. He used to express any substantial undertaking of a mathematician in those four words (strictly speaking, in four corresponding Chinese characters). 'Effortless' was a word alien to his mathematics at least from his viewpoint, though it may have looked differently to others, and he must have found immense delight in such 'fighting and struggle'.[38]

I was in my period of hard fighting and bitter struggle and I did find like Taniyama some joy in these struggles; I felt that at last I was getting somewhere in my graduate work.

∞

Over the next couple of weeks of thinking, I had a growing conviction that the group theory statement I needed to verify had to be true. I had tested it against putative counterexamples and it had stood up against them. But I had still found no clue to prove it. I fantasized that the growing conviction might be getting me closer to proving it. I kept hoping that I could add a small piece of evidence in favour of André Weil's dictum that theorems were proved by people who believed in them. Belief preceded proof perhaps, even if absolute belief could only be vouchsafed after absolute proof.

One Sunday morning, after two weeks spent getting nowhere, I had a realization as I did my morning stretches. I had taken to running on the track near the Caltech gym. Doing exercise streamlined my body and mind and made me think better.

The realization was that something I had spent a few desultory weeks studying a year ago was exactly what was needed to answer my question. Modular symbols were created and studied in the 1970s by Bryan Birch at Oxford, Peter Swinnerton-Dyer at Cambridge, Yuri Manin in Moscow and Barry Mazur at Harvard, not always working together, but led to similar constructions motivated by the slightly different problems they were looking at. I had studied in my meandering path through the literature a paper that used modular symbols in the context of congruences. I had taken delight in understanding the paper, and liked its group-theoretic way of looking at congruences.

The paper included a concise description of modular symbols. Modular symbols are an elegant tool – they turn the continuous into something discrete. I realized when doing my stretches that morning on the running track that if I used modular symbols in the context of my question, the answer became apparent.

Reinterpreted in the language of modular symbols, the answer to my question was obvious. I had found the missing key to my problem. Rather than a leap of the imagination, it had taken a nudge from the subconscious to make me reach for something I had read that could be relevant. It was like being moved to pull a book off a shelf in the library that one had borrowed in the past, read parts of with fitful attention, led back to it by the tantalizing memory of a paragraph in it – one could even visualize it situated in the middle of a page, halfway through the book – that might conceivably address one's predicament. Just to utter the phrase modular symbols was enough to answer my question, such was its incantatory power in my situation. The solution seemed too facile, and together with a bubbling excitement, I also initially felt a bit doubtful. But after pacing around, sitting down on a bench, wiping the sweat off my face with a towel, I was convinced that this had to work, the fit of the key provided by modular symbols was perfect.

Ramanujan symmetries have been studied intensively since the nineteenth century. The subject seems to have the gift of eternal youth: there is still something new to be discovered about them. Modular symbols were invented quite recently, as late as the 1970s. In mathematics – a subject with a written history of more than 4000 years – an idea that is two decades old, as modular symbols were then, might still be considered a new kid on the block. Once proved, a theorem remains true forever. Theorems proved by Euclid or ideas discovered by Aryabhatta are still relevant. Mathematics discovered in the eighteenth century, for instance the mathematics of Gauss, is not only valid and non-trivial (a mathematician's way of saying something is deep or at least interesting), but can also still provide inspiration for vital new ideas. Generations of mathematicians have worked on various aspects of Ramanujan symmetries, building a powerful and rich theory that has solved classical and very hard problems in other parts of mathematics.

Mathematical ideas and objects can in theory be abundantly created. But in practice the ones that exist, surviving over decades or even centuries as viable creations, are so precious that even the tiniest part of them cannot be wasted. In Kerala every part of a coconut is used: its water to drink, its *malai* (tender meat) to eat, its shell to make coir mats. Ramanujan symmetries are to number theorists what coconuts are to a Malayali. As a community, mathematicians are abstemious and ecologically conscientious, using every last scrap of an idea. I marvel at the way mathematicians optimize ideas by making strenuous efforts to wring out every last drop of use from them. This is done by finding the right context for the idea, developing formalism and notation that capture the idea as succinctly as possible, and finding its most general and powerful form. Mathematicians are good citizens of the world of mathematics, conscientious about its resources, and conserving and husbanding them with great care.

∞

I had to now harvest the fruit of my efforts by writing down my proof. I had bent a fruitful branch of an apple tree towards the ground after some effort and now I had to gather in the apples, hopefully bushels of them. This promised to be doable work, but it still remained to be done. The next morning I came in early to the department and started typing out the proof on the laptop I had recently purchased.

I had become aware during the writing of the joint paper with Dipendra of the spell a typed-up manuscript with perfectly typeset equations could cast on me, making the arguments appear more solid than they actually were. Often after typing up a proof and admiring it as it swelled like a symphony on the page, I would detect a fatal flaw in a detail that had seemed obvious. I had worried about a subtle point in the argument, while overlooking a logical flaw in a part of the proof that had seemed more like connective tissue.

Once the argument of Ribet was made to work in my setting of wild congruences, it was like having a pump at my disposal that I could prime to make the wild congruences proliferate and fill up nearly all of the island of congruences. To make them proliferate to their fullest extent I also used an argument that I had read in the short paper written by Henri Carayol and published in the Duke journal in 1989, so around five years earlier. During the time I wrote my thesis, I did not delve too deeply into the ideas of Carayol's paper, merely using his conclusions and theorems.

In the few weeks that it took to type up my results and their proofs that would form the main chapter of my thesis, I stayed in the department from morning till late evening, often close to twelve hours at a stretch. There were deficiencies in the writing I had done during the day that would flash in my mind as I walked back home, rustled up a simple meal and made conversation with my roommate.

As soon as I entered my office the next morning I was ensnared by the work that I had identified as needing amendment after having left my office the previous evening. I had to write up some lemmas and sequence them so that they would by logical concatenation produce the desired result about wild congruences. The writing of the paper drew me in, and I could not tear myself away from my desk till it was well after lunch. I sometimes felt like the character Abhimanyu from the Mahabharata who had been taught to break through and penetrate the enemy's armoured formations, but had not learnt how to get out once he was encircled by the enemy forces.

The easy fix for the empty stomach that growled within me was to wait for teatime in the department lounge around 4 p.m. In the early days of my graduate study I had struggled to stay in my office and work even for an hour continuously. I would oscillate between the department and my student apartment several times a day. The hard work now was possible as it was not an act of the will, but almost involuntary, the only type of hard work that I seemed capable of.

∞

My work had now progressed to a point that I could email some experts a draft of my manuscript. I first sent the draft to Richard Taylor whom I had messaged a few weeks ago about my Sapporo question, before I started thinking obsessively about it. I wrote in my email the caveat that this was still work in progress. Taylor was an expert in the subject, making a name for himself, younger than Ribet, and around five years older than me. I think he was working in Cambridge at the time I emailed him. I figured that once I told Taylor about how I had invoked modular symbols he would know in a flash the entire structure of my proof.

To my relief, Taylor replied within a week and had nice things to say about how far I had got with studying congruences in the wild case. It surprised him. He agreed that just an off-the-shelf use of Carayol's result would not have given me the results I had obtained. He made particular reference to the use of modular symbols in my proof, which I had brought in like a *deus ex machina* when all else had failed in proving my group theory property. It worked like a charm, just like tangled plotlines in a Greek drama are straightened by the device of an actor playing God descending from up on high and imposing order by decree. Taylor asked me if I had thought of the idea of using modular symbols myself. I decided that this showed that the idea was nice and unexpected and I was happy that it had surprised an expert.

Taylor also wrote to me that Andrew Wiles had new ideas about congruences in his work on the elliptic symmetry conjecture. The gap in Wiles's strategy had been fixed. Two manuscripts would be released shortly containing the complete proof. The second, shorter, manuscript was written by Taylor and Wiles. Wiles had called upon Taylor's help to plug the gap in his proof. These manuscripts were not available as yet. Taylor advised me to try and publish my results quickly because of the partial overlap with Wiles's forthcoming work.

Wiles, in reply to an email I sent him, said that he did not have any especially new ideas about congruences in his work. Later when the manuscripts became available, I did see that my work intersected with a small part of Wiles's work, but I was relieved to see that his work did not make my efforts redundant. There was a lemma in his paper that could be used to prove my group theory statement by a proof that was less baroque than my proof that used modular symbols. But I thought my proof had an element of surprise to it which I liked. It was also reassuring to see that my ideas overlapped partially with a work as monumental as Wiles's proof of FLT, showing that the issues I was thinking about were alive, contemporary and at the cutting edge of current research in mathematics.

Wiles overcame the gap in his earlier approach announced in Cambridge in 1993 by a totally unexpected argument. He wrote in the introduction of his paper that he came to a 'marvelous revelation' that made his proof work approximately a year after the flaw in his earlier proof had emerged:

> In doing this I suddenly came to a marvelous revelation: I saw in a flash on September 19th, 1994 that de Shalit's theory, if generalised, could be used together with duality to glue the Hecke rings at suitable auxiliary levels into a power series ring. I had unexpectedly found the missing key to my old abandoned approach.

There have been several instances of mathematicians coming very close to a solution of a famous problem, faltering at the last step, but still recovering to fix their solution; the intuitions they built up thinking hard about the problem for years were able ultimately to overcome the final hurdle at which their technique had come up short. There are examples that go the other way too, but Wiles's revelation did indeed overcome the last hurdle in his path, or rather circumvented it by finding a brilliant detour that led him to the solution. Wiles narrowly missed getting a Fields Medal on account of the associated numerics, as by 1998 when the International Congress was held in Berlin, Wiles had already crossed forty. The historic importance of Wiles's work made his missing a Fields Medal seem insignificant, in fact almost an irrelevance. He got many other prizes for his breakthrough. One of them was the Wolfskehl Prize which was instituted in the early twentieth century with prize money of almost a million pounds to be given to the person who solved FLT. By the time it was awarded to Wiles in 1997 the value had reduced to 30,000 pounds partly on account of the hyperinflation in Germany after World War I.

Wiles's phrase 'marvelous revelation' echoed Fermat's claim in 1637 that he had a marvellous demonstration of his theorem that the margin of the book of Diophantus he was reading at the time was not wide enough to contain. The news of Wiles's revised proof made less of a news splash in the fall of 1994 as compared to his first announcement a year earlier. But within the mathematical world the proof was sensational. The new argument was simpler than the original flawed proof, and introduced a dazzlingly original patching method to complement the ideas that he had discovered earlier. The proof was quickly endorsed by experts. Wiles had escaped the Fermat curse that had doomed all earlier efforts to settle his problem! These earlier efforts had played their part, leading to developments in number theory that were part and parcel of Wiles's approach.

Wiles's solution was a synthesis of many different techniques and was amazingly intricate and ingenious. Wiles had silenced doubting Thomases like Abhyankar by performing the miracle of his proof. No one could deny Wiles's victory over the most famous problem in all of mathematics, and the efficacy of the tools of modern number theory that he had so brilliantly marshalled to solve Fermat's seventeenth-century problem. Wiles's work turned the Galois symmetry arising from elliptic curves into a Ramanujan symmetry, a feat almost as miraculous as turning water into wine.

Now Wiles's 'modularity lifting' technique was on firm ground. It was to be the main engine in our proof of Serre's conjecture a decade later. A p-adic Galois symmetry is like a skyscraper standing on the base of its mod p 'reduction'. Wiles's technique was like a feat of levitation: it 'lifted' the Ramanujan property from its base, its mod p reduction, to the entire skyscraper.

For me there was the added marvellous coincidence that around the same time as Wiles's revelation, I had the breakthrough in my thesis work about congruences between Ramanujan symmetries. The theory of such congruences was at the heart of Wiles's twentieth-century proof of Fermat's seventeenth-century problem. My revelation was objectively far less marvellous than that of Wiles, but for me personally it was a thrilling breakthrough moment four years in the making. Wiles later compared his moment of revelation to a light being suddenly switched on in a dark room. The piecemeal sense of the room one gets by stumbling against pieces of furniture in the dark is clarified into knowing clearly the room's entire layout when the light comes on. My far more modest realization was like a door that I was pushing against suddenly giving way, making me stumble awkwardly into the room on the other side.

∞

There still remained a stumbling block to overcome, before I could have a complete analysis of wild congruences in the bag, that stymied my efforts for a while. I had shown that my wild congruences grew abundantly in the island of congruences between Ramanujan symmetries, but there was a patch of the island that I could not gain access to. I suspected that the patch was barren, there were no wild congruences growing in it, but I could not be certain. These were congruences between Ramanujan symmetries of weight 2 and levels p and level p^2. Here I was bumping into the difficulty that I still had no way to figure out a priori necessary conditions for the existence of wild congruences. If I had access to necessary conditions, then I could have reasoned that the acidity of the soil in the patch made it inhospitable to the wild congruences. Thus far I had been able to empirically establish congruences all over the island. I had ducked the issue of finding necessary conditions for the wild congruences by showing that they were omnipresent except for one patch. My methods failed to prove the existence of wild congruences in this patch. But that was not enough evidence, even less a complete proof, that there were no wild congruences growing there.

I was at a loss. The one paragraph in Ribet's Warsaw paper that dealt summarily with necessary conditions for congruences in his tame case seemed to be of no help in my wild case. Like in the case of the group theory statement that had stumped me, when I felt paralysed as it did not seem possible to make incremental progress, this problem of showing the non-existence of wild congruences in one patch that was surrounded on all sides by a forest of wild congruences, seemed beyond me. There seemed no way of stealing upon the problem and catching it unawares. It would need a frontal attack. I would need to find an argument for this by myself. There was no model to follow, and it seemed like an all-or-nothing situation.

I kept working on this problem even as I continued writing and editing the other parts of the paper. I carried the problem in my mind on the bus journeys I made to see my adviser at UCLA. I tried to find inspiration by looking at papers related to p-adic Hodge theory that I carried in my backpack. I would sit with a paper open on my lap while I looked outside the window of the bus, at the moving urban landscape that scrolled by. I felt discouraged looking at these papers. They were impenetrable to me, and if I had to build on these results before I resolved my issue about the seemingly barren patch, I was doomed. I despaired of succeeding in establishing the barrenness of the patch. If I could not come up with an argument, I would just leave this issue unresolved in my thesis. But I was not happy to be doing this.

As I walked on the streets of Pasadena – down Lake Avenue, turning into Colorado Boulevard – preoccupied with my mathematical conundrum, the cityscape would pass by in a haze. I passed by people I never saw again: like apparitions who were absorbed into distance, diffused into sensation. The problem seemed to resist all my efforts.

∞

In these last few months before I defended my thesis in December of 1994, I had made much greater progress than I had ever hoped to. Through all my failures over four years, through the despair of ever proving a real theorem and writing a satisfactory thesis, I had kept trying to work, kept reading mathematics that appealed to me, like Ribet's paper that I obsessed over for months, not getting a complete, systematic understanding of it, but developing a sense of its arguments, layering my mind with the intuitions I acquired from mulling over the paper.

I had made it thus far on the courage of my despair, or a despairing courage. I call it a despairing courage because my persistence was not built on confidence. At least not a robust, calm confidence. Perhaps in its stead there was something much more muted and implicit, a sense that I had something in me – hard to measure and not likely to register on any scale – that, if I were able to draw upon it, would lead me to a breakthrough in my work. The four years had tested me, found me wanting, justifying all the self-doubts that had been my constant companion since childhood.

During the weekly RTD bus journeys after making the breakthrough on my Sapporo question, travelling between Caltech and UCLA, I had a pressing sense of my mortality. I felt it was imperative that I not die before I had completed writing out my investigations of wild congruences. This was logically a ridiculous way to feel – it was extremely unlikely that I was going to die in my twenties, in good health. The enhanced sense of my mortality was all the more preposterous because although I had some confidence that my thesis was an interesting piece of work and that I had created some novel mathematics, I also knew that it was not a great breakthrough. In my own personal context it was a big breakthrough, the first theorem I had proved in my life, my first creative work in mathematics. In a larger context it was just an interesting piece of work, the work of a beginner. The project had been kick-started by asking a good question, and I had for the most part emulated known methods to answer the question, mainly combining known ingredients in novel ways. I also felt, almost as ridiculously as fearing death, that I should write up my results quickly, or else I could be beaten to proving my theorem about wild congruences.

But I was not quite at the finishing line – there was still the unresolved question that haunted me. The missing piece of the analysis of wild congruences nagged at my brain. It was at the back of my mind constantly. One day on the way back from UCLA, alighting from the bus's darkened interior on to Lake Avenue that was awash with the mellow light of the descending sun, I saw what could be used to prove that the patch of the island I was focusing on was indeed barren. I could use a theorem of Carayol from his long and difficult paper 'Sur les représentations ladiques associées aux formes modulaires de Hilbert', the one that had emerged from his seven-year penance, and derive a logical contradiction if there were any wild congruences in the patch. The paper of Carayol was published in the prestigious French journal Annales *Scientifiques de l'École Normale Supérieure*, founded in 1864 by Louis Pasteur. I remembered the result of the paper, but the proofs I had only a general idea about. I was quite willing to black box results, that is, use theorems from the literature whose proofs I did not understand completely, even after having spent quite a bit of time studying them. A mathematician made of sterner stuff would perhaps not be ready to black box results, but in my case my technical limitations left me little choice.

If I used the 'local-global compatibility' property that Carayol had proven, I could argue in a way that was, in fact, not very distant from how Ribet had used general principles to rule out congruences in the tame case, in the one-paragraph argument of his Warsaw paper. There was still some novelty in the argument I devised. I also drew upon Kummer theory, a basic tool of algebra that is taught in first-year graduate courses. Kummer was one of the most prominent number theorists of the nineteenth century and had developed powerful tools in algebraic number theory partly in an effort to attack FLT. Kummer theory in conjunction with the deep results of Carayol's paper produced a contradiction if one assumed that there were congruences between Ramanujan symmetries of levels p and p^2. The inaccessible patch had to be barren, something I could now deduce by pure thought, sight unseen!

∞

The experience of discovering the final clue to solving the problem about wild congruences – the idea occurring at the exact moment when I stepped off the bus when it arrived at my stop near Caltech, the terminal stop for the bus route – reminded me of a famous story of how the great French mathematician Henri Poincaré discovered Fuchsian functions:

> For fifteen days I strove to prove that there could not be any functions like those I have since called Fuchsian functions. I was then very ignorant; every day I seated myself at my work table, stayed an hour or two, tried a great number of combinations and reached no results. One evening, contrary to my custom, I drank black coffee and could not sleep. Ideas rose in crowds; I felt them collide until pairs interlocked, so to speak, making a stable combination. But the next morning I had established the existence of a class of Fuchsian functions, those which come from the hypergeometric series; I had only to write out the results, which took but a few hours. Then I wanted to represent these functions by a quotient of two series; this idea was perfectly conscious and deliberate, the analogy with elliptic functions guided me. I asked myself what properties these series must have if they existed, and I succeeded without difficulty in forming the series I have called theta-Fuchsian. Just at this time I left Caen, where I was then living, to go on a geological excursion under the auspices of the school of mines. The changes of travel made me

> forget my mathematical work. Having reached Coutances, we entered an omnibus to go some place or other. At the moment when I put my foot on the step the idea came to me, without anything in my former thoughts seeming to have paved the way for it, that the transformations I had used to define the Fuchsian functions were identical with those of non-Euclidean geometry. I did not verify the idea; I should not have had time, as, upon taking my seat in the omnibus, I went on with a conversation already commenced, but I felt a perfect certainty. On my return to Caen, for conscience's sake I verified the result at my leisure.[39]

Poincaré had got his idea stepping on to a bus in Coutances, I got mine stepping off a bus in Pasadena. The idea of Poincaré was far more consequential for mathematics than my idea to rule out congruences between symmetries of level p and level p^2. But I did feel the same certainty about the correctness of my idea as Poincaré, and a surge of joy on hitting upon it in the magical light of a southern California evening, just when I was on the point of giving up.

In a related and more contemporary vein, Serre gives a description of finding the key idea for his celebrated thesis in the 1950's:

> I prefer to close my eyes when I think about mathematics. The best work is done by night, in half sleep. Sometimes I go to bed thinking, 'Ah, I have a nice lemma to prove–or disprove.' (Should I explain what a lemma is? A mountain climber needs holds to get from one level to the next one. Lemmas are the holds of a mathematician.) Of course one has to write down things later, if only for publication. Sometimes you then find out what you have thought was wrong, but that's rare.

> My thesis is a typical case. There was a simple looking but rather powerful new idea (the 'loop space fibering', found at night, on a train). This basic idea was not enough: there was a technical part which required a rather difficult lemma. During three days I could only see the proof of the lemma when I was flat on the bed, my eyes shut. After that I understood it clearly enough so that I could write it down and my thesis was essentially done.[40]

I defended my thesis in a small room in the mathematics department at Caltech, the same room in which I had failed my topology exam three years earlier. Professor Hida came from UCLA to attend my defence. There was a celebratory air, and I felt an overwhelming sense of relief. I submitted my research paper on congruences in the wild case to the *Duke Mathematical Journal*, where it was accepted after a few months.

I skipped my graduation ceremonies at Caltech and headed to Bombay.

7

At a Hospital in Bombay, at Work in TIFR*

I went straight from the airport to Jaslok Hospital in South Bombay with my sister Padmini. I was very moved when I saw her smiling face at the airport. She had to shoulder a lot of the responsibility of taking care of my mother in addition to now becoming the mainstay of my father's firm. The streets we drove through were patchily lit and there were milkmen out on deliveries, balancing containers on bicycles. We crossed a bridge where piles of the morning newspapers lay awaiting distribution. The predawn hours felt like a hiatus before the city resumed the thrum of its daytime routine. The hospital was deserted and in the dimness of the lobby I saw outlines of figures of people swaddled in blankets lying on benches. The dim lighting combined with the eerie calm of the lobby, a hive of activity in the daytime, made these sleeping figures seem like mummies.

When I entered my mother's room it was dark with just a night lamp burning. She was sleeping on the surgical bed in the centre of the room. My father was snoring lightly on the sofa. There was

* Some parts of this chapter are based on my article 'TIFR and a conjecture of Jean-Pierre Serre' published in *Bhāvanā*, Volume 7, Issue 3, July 2023.

another figure of a bearded man sitting on a chair next to the bed. Our footsteps woke my mother. I rushed to touch her feet and hugged her, feeling all the warmth of being back home. Her eyes were puffed with the edema her liver disease caused. My father woke up and I touched his feet too. 'We have been waiting for you, Sakhar,' he said using his Marathi nickname for me which meant sugar. 'You have won this important battle with yourself and mathematics. Now as a family we look forward to many other things from you!' The bearded man had come into my family's orbit as an electrician. But over the last few years he had become an assistant of my mother's, carrying out various tasks, mainly centred around charitable giving to people across Bombay. My mother was much impaired by her illness, but even from her bed she could keep a whole army busy.

∞

I had returned to Bombay to be with my mother, but I also needed a job. I was elated when I secured a position as a Visiting Fellow at the Tata Institute of Fundamental Research (TIFR), an institution I had held in awe as a schoolboy. It was a temporary position with a tenure of two years during which one could apply to be a Fellow, which was the lowest rung of the more permanent (tenure-track) faculty ladder. There was no strict yardstick to measure progress. One would have to show some degree of productivity by writing papers and maybe getting a couple published. I did not worry too much about the year ahead. I was just happy to be back in Bombay with a thesis in my bag.

TIFR lay at the southernmost tip of Bombay. It was in an area known as Navy Nagar, built on reclaimed land. It had a dramatic setting, on the Arabian Sea, away from the noise and chaos, churn and energy of the city. It had been born in a remarkable set of circumstances. Its founder, Homi Bhabha, had been a distinguished physicist. He was charismatic and had a persuasive vision, as well as the skills, tenacity and connections needed to realize it. His vision was that India should draw upon its rich human capital to leapfrog into modernity. Science would be the leading edge of this thrust. He wanted to develop nuclear energy for India as an abundant resource available for its development, and at the same time make possible research in the pure sciences in the country. In his mind technology and the pure sciences were part of a common ecosystem; they were mutually dependent and one could not have one without the other.

Remarkably, Bhabha persuaded the leadership of the newly independent and resource-strapped country – one that had just thrown off the yoke of centuries of debilitating British rule, and had many pressing problems on its hands – to allocate resources for intellectual activities like pure mathematics. This would not directly solve any practical problems, but could still contribute to the intellectual temper and growth of the country, undergirding scientific progress. The institutions that he built (TIFR and the Bhabha Atomic Research Centre) represent a synthesis of three elements: a single person's vision, a government that was sympathetic to science and learning, and a private company Tata, that was willing to do its bit for science. These were long-term bets and investments which paid rich dividends.

Leading mathematicians from all over the world came for periods of three months at a time to give a course of lectures on different topics at the frontiers of research. The research scholars took notes that were written up as books. In the decades of the 1950s and 1960s young mathematicians at TIFR were sent on deputation to centres like Paris to learn directly and first-hand the latest developments in fields of pure mathematics, such as algebraic geometry. They came back and proved deep theorems that made the world sit up and take notice. It was a remarkable flowering of mathematical creativity in the newly independent India. The work done at the School of Mathematics at TIFR from the 1960s onwards started a seminal period for the pure sciences. I felt very excited to work there, and to try and make headway with my research.

∞

Over the next few years (from 1995 to 2002) my work at TIFR was interspersed with many hours spent at hospitals attending to my mother. My mother was in and out of hospitals. The hospitalizations became almost routine and played to a known script. They usually followed several days of uncertainty at home, when my mother's blood values seemed headed in the wrong direction because of her malfunctioning liver. She could be given higher doses of diuretics when under hospital care. While in the hospital, the fluid in my mother's stomach could be tapped, and at the same time she could be given albumen to compensate for the proteins she lost after the fluid in her stomach was drained.

I spent long afternoons in Breach Candy Hospital in my mother's room overlooking the sea. She had been admitted there after a crisis in her health a few months after the spell in Jaslok. My job did not require me to punch a timecard, so it was not hard to spend time with her. Although we did not speak much to each other in the afternoons, there was a sense of being in silent communion. She would lie for prolonged periods with her eyes closed, not asleep, and I would watch her from the maroon, rexine-covered sofa pushed against the wall. I felt calm sitting by her bedside in the hospital room. I would go to her bed to adjust the blanket that had slipped off her feet or shift the pillows so that she was more comfortable. I would massage her feet. I slept nights on the sofa using bed sheets and a blanket provided by the hospital.

∞

Some days my mother would be hooked on an IV drip, getting infusions of albumen. The albumen had to be infused very slowly into her, to avoid an overload that her body would not be able to tolerate. I lost track of the time spent staring at the albumen dripping into the transparent chamber of the IV. I would think of the unresolved research problem that was dogging me. Thinking of it was a way of allaying the anxiety I felt about my mother's health and about my career. It was also a way of tackling the boredom of a long quiet afternoon.

I passed a lot of time in the hospital musing about the problem in mathematics I was stuck on. The way one thought about a maths problem seemed rooted in the subjectivity of the person doing the thinking. Even the random and seemingly irrelevant details of my life – like thinking about it in Bombay, in a hospital room watching the albumen fall drop by drop, sitting by my mother's bedside – might make me look at something from a novel perspective that engendered a new insight. Actively thinking when trying to solve a problem brought concepts and definitions alive that had seemed inert on the page. Even if the definition might be unambiguous and prescriptive on the page, one's inner experience of a mathematical concept could be unique to oneself, enabling one to see a facet hidden to others and thus leading to a new observation or even breakthrough. This was not dissimilar to how different devotees of Krishna might think of the god, leading to devotional poetry and songs of different moods. In the bhakti tradition, the way Mirabai imagined Krishna was different from how Surdas did, affecting their imaginative and literary response to the Krishna they knew. The Krishnas of the lyrical devotional poetry they wrote were different avatars of him.

Doing mathematical research in Bombay, the city I had grown up in, felt different than doing it abroad. In Bombay I was more than someone trying to do research in mathematics: I was a son, a brother, a nephew, a citizen of India. I was a more full-fledged inhabitant of this city than I had been of Pasadena. Streets that I walked in had past resonances. Wandering through some areas of the city around Victoria Terminus station and near Churchgate was like walking through my past. The cityscape had not changed much in these areas in South Bombay, where colonial buildings held greater sway. As a child I had not been conscious of the British names of railway stations and precincts. Now there was a political movement to rename these structures, erase the colonial nomenclature and baptize them after Indian heroes, like the ubiquitous Chhatrapati Shivaji Maharaj. Confusingly, both the airport and the principal railway station were named after him. Hundreds of years after the historical Shivaji had controlled traffic in the Western Ghats, he was back in control of modes of transport in Bombay. Bombay was officially renamed Mumbai. I continued calling my city Bombay when speaking in English, and Mumbai when conversing in Marathi as I had always done. To call it Mumbai in English or Bombay in Marathi distanced the city from me.

∞

My father came at the end of a long day at the office to the hospital, his arrival delayed several times through the evening. There had been revised updates of when he would arrive. 'How is Aai?' he asked, referring to my mother. He looked around for any signs of food forbidden for my mother, like a customs official on the lookout for smuggled goods that he could seize. 'Did the doctor come? What did he say?' My father's flourishing accounting practice kept him very busy. He worked long hours. He managed to find his way past the stationed guards even if he came well after visiting hours were over. In his accounting practice he was principled, trusting that the quality of the work his firm did and what he brought of himself to the work – passionate engagement, intelligence, a grasp of the fundamentals of business and accounting – would lead to growing prosperity. Each year was better than the last. He had clients who had come to him after trying several other firms and then stayed with him for the long term. My father felt that one of his strengths as a person, and particularly as a professional, was that he knew his weaknesses. He thought I had some of that quality as well. It was like the ability to hear oneself when singing and know when one was going off tune. If one could not hear that, it was impossible to come back to being in tune.

We were all immersed in the minutiae of caring for my mother. While at the hospital, my mother's fluid input and output was measured and recorded. Nurses came in periodically through the day to ask for the latest records. We maintained our own balance sheet of the daily input and output, not trusting the hospital staff to get it right.

My father sometimes smuggled in other doctors – homeopathic, Ayurvedic, along with the usual kind – to see my mother. One of them made a special trip from Chennai to see my mother. I picked him up from the airport. He had just come back from a visit in which he had taken a dip in the icy-cold waters of the Ganga somewhere up north. He told me: 'For a few moments, after coming out, I ceased to exist!' My mother needed a blood transfusion in one episode of her illness. My blood group matched hers and the blood I donated could be used by her. I went to the lab in the hospital. The pathologist was someone I knew from our building growing up. She came from a conservative family and I was surprised to see her at work in the modern setting of a lab in Breach Candy Hospital. In Bombay, worlds often collided.

∞

My mother's hospitalizations were intermittent and most days I would be at TIFR trying to make progress in my research. I was studying Carayol's paper 'Sur les représentations Galoisiennes modulo l attachées aux formes modulaires' one of the papers that I had used for my thesis work. It was short, weighing in at a slender 17 pages. I sat at my desk in my office in TIFR turning its pages back and forth, looking for inspiration. I shared the office with a colleague who was slightly older: he had not come in as yet. We had desks set at right angles to each other.

For long periods I just sat staring at the paper, mind partly adrift, partly ruminating, chewing the cud of the mathematics I had read in the paper. I had picked up enough French to read maths papers written in the language, primarily by reading other maths papers written in French. I had read Hida's French notes based on the course he gave in Paris on his theory of p-adic Ramanujan symmetries early in my graduate student days. The vast majority of Serre's papers in his Collected Works were in French. French at worst aggravated slightly the intrinsic difficulties of understanding the mathematics. There was inevitably some loss involved because of not knowing the language, and thus at times losing out on the nuance of a remark, or the flight of a speculative thought in the introduction. But one got the general drift, with effort could fill out gaps in one's understanding, and in the end figure out the logic of a proof.

Paris is a great center for the kind of number theory I work in. It has historically been very important, and continues to exert its influence. While English has become the new *lingua franca* of mathematical exposition, replacing the Latin mathematicians used in Fermat's time, French mathematicians have resisted the Anglicizing wave to an extent. Thus it is commonplace for someone in my subject to have to come to grips with a math paper written in French.

∞

I wanted to deepen my thesis results. I had made a morphological analysis of wild congruences and shown their ubiquity. But I wanted to go further and prove more structural properties of the wild congruences and analyse their genetic code that led to their morphology that I had mapped out completely in my work at Caltech. This would give a higher level explanation of why these congruences existed. Once I posed this question to myself, it was quickly apparent that the methods I had used in my thesis would not suffice to answer the question. The decisive turn in my thesis had been to pose the right question. I now hoped that the question I formulated would lead to an interesting generalization of my thesis work.

Carayol's paper seemed to hold the key to proving the generalization I was seeking. There is a crucial lemma – an interim result – that has come to be known as Carayol's lemma, and is the engine that drives the paper. It is formulated and proved in Section

3 of the paper, entitled 'Un lemme'. The main theorems in the paper are deduced from the lemma of this section. The lemma seemed to suggest a natural extension of itself, and if one could push it through to its next-generation version, it looked very likely that this would help prove a satisfying generalization of the theorem of my thesis. My ideas were still at a very tentative stage.

Lemmas are typically not as prestigious as theorems. They are often just used as stepping stones in the proof of a theorem. In a textbook I read as an undergraduate, a particular lemma had been referred to as 'always a bridesmaid, never the bride'. This expression had not aged well, and was equally off the mark about bridesmaids as about lemmas, and about brides as about theorems. The implied lower status of a lemma as compared to a theorem was not true of many a lemma: sometimes a utilitarian lemma of a paper became more widely cited than its main theorem. Carayol's lemma was a case in point: a clear-eyed, hard-edged insight at the centre of the seventeen-page paper, which one could seek to exploit in situations that are quite distant from the one studied in this paper. In my own work I often craved for at least a lemma that I could prove and make modest progress in my research. A lemma every few weeks kept the blues away.

There were symbols used throughout Carayol's paper that were part of the universal vocabulary of mathematics. These served as signposts when reading the French prose of the paper. Equations recurred like refrains throughout the text. The prevailing model of mathematical exposition was to be terse, say no more than necessary, set up the needed definitions formally, break the proofs down into lemmas and propositions that carried the brunt of the argument, making them ready for off-the-shelf use throughout the paper and easily citable in other works as well. This style of writing, added to the fact that the mathematical objects interacting with each other in the paper were known protagonists in this type of mathematics, made one's lack of language expertise less of a handicap.

The ratio of ideas to length of Carayol's paper was satisfyingly high. The author had written clearly, with elegance, solving a very precise problem that clarified certain exciting developments in number theory. It was published in 1989, just before my days as a graduate student began. Often when I reread it, or just parts of it, like rewinding or fast-forwarding an audiotape to the point where one felt moved to listen to it again, I realized I had not understood a subtlety, or misunderstood a piece of notation, which sowed the seeds for misinterpreting an argument that occurred two or three pages later.

∞

My reading of Carayol's paper was marked by periods in which I was intensely focused on the paper, with the mind engaged in the details of the proof of a lemma in the paper, closely following the logic of the proof, right to its conclusion till the claim made in the statement of the lemma stood proved. The proof was a few lines long, and the difficulty was in understanding the objects being talked about that had been introduced in the previous sections. At other times my mind wandered, and I lifted my eyes from the paper to the blackboard in front of me. The blackboard was covered with chalk marks; stray mathematical symbols and words peeped out from underneath the foliage of less decipherable symbols that were half erased.

The closest mathematicians got to physical labour in the course of their day job was working at blackboards, either in private settings discussing ideas with colleagues, or lecturing in a classroom, covering them with symbols, creating modern black-and-white *rangoli* that would be wiped out to create new ones. It brought to mind waves advancing and retreating, leaving white evanescent surf scrawled on the sand in their wake. When working at a blackboard, mathematicians got dusted by the crepitation of chalk pressed against the slate or glass of the blackboard, sometimes getting covered with a white film of chalk dust, like construction workers at a building site, or like bakers powdered lightly with flour. Getting one's hands dirty was the expression used amongst mathematicians for an argument full of calculations; proofs which were 'pure thought', conceptual and carried out with a minimum of calculation were prized. Such proofs telescoped hours of thought into aphoristic brilliant arguments with no residue of the intellectual labor which went into crafting them.

Behind where I sat there were large wooden bookcases, with my collection of books, or a part of my collection. The collection was scattered over different parts of the city: some of it here in my office, some of it in my parents' flat. My attention drifted to the window through which one could peer down on to the East Lawn at the front of the institute. Like a heliotropic plant or like an insect buzzing against the pane of a shut window on a hot day, I was drawn to the sealed window – windows in the offices could not be opened, the entire institute was centrally air-conditioned by ageing equipment, wheezing out cold air from its lungs – and stared out at the sky which was losing the fresh blue colour of early morning in the rising heat of the day.

I decided to go for a walk in the institute, setting out without a fixed idea of where I was headed, either to the seaside by the West Lawn that bordered it or the colonnade at the front of the Institute, which would be quiet at this time of the morning. The colonnade was by the East Lawn with a massive tabebuia tree at its centre that I could see from my office window. Alternatively, I could wander to the almond grove, the atrium of the auditorium, or just walk the grey-walled corridors of the institute, with paintings on the walls. This would be a way to clear my head, get some momentum in thinking about the paper and figure out if the key lemma in the paper which I was focused on could be generalized to be used for what I had in mind. It promised to be the key to deepening the results of my thesis.

I justified taking a walk as a way of thinking about the paper without being distracted by its presence as a physical object on my desk. I would risk trying to recall the arguments in the paper from my mental construct of it, shuffling through its suite of ideas, stumbling at points where I would have to try and find a patch, an ad hoc argument if memory failed to recall how the author had worked his way around it, panicking about points that seemed obvious when I was physically with the paper, but now seemed less clear. Exposing one's sense of the paper to hazard in this way might enable a closer understanding and even engender new insights occasionally.

Reconstructing the paper in my mind in this manner was a bit like a painter looking away from a landscape to realize for themselves the values of what they had been looking at, what the scene meant to them, the stand of trees nearby, the low horizon, the upward sweep of the ground to a cluster of houses on the far side. They had to schematize what they saw and decompose it into its elements before realizing the landscape on a canvas.

∞

I walked along the paved path by the Arabian Sea, which was a couple of hundred metres in length. I walked to and fro for about twenty minutes. In one direction, I could see Malabar Hill on the horizon, a posh part of the city. There was a cluster of highrises, and beneath it right on the shore the governor's bungalow with its extensive grounds wrapped around a turning in the coastline. The scene shimmered in the haze of the heat. My parents' house was beyond the outcrop of buildings, as were the hospitals that my mother had to recurrently be taken to. The walkway lay between the sea and the West Lawn that extended to the main building of the institute. It had at one end – the end from which you walked towards the city on the distant horizon – a grove of casuarina trees, growing unkempt and wild, much less orderly than the almond grove, well adapted to the coastal environment, backing up to a wall that marked a boundary of the institute. Beyond the wall lay land under the jurisdiction of the Navy. One could hear, early mornings and late evenings, bells ringing from across the wall. There was a Shiva temple there that I had yet to see for myself.

The gardeners were busy at work on the West Lawn. It was said, half-jokingly, that the gardeners were more diligent than employees in the other departments – maths, physics, molecular biology – of the institute. The gardeners were filling quaint-looking small wheelbarrows with their prunings. I felt a twinge of guilt, loafing around at the beginning of a working day. My pace quickened slightly as I passed them. I could justify all I had done during the day as work, but not entirely convincingly, as even to me it did not quite feel like solid real work. I was not sure if I could shake hands with the gardeners on an equal footing, as comrades-in-arms, doing our bit for the institute. But we did have a bond, of sorts. The gardeners were local, from Bombay, Marathi-speaking, while the faculty came to work here from all across the country. As a local, Marathi-speaking boy myself, this forged a natural connection with the staff working here – the security guards at the gate, the secretaries in the maths department, the gardeners and staff working in the maintenance department. When I came to work I exchanged greetings with the guards in Marathi. I was waved in without having to produce my ID card.

Bhabha had been as attentive to landscaping as other aspects of the institute. There were photographs of him with a team of gardeners surveying the grounds. He would even send back photographs from his travels of gardens he had liked, to be used as a basis for ideas about what could be done here. In the centre of the West Lawn there was a grouping of plants and shrubs which was known as the Amoeba. As I headed back indoors I passed an outdoor stone sculpture of Vishnu near the Homi Bhabha Auditorium. It was a few centuries old and had been presumably bought by Bhabha as a work of art. The context for its presence in this institute was secular rather than religious. But one did see on occasion flowers placed at the feet of the statue. Especially on days of religious significance in the Hindu calendar there would be an abundance of bougainvillea blossoms, marigolds and hibiscus flowers placed on the lap, and at the feet, of the seated deity. Bhabha might have frowned at this type of attention and tribute paid to the sculpture that kept alive its sacred dimensions, moving it out of the purely aesthetic realm which it probably inhabited in his eyes. Inevitably, other eyes saw it differently.

I stepped back into the air-conditioned comfort of the institute. Just past the sliding entrance door, near a pillar, there was a floral arrangement. Each weekday there was a fresh arrangement. There must have been a team of gardeners dedicated to making these skilful arrangements displayed in different parts of the institute. If one were distinguished enough, one might even have these brought to one's office. These were as much a hallmark of Bhabha's style as TIFR's art collection. It was an everyday occurrence to walk past paintings by a stellar cast of artists, most of them unknowns when Bhabha collected them: M.F. Husain, V.S. Gaitonde, K.H. Ara, Raza, B. Prabha, Mohan Samant. The Tata Insititute of Fundamental Research is almost unique amongst its peer institutes across the globe for its remarkable art collection, mostly mid-twentieth-century Indian art.

Bhabha, himself a competent artist, had managed to have a budget allocated for the acquisition of works of art and had personally curated the art collection for TIFR. He had chaired a committee that chose the promising young artist M. F. Husain's entry in an open competition for the commissioning of a mural for TIFR. Most of the artists had interpreted their mandate narrowly and produced work that would resonate with the scientific temper of the institute. Husain won the competition by instead trying to capture the energy of a newly independent country, with its ancient traditions, but ready to stride into the modern world. Bhabha selected Husain's entry even though it was perhaps the most lightly sketched and least developed of the entries. He saw its potential and appreciated its metaphoric quality. The mural, entitled 'Bharat Bhagya Vidhata', is on the mezzanine floor of the institute, just outside the Reading Room, and it is one of Husain's most celebrated works. The mural depicts a Rajasthani landscape that bristles with energy. Camels and elephants and human figures populate the mural in an open democratic spirit. There is a debate about whether mathematics is more of an art or more of a science. In the art-filled surroundings of TIFR one felt that maths was as much art as science.

The art collection was in keeping with the goal of the institute to be in the avant-garde of scientific research. I read somewhere that after Bhabha acquired a painting he would hang it in different places in the institute and see how it affected the mood of the place, the movement of people in that space, if people noticed the painting there, and whether some stopped and stood before the painting. The paintings were later placed more lastingly in various parts of TIFR so that people would encounter them going about their daily work routines: in computer rooms, above photocopying machines, in corridors, seeping into the atmosphere of the entire institute. Bhabha wanted people who came to TIFR to be inspired by their surroundings in ways that they might be only partially conscious of. Quality art on the walls, a striking location, the architecture, modern but monumental, would hold the people working in the institute to a standard that they could measure their work against. As I worked there, over time, I became grateful for the founding vision of the institute that wove in a spare aesthetic – represented in the modern architecture, paintings, sculptures, the landscaped lawns – into the fabric of the institute.

∞

Thinking of Carayol's paper without having it in front of me, taking away that crutch, was a bit like someone trying to learn a passage of text by heart and then shutting the book, and seeing if they could recite it cold. Although here the purpose was to see if one could recreate the logic of the paper for oneself, or blur the edges of the maths of the paper, so that the ideas of the paper – and in particular Carayol's lemma – would become less bound to the results proved, freeing them from their immediate context like cutting balloons free to float away into the blue skies, enabling one to see the essential point of the arguments in the paper.

I needed to look at a book in the library. It was in another part of the institute that was secluded and did not attract much traffic. The entire institute always felt cold, one needed a sweater sometimes, even if the city was in the grip of stifling October heat, but it felt much colder in this library. If the institute was like a refrigerator, the library was its deep freezer section. Journals were kept in the Reading Room, which was a long corridor away. The Reading Room was dotted with desks, with current issues of journals on racks along the far wall. Many of the desks were piled high with books by graduate students who studied there intermittently, the piles of books acting as sentinels, guarding the desks in their absence. Some of the desks in the prime location right against the picture windows nearest the ocean were permanently reserved, and if one went and sat there to read one felt like a squatter, always on the lookout for the return of the person who had reserved the desk, and prepared to be evicted at short notice.

Near the entrance of the Reading Room there was a smaller section with a few upholstered chairs, which had the newly acquired books on display as well as a few journals of general interest. I would often come here to escape the confines of my office on the pretext of checking out the newest arrivals. I wandered into the stacks at the back of the Reading Room in which older bound journals were kept, looking for a paper that had been referenced in something I was reading. It was like drifting into the back of a shop where merchandise that was not on display was stored. The paper I was looking for was from the 1970s; I felt it might help in finding a good way to generalize Carayol's lemma.

In thinking about Carayol's paper, I was trying to derive inspiration from a mathematics paper to try and write a paper of my own, to see the ideas in it in their barest form, and check if they could be adapted for my own ulterior motives. It was like an artist looking at a painting on the wall of a small room of a museum, one they returned to every so often, viewing it from different points of the room, understanding a little more with every visit – and through the thinking which went on in between the visits – coming back for the pleasure of viewing, but also because they did not quite know what they sought from the painting, slightly tormented by the thought that they had still not grasped what the painter had done.

∞

As I got to know the art at TIFR better, I noticed that the work of V.S. Gaitonde stood in counterpoint to Husain's work. His work was much quieter and had grown in esteem to rival the louder fame of Husain. Large Gaitonde canvases hung in several spaces in the institute. They were enigmatic, some of them resembled seascapes, like a Turner painting of a storm in which all the storminess had been sublimated: flat planes of paint with squiggles. There were calligraphic strokes on some of the canvases, which in the quietness of his painting stood out almost like graffiti. Artists revered his work. My office-mate told me that he had seen an artist come and prostrate himself in front of a Gaitonde canvas; the artist sensed a mastery in Gaitonde's handling of brush and paint, a perfection in his line that my untrained eye could not see. Gaitonde's paintings had a zen quality. He called his paintings 'non-objective' and his work was influenced by the Buddhist paintings at Ajanta. The reticence of his paintings, their minimalism, reminded me of a quote by the well-known algebraic geometer David Mumford about the work of Alexander Grothendieck who aimed to strip a piece of mathematics so that what remained was almost nothing, but yet from that state of almost emptiness, the entire structure could be invoked.

> ... He would always look for some way of formulating a problem, stripping apparently everything away from it, so you don't think anything is left. And yet something is left, and he could find real structure in this seeming vacuum.

A Gaitonde canvas hung in the lobby of the Homi Bhabha Auditorium of the institute. Some areas of the canvas seemed heavily worked on, impasto and explorative, mute and enigmatic; it was as if the artist was struggling with something, almost groping towards the foundations for the painting. They were like passages at the beginning of a Hindustani vocal recital, the voice exploring notes in the *mandra saptak* (lower octave) and finding structure in something that was still forming. The subtle variations in the colour, shade after shade, a result of layer upon layer of paint, were like the open-ended passages at the beginning of a vocal recital. These passages of the art or the music seemed to replicate for the artist what one experienced upon entering a dark room: if one stayed long enough, after moments in which the eye could see nothing beyond the initial empty blackness, one began to discern shapes and sense the layout of the room.

The works of Husain and Gaitonde seemed like antipodes in the TIFR art collection, contrasting worldliness with inwardness, exuberance with restraint. When I looked at paintings of Gaitonde and others I never felt that I went beyond their periphery. I had to be told of their importance, and what place they held in the development of art, before I was moved to look at them carefully. This reminded me of a quote of Grothendieck, who had been guided by Serre as he took his first steps in the field of algebraic geometry in the late 1950s. Grothendieck said in his memoirs that a piece of mathematics, that might have left him indifferent reading it on a page, would come alive to him after Serre explained it to him:

> The essential thing was that Serre each time strongly sensed the rich meaning behind a statement that, on the page, would doubtless have left me neither hot nor cold – and that he could 'transmit' this perception of a rich, tangible, and mysterious substance – this perception that is at the same time the desire to understand this substance, to penetrate it.[41]

I read biographies of artists, mathematicians, and composers. I was drawn to artists who were not successful to begin with. My saints were the dogged ones, like Cézanne, who grappled with his art and found his style after a long struggle. He painted Mont Saint-Victoire throughout his life, groping his way to new painterly truths, returning to his motif as he was never done with it, never satisfied. Not like Mozart whose music could seem effortless, although of course great talent and genius was a gift as well as a burden – it too pushed one to excesses of efforts.

I imagined an artist who is a poor draughtsman and struggles at drawing with verisimilitude – a landscape, a portrait, a still life – their perspective is all wrong. Their limited technical abilities force the artist to be like a subsistence farmer cultivating a small parcel of land; lacking the skills of their more talented peers, and unable to practise shifting cultivation by moving to greener pastures, their limitations tether the artist to a tiny plot of land. The etched failures of their apprenticeship give them a style that they become known for; not a wide renown, but nevertheless their work attracts a small circle of admirers. Their pictures hang in museums. They are not a great artist, but someone known for a point of view: bow-legged chairs, teetering tables, dented fallen fruit, catching the glint of something nouvelle. The artist tends to be inept in front of an easel before a model. But they return late at night to the studio to work after everyone has gone home. With the model not in front of them, the artist works from memory. The portrait becomes psychological, the hollowed eyes, the askew stance, an untamed ferocity that characterizes the artist's style. Could I be such a minor artist? Not consummate, but specialized, ploughing a narrow furrow, but turning up discoveries by dumb luck and persistence? A furrow that turns out to be a surprisingly inexhaustible mine of discoveries. Another furrow would have yielded nothing.

I drew comfort from a quote attributed to the well-known mathematician Raoul Bott: 'There are two ways to do great mathematics. The first is to be smarter than everybody else. The second way is to be stupider than everybody else – but persistent.'

After several weeks of thinking about Carayol's lemma, I found a version of if it that would be adequate for generalizing my thesis results. I started writing down a draft of my ideas. It took me several months of work to get this into a shape that looked reasonably complete, although a satisfactory way of writing all this up eluded me for even longer.

∞

I had shipped Serre's Collected Works, along with all my other earthly possessions, when I left Pasadena. A few months later, I got a notice that the shipment had arrived in Bombay, and I went with my customs agent to clear it at the Bombay Customs House. It was located in a surprisingly quiet area of Bombay; all round it was the pell-mell and chaos of the city.

Indian customs was feared by Indian travellers returning from trips abroad. I remembered being stuck in customs for hours after coming back from a holiday in Europe with my mother and sister when we were still at school.

This time around, getting the shipment of books and a stereo system released from customs proved less arduous. The economy had just been opened up by the Narasimha Rao government; Finance Minister Manmohan Singh had announced a series of reforms. Perhaps my getting out relatively quickly from the Customs House was partly a result of those economic reforms. The atmosphere still seemed saturated with bureaucracy – we had to go with our forms to three different officers to get their signatures – but there was a certain decorum and calm compared to my childhood experiences of customs. Those memories were of eviscerated suitcases, with their entrails left lying all over the place, like a forensic lab after a particularly thorough post-mortem on an unfortunate cadaver. The atmosphere now was like the outpatient department of a government hospital: the surroundings were not plush, and one was surrounded by people waiting their turn patiently, sitting on plastic chairs, or walking around, with nurses calling out the number of the next patient to be examined by the doctor, sometimes cursorily, or patients leaving with medicines, hopeful that they would feel better as a consequence of the visit.

The customs officials seemed disappointed that I was bringing back so little after so many years abroad. After a couple of hours of powwowing with the officials – who seemed to be almost toying with us as they waited to catch bigger fish – the shipment was released and I was reunited with the three volumes of Serre's Collected Works, and my entire book and music collection.

8

Prospecting for Gold

The breakthrough in my thesis at Caltech occurred after I began thinking about a problem that was more open-ended after having come a cropper trying to solve the more technical questions that my adviser had initially suggested. Now again as an early career researcher, fresh out of my PhD, I wanted to try and work on something that was open-ended. This, I reckoned, enhanced my strengths and mitigated my weaknesses, giving me the creative freedom I needed to find my own path, as compared to working on problems that were more narrowly defined and engaged with best at a more technical level. Thinking about such questions had the added dividend that any progress one made had the potential to make a big impact. This prompted me to start thinking, soon after I joined TIFR, about the most central question in my field: Serre's conjecture. By its very nature this would be chancy work, almost like panning for gold.

No one had a strategy to prove Serre's conjecture. The work of Wiles on the elliptic symmetry conjecture had introduced a powerful set of methods to relate Galois and Ramanujan symmetries. This had started a gold rush to try and prove more such relations. But

Wiles's work seemed to make no direct impact on the conjecture: in fact he had used known cases of Serre's conjecture for 'small Galois symmetries' to prove FLT. The general question raised in the conjecture about relating Galois and Ramanujan symmetries seemed wide open and challengingly, almost irresistibly, inaccessible. By temperament I was drawn to tilting at windmills. I was averse to short-term risk – I could never be a day trader or take the risk of climbing up perilous mountainsides – but I did have an appetite for long-term risks; my whole mathematical career was like a lifelong gamble. This aspect of my temperament was partly what led me to work on Serre's conjecture.

Even if risky, it was a calculated risk. Serre's conjecture was a very central problem, and so, even if one fell short of proving the conjecture, working on it might lead one to discovering interesting and new mathematics. Wiles's 'modularity lifting' method provided stunning affirmative answers in many cases to the question 'Which Galois symmetries are Ramanujan?' Serre's conjecture asked the same question in the mod p setting. In spite of the logical conundrum about Wiles's method needing Serre's conjecture as an input, there was still inchoate hope in the air that his methods could be repurposed to make an impact on Serre's conjecture.

I broke off the conjecture into smaller parts and instead of thinking directly about the conjecture focused instead on trying to prove its implications. Some of the implications of Serre's conjecture were surprising enough when viewed in isolation as to seem almost incredible. Believing in the conjecture was like incurring a debt, taking a loan that was sanctioned only because Serre backed the loan as guarantor, staking on it his stature as a mathematician. But conversely, believing in Serre's conjecture in a sense made one also its creditor. It had to survive all the spot credit checks one made

– none of its implications could lead to contradictions. The fact that Serre had gone to great lengths to formulate an optimal and exacting conjecture, making it as falsifiable as possible, meant that if there was a default on the debt repayments it would be flagged immediately.

One of the implications of the conjecture was related to lifting of mod p Galois symmetries. Pierre Deligne had raised an objection when Serre made his conjecture in the 1970s: it implied a very surprising lifting property of mod p Galois symmetries which seemed inaccessible, like a glass wall which offered no footholds to help scale it. It predicted that a mod p Galois symmetry lifted to a p-adic Galois symmetry.[42] Lifting mod p Galois symmetries is related to lifting mod p numbers to p-adic numbers that we talked about in the context of Serre's *A Course in Arithmetic*, but much harder, as now one had to lift symmetries rather than just numbers.

This was an astonishing prediction, akin to saying that something tiny one could perceive like the mod p symmetry was merely a corner or fragment of something much vaster, namely its p-adic lift, that was almost totally hidden. One would not have believed the lifting statement were it not for the fact that it had come from Serre. As a colleague said: 'If it were Bob's conjecture, I wouldn't have believed it!'

I decided to think about the lifting question. An attractive feature of the problem was that the techniques that could be used on it were rather limited. If it could be done at all one would simply have to hit upon a brilliant idea! One hoped for a magical moment like a player in a game of soccer when the ball comes to him and he fortuitously finds a line of attack, the ball almost attached to his foot with a string, dribbling past defenders, leaving them flat-footed, and in a burst of speed and energy and creativity he swerves the ball into the goal. One of the qualities a researcher needs to have is a sense of what are the most interesting theorems that are provable given the current state of mathematics. As a novice I had no such reliable intuition to fall back upon: I was drawn to thinking about Serre's conjecture in Bombay, and hoped optimistically that I could make incremental progress towards it given the recent developments in number theory.

Serre's conjecture had the tantalizing appeal of something hovering at the edge of the known and unknown.

∞

Thinking of lifting Galois symmetries in the context of Serre's conjecture frustrated all my efforts. However, thinking of liftings did lead me to a small interesting result. I got the idea on a trip to Allahabad that I made in the year 1995, a few months after I returned to Bombay. Dipendra had offered me a permanent job in the Mehta Research Institute (now called the Harish Chandra Institute) whilst I was still struggling to finish my thesis in Pasadena. It was a little more than a year since my first visit when I was still a grad student. During the previous visit I had been anxious and despondent about my prospects as a mathematician, but I was more confident now that I had some results under my belt. This second visit to the city was to check out what life would be like working there.

My mind refreshed by the change of scene, as soon as I arrived in Allahabad I realized that there was a lifting question to be addressed even in the case of 'one-dimensional mod p Galois symmetries'. Serre's conjecture was about mod p Galois symmetries in 'dimension two', so the one-dimensional case was like a toy case. One-dimensional symmetries were well-understood objects and the lifting question for them was settled. But if one asked for a stronger type of lifting result for special infinite collections of one-dimensional mod p Galois symmetries called 'compatible systems' then it was not obvious if they existed.

The notion of 'compatible systems of Galois symmetries' was first formulated in a paper of Yutaka Taniyama from the 1950s. We have encountered an example of compatible systems of Galois symmetries, those arising from the Ramanujan Δ-function, in Serre's work to understand Ramanujan's fantastic observations about Δ. Taniyama's paper was an important influence on the yoga of motives that had emerged in the work of Grothendieck and Serre. Motives gave rise to compatible systems, and compatible systems led one to think that there was a motive lurking behind them. Taniyama, after defining this notion in his paper, had studied one-dimensional compatible systems of p-adic Galois symmetries and showed that they always arise from 'motives'. An answer to my question would imply Taniyama's theorem, and was a priori stronger, as it did not follow from Taniyama's work.

I mused about this question during my month-long stay in Allahabad. I could not resolve the question when I was there, but on coming back to Bombay, one evening in the Worli flat, I finally realized what I needed to prove the lifting statement I was after. If I could answer another question that was seemingly unrelated I would have lifts of 'compatible systems of one-dimensional symmetries' in my bag. Serendipitously, when I asked Ribet this question by email, he told me that it had been answered in a recent paper. Mathematical research is often just about asking the right questions and making the right connections. Even with this small success, the problem of lifting 'two-dimensional mod p Galois symmetries', the case which was relevant for Serre's conjecture, remained intact.

Travelling to Allahabad might have helped in doing this new piece of maths. Just entering and exiting airports or railway stations could be inspiring! I had been led to define compatible systems of mod *p* Galois symmetries, a definition that was almost there in the literature but not quite. Making the definition naturally suggested looking at it in the simplest of all cases: the one-dimensional case. This turned out to be an interesting tractable case in which one could still do something new. My work generalized Taniyama's result and in fact proved it in a more satisfactory way, giving a complete version of his original theorem.

I wrote up my results as a note and sent it to Serre in his role as an editor of the journal *Comptes Rendus Mathématique de l'Académie des Sciences*. I did so with some trepidation, and my fears were justified as he sent me an email rejecting my paper, admonishing me for having too much advertisement in it for my definition of mod *p* compatible systems. He wrote that the notion was not particularly novel, but he lifted my spirits by ending on a positive note. If I cut down on the advertising and wrote a shorter paper concentrating on my results showing that such compatible systems in the one-dimensional case arose from 'motives' then he would consider my note for publication.

The fact that Serre responded with a mixture of admonishment and interest to my small paper suggested that he engaged with what other people did, and responded to even small results, if there was something in them which struck him as new and worthwhile. I was to benefit later too from his reactions to a few pieces of work that I sent him. Serre was unusually generous in this regard, as typically mathematicians did not respond to such small observations. It helped that Serre had a wide mathematical culture and was quick-thinking. I cut down the paper to a third of its length and Serre accepted it for publication.

∞

Lunch at the Tata Institute was a highlight of the day, something one looked forward to as one worked through the morning in one's office. One did take breaks for coffee, walk around the institute and sometimes knock at a colleague's door to chat, ask them a maths question or relay some idle gossip. However, we were mindful of not indulging in too much chit-chat, as otherwise, we would never get any work done. In the institute, the rule was that mathematics always took precedence: if one was chatting with a colleague, just shooting the breeze, and someone walked in with a mathematical question or thought, one was meant to declare pre-emptively 'Let's talk later again, I will leave you guys to the maths', and slink away. But lunch was a respite from all that, if not from the inner workings of one's mind. Soon after noon I knocked at the doors of my friends' offices on the third floor to see if they wanted to go for lunch, and the three of us took the lift down from the third to the ground floor. The lift was one of the fanciest spaces in the institute, wood-panelled and sporting brass fittings. I could completely imagine Homi Bhabha mulling over these details. Sometimes one rode the lift with someone busy polishing and buffing the wood and brass. When in the lift, especially if one was travelling solo in it, one could pretend that one was in a five-star hotel rather than a government-run research institute.

The lift was crowded at this time. For many of the faculty who stayed across the road in the TIFR's housing colony, this was the closest they came to travelling with a crowd, which was the daily lot of those who lived further away. At rush hour the Eastern and

Western train lines which carried people from the suburbs in the northern part of the city to the office area in South Bombay were famously overcrowded and could intimidate a newcomer to the city. More people were jammed into compartments than one would have imagined to be allowable by Pauli's exclusion principle (that no two particles can occupy the same quantum state). One was held in place by the people pressing against one's body. You could enter or leave the compartment only if you positioned yourself so that you were carried by the tides of commuters moving in and out.

Lunch was either at the West or East Canteen. The names were literal to a fault. The West Canteen faced west and the lunch was Western-oriented, the East canteen faced east and the lunch was Indian. We decided to join the line at the West canteen. There was a certain relief at being amidst people after having spent time with oneself, trying to concentrate, forcing the mind to think through a piece of mathematics. When trying to do a new piece of maths, it sometimes felt like walking on eggshells, one was not sure if an argument would hold up or crumble and be undermined because of the flawed logic of one of its steps. One could lose a theorem instead of gaining one in the course of a day. In this fraught situation, being in company, chatting about the latest movie or a surprising election result, getting out of one's mind and office and into the world came as a release.

Through the picture windows of the West canteen, one could see the Pelletron, a tall structure that I had often considered climbing to the top of to view the bay from there. I wondered if it loomed like a lighthouse when glimpsed from the open sea. It was a heavy ion accelerator used by some of the experimentalists working at the institute. I wondered if one would be able to look down from its top on to the Shiva temple, which lay beyond the casuarina trees and the wall of the institute, with rusted barbed wire atop it. From the top of the Pelletron I fancied I might see a segment of Marine Drive, at least on a clear day, when the haze from the heat and the pollution did not hang palpably in the air. Thinking about these things was more appealing than actually climbing the Pelletron, which I never ended up doing.

At lunch, the three of us talked about a recent result which had made mathematical headlines. We gossiped that it was striking but not particularly deep. At a neighbouring table there were a pair of mathematicians who had been constantly together for the last few weeks. They were inseparable, having coffee together, at lunch at the same table, taking walks together in the colonnade, along the shore, in the almond grove, lost in discussions. This was a sure sign that something was cooking and they were working together on an idea or project or paper. After a period such a pair might drift apart, and new pairs might form. Another collaboration was afoot!

The proximity of staying and working in the same place – the housing colony was just a few hundred yards away – and a certain commonality of mathematical interests led to a high degree of collaboration among the faculty working here. The number of people doing serious research in mathematics in the country was very small, especially given the size of India, and TIFR had many of the best mathematicians in the country.

A foundational theorem proved in the 1960s by two young mathematicians M.S. Narasimhan and C.S. Seshadri working at TIFR, in the area of 'vector bundles to Riemann surfaces', had put TIFR on the world map of mathematics. The School of Mathematics had become a centre for the study of this speciality which lay at the crossroads of algebraic geometry and Riemannian geometry, two prominent fields in pure mathematics. Bernhard

Riemann was a nineteenth-century German mathematician who had revolutionized the concept of space in mathematical analysis through his theory of 'manifolds', just as Grothendieck was to revolutionize the concept of space in algebraic geometry through his theory of 'schemes' a century later. Riemannian geometry was at the heart of Einstein's theory of general relativity, a spectacular example of the 'unreasonable effectiveness of mathematics'. Einstein in his thinking about gravity and the structure of space–time realized that gravity is an intrinsic property and effect of the curvature of space. Riemann's ideas which predated Einstein's work by several decades turned out to be exactly what Einstein needed to flesh out his theory. Einstein collaborated with the mathematician Marcel Grossmann: it was Grossmann who told Einstein that Riemannian geometry was what was needed and supplied the mathematical expertise to work out the equations of Einstein's theory of general relativity. The Narasimhan–Seshadri theorem has been used in later developments in theoretical physics related to Einstein's theory.

One of my friends at the table seemed preoccupied and morose. It could be hard to keep up social appearances when one was distracted, and worrying about some piece of mathematics, which was presently stuck like a piece of furniture being piloted through a narrow doorway. In other settings one would attempt to hide one's preoccupation, but in a research institute that was not necessary. Preoccupation was de rigueur, almost part of the job description. I was also preoccupied myself, wondering about an email from Serre.

∞

I had returned a few weeks ago from a conference in Bangalore on FLT. Wiles's work on it was just about a year old. I was asked to give the last few lectures of the conference on the methods introduced by

Wiles in his proof of FLT. During the conference one of the experts who had come from abroad asked me a question about Serre's conjecture. He asked whether Serre's conjecture implied another famous and older conjecture in the subject called Artin's conjecture. Emil Artin, an Austrian mathematician of Armenian descent, had proved his famous reciprocity law in the late 1920s whilst working at Hamburg. This was one of the great achievements of number theory in the twentieth century: it was a big generalization of Gauss's law of quadratic reciprocity. Artin had been led to his reciprocity law when proving the 'one-dimensional' case of what later came to be called Artin's conjecture. The Artin conjecture was one of the most important conjectures in number theory. Trying to find the right setting for Artin's conjecture had been a key motivation for the grand conjectural unification of number theory envisioned by Robert Langlands in the 1960s.

My initial reaction was that the question was unlikely to have an affirmative answer. Artin's conjecture is about very different types of symmetries than the symmetries in Serre's conjecture that are described using mod p numbers. Artin's conjecture involves Galois symmetries described using complex numbers. As these two kinds of numbers are as different as chalk and cheese, one's first thought was that there should be no connection between the two conjectures.

However, my recent work on compatible systems made me think of the question I had been asked in that setting. Doing this almost immediately established a viable connection between the two conjectures, apart from one wrinkle that kept bugging me. The Artin conjecture was related to an edge case of Serre's conjecture, and there was an issue of 'non-liftability' in this edge case. But thinking of this difficulty in the light of compatible systems suggested that one could vary the prime p. One of the oldest theorems in number theory is Euclid's proof that there are infinitely many primes. If one threw out finitely many 'bad' primes, one would still be left with infinitely many primes, and for these remaining primes the 'non-liftability' was not an issue.

I excitedly emailed Serre to say that I could show that his conjecture implied the particular (two-dimensional) case of Artin's conjecture which I had been asked about. I even sketched the argument as it was very short. Serre almost immediately wrote back saying that he did not believe my proof. This punctured the balloon of my confidence, and I tried to go over my argument and see where I had made a mistake. I could not find a definite flaw in my proof although there were points I was tentative about. Telling myself I could live with another blow to my confidence, if that was how it turned out, I replied to his email explaining my proof again, and pointing out that the argument was very close to how he had deduced the elliptic symmetry conjecture from his conjecture, save for an additional wrinkle. I tried to explain again how one could get past that last obstacle using a general argument that he would know better than me. At lunch, and on a walk later in the almond grove at TIFR, the question of how Serre would respond, was at the back of my mind.

After lunch I found he had replied. He now believed my argument. My persistence had been worth it. Serre was in fact pleased at the end of this exchange because it showed how strong his conjecture was: it implied the two-dimensional case of Artin's conjecture. I later learnt that Artin's conjecture was one of the motivations that led to Serre making his own conjecture. Thus it must have been satisfying for Serre that his conjecture in fact implied that of Artin in some key instances. My observation was quite small, but had been missed by experts: this showed how the subject sometimes progressed via small nudges and pushes, and small shifts in perspective that revealed something new. My result, relating the conjectures of two famous mathematicians, probably helped me get nominated for a prize for young Indian mathematicians. I had to travel to New Delhi to be interviewed and ended up winning the prize. The prize money was modest. I was touched that my father, despite his busy schedule and my mother's illness, made time to come to Delhi to see me receive it.

∞

As a fledgling researcher one had to periodically give talks about one's work. Thus, I had to craft a talk about my work which had now started focusing on Serre's conjecture. In mathematical seminars and colloquia, one still gave blackboard-and-chalk talks, and they were useful props for nervous speakers. I had not started out life as a good public speaker. When I was ten, at an elocution competition in St. Mary's, the weeks of practice had just melted away when I began speaking, and all I could think of was wanting to run away from the stage. The elocution piece, which should have taken two or three minutes to deliver, was over in less than half a minute. Now, as a researcher, I would cram in too many things into the lecture, write too much on the board. My initial talks were not very good, but I gradually improved.

One of the talks I had to give was a colloquium that would be accessible to a broad mathematical audience, and thus I had to introduce in general terms my research area to non-specialists. I talked of the quest of number theorists like myself to understand symmetries of the solutions to all polynomial equations with rational coefficients. (An example of such an equation is $3X^{89} + \frac{5}{13} X^3 + 22 = 0$.) This controls a lot of number theory, and hidden in its belly are answers to many questions number theorists care about, such as FLT. Serre's conjecture encodes this rich information in terms of mod *p* numbers, at the cost of losing a lot of information (many integers are $\equiv 6 \pmod{11}$ for instance). But varying *p* through infinitely many primes, we don't lose any information. For instance, if two numbers *a*, *b* satisfy $a \equiv b \pmod{p}$ for infinitely many primes then $a = b$ as their difference $a - b$ is divisible by infinitely many primes *p*, and the only number with this property is 0! This simple logic underlies many of the applications of Serre's conjecture, ranging from it implying the elliptic symmetry conjecture, to my argument showing that it implies Artin's conjecture.

In my talk I introduced Galois symmetries and Ramanujan symmetries as symmetries arising from completely different sources, like rivers springing from different mountain ranges. I wanted to emphasize that the mingling of these symmetries is miraculous and had played a crucial role in the development of number theory. I started with a simple example of Galois symmetries, those arising from the solutions of $X^2 - 5 = 0$. This is the setting of the law of quadratic reciprocity, historically the first instance of the mixing of such symmetries.

The Galois symmetries arising from one-dimensional settings had been completely understood, I told my audience, by the 1930s, because of the Artin reciprocity law; this law is a comprehensive and satisfying generalization of the law of quadratic reciprocity. The evolution from quadratic reciprocity to Artin reciprocity took over a hundred years: it typifies how mathematics develops, moving from the particular to the abstract, making a particular and brilliant insight more general, almost unrecognizable in the new formulation, and yet more powerful, each turn of this path from the particular to the general needing new concepts and viewpoints.

The way Artin's reciprocity law implies quadratic reciprocity as a corollary would have pleased Gauss: he had sought a 'natural' proof of his theorem (which he called his *theorema aureum*, his golden theorem) throughout his life. From a modern twentieth-century viewpoint, Gauss's nineteenth-century law of quadratic reciprocity could be formulated as saying that one-dimensional Galois symmetries arising from an equation like $X^2 - 5 = 0$ are of Ramanujan-type. The next frontier, I explained, was that of two-dimensional Galois symmetries, which brought us to the setting of Serre's conjecture. At this point the talk became more technical and I got into the statement of Serre's conjecture and sketched its many strong consequences.

Talks made one reflect on the trajectory of one's work. Preparing for a talk clarified one's thoughts and could even at times lead to a tentative new idea.

∞

Belief in a famous well-established conjecture in mathematics is almost like belief in a theological statement made by a great religious authority. Both beliefs have niggling doubts lurking in them; believers invariably seek greater certainty. We were all believers in Serre's conjecture in my area of number theory; it shaped our behaviour and our mathematical agenda. Yet we all craved a proof to convert belief into incontrovertible certainty.

Talking about my work on Serre's conjecture led me to think of another implication of it. The question was whether we could prove the conjecture for mod p Galois symmetries when one knew a specific weaker version of the desired conclusion; I'll call this the 'restriction problem'. If I could solve it even in particular cases, it would be another piece of evidence in favour of Serre's conjecture, strengthening one's belief in it.

The experience or expertise I had built up in writing my thesis did not seem relevant here, and I struggled for months on this question with little to show for it. I now had two subproblems both arising from Serre's conjecture to think about: lifting mod p Galois symmetries to p-adic Galois symmetries, and my restriction problem. The two problems were on opposite sides of the chasm bridged by Serre's conjecture. There seemed to be no apparent relation between the problems. I was at a loss to make progress on either of the problems. A nice feature of these problems was that they were easily stated and there was not that much in the literature that seemed useful and relevant to solving them. So one could carry them in one's head and just think about them, hoping to strike gold.

In the real world, I lived in three dimensions; in my mind I lived in the world of two-dimensional Galois symmetries. The real world was messy and complicated. In my mind, the problems were challenging, but yet there was the tantalizing possibility of making decisive progress by thinking about them.

∞

Weeks or even months in Bombay would pass by without my doing any productive work. But I was certainly discovering the city. On one of my walks in Bombay, I visited a predominantly Muslim area of the city. Growing up in Bombay, despite the seeming cosmopolitanism of the city, life was still lived mainly well within the community one belonged to. I was thinking at the time about lifting a mod p Galois symmetry to a mod p^2 symmetry, a first step to lifting to a mod p^n symmetry for all n which would yield a p-adic lift, answering Deligne's question. I was preoccupied by a lemma that reformulated the problem. I found myself in a narrow street full of furniture and antique shops. The area I was wandering in was called chor bazaar, which literally translates to 'a market of thieves' – antiques of dubious provenance were sold that had sometimes just been minted the other day. In this very different world, people seemed to live, work and worship all in one place. I walked along a narrow street, passing weathered-blackened buildings, tottering with age, propped up by scaffoldings. Wood-framed windows, clothes hanging outside, darkened rooms. A couple of goats were being driven through the middle of the street, fright making their feet fall crookedly, quite possibly on their way to an abattoir. I stepped into a shop filled with pieces of furniture in various states of being. Broken legs, tilted tables, patched together chairs, huge chests, wrought-iron benches. It looked like an orphanage of abandoned pieces of furniture. The shopkeeper, his mouth coloured a deep red by the paan that he was chewing, took out a lamp with pride. He said it was more than a hundred years old, throwing a gauntlet to disbelief.

After several months of being stuck on both problems, pushed by my failed attempts on the restriction problem, I tried to unify the problems: could lifting mod p Galois symmetries to mod p^2 Galois symmetries be done whenever it worked in a weaker sense related to my restriction problem? In the context of lifting Galois symmetries there was one simple situation in which I could answer the question by adapting an argument which I had used in the final step of my thesis. I had carried out the first step of the lifting problem, namely lifted the mod p Galois symmetry to a mod p^2 Galois symmetry. The mod p^2 lifting argument I discovered was very simple. It had taken me many months to stumble upon the argument that worked. I would not have thought of this argument if I had not been thinking simultaneously about the apparently unrelated restriction problem. Both the problems had been suggested by thinking about Serre's conjecture. Their cohabitation in my mind might have caused one problem to impact the other.

I had read mathematicians say that after they proved a theorem, the thrill of discovery is replaced by a dull indifference to something that was now understood. To me a discovery was accompanied by wonder that I had managed to make the observation on which the problem had turned.

∞

Serre's conjecture seemed to be a problem that one could not think about only from one point of view. One had to attack it from all sides. One could think of it geometrically, or from the point of view of algebra, or from other points of view. I was not committed to any one approach. Unlike my thesis where the problem I solved was already cornered in a very definite nook of the subject, Serre's conjecture seemed to be out in the open. Thus one had to throw everything one had at it, in the hope that something might stick.

I wrote to Serre about my argument for mod p^2 liftings. Serre responded enthusiastically within a few days. He told me that in fact my argument applied more generally than I had thought. The argument produced an example of something that he had defined in a course at Collège de France. He gave a course every year spread over two months; every time he had to present new mathematics. I knew nothing about his prior course, but my argument nevertheless illuminated something about it.

I wrote up a short paper about my mod p^2 lifting result. I was excited by the paper; it was just a small observation on a question I had been thinking of for a few months, but the observation was surprising. The result seemed counter-intuitive, a little too good to be true. If someone had asked me if I believed such a result to be true before I proved it, I would have been very sceptical. I felt very encouraged by Serre's response and thought hard for the next few months about trying to take the next steps in the lifting problem. I had only done the first step.

I kept musing about questions suggested by Serre's conjecture during these years in Bombay, carrying them in my mind, experiencing mainly frustration, but also small eureka moments, making small observations that I wrote up as short papers. It was a little like kicking the ball around on a field, with the goalposts obscured by a thick fog. As there was no reasonable way to aim to kick at the goal which stood smothered in the fog, one just kicked the ball around and chased after it in bursts of somewhat random and sporadic, but still intense, activity. The small results I proved motivated by Serre's conjecture did not make any direct impact on it; the conjecture still seemed infinitely far away. I would have to wait for almost a decade after I had begun to focus on the conjecture, from the mid-1990s to the early years of the new millennium, before I could prove any decisive results towards it.

9

Honeymoon in Paris

My father had provided my details to a few matrimonial agencies. His office assistant was placed in charge of sorting through the responses, and axed most of them. I didn't take much interest in this operation, which was being mounted with my father's usual efficiency. My default position, like that of most of my friends, was that I didn't really want an arranged marriage. But I went along with my father's outsourced efforts, with an attitude of 'let's see what happens'.

One day, my father announced that there was a promising proposal from Pune, and suggested that he and I travel there to meet the young woman and her family. It turned out two of my aunts had already met them, and I felt encouraged when I heard the more 'modern' of the two had taken an instant liking to the young woman. I too was charmed by Rajanigandha when I met her at her parents' flat. We were already there when she came in, a few minutes late, in her white doctor's coat from a nearby hospital, where she was doing her medical residency. I found her natural and unaffected, at ease with herself and her environment. She was very different from me, and that was part of our attraction for each other – differences in taste, temperaments, professions. She listened mainly to Bollywood songs, but good sport that she was, cheerfully accompanied me to a Kishori Amonkar concert in Pune soon after we were engaged – and that too at the crack of dawn. Kishoritai had announced this as a free Diwali concert, and had scheduled it for 4 a.m. so that she could sing early morning ragas.

Kishoritai as usual did not begin the concert on time. The audience waited and waited and it was almost 6 a.m. before she began to sing. Even after she came on stage, she spent the next twenty minutes tuning the tanpuras. She sang Bahaduri Todi, a complex and sombre raga of this time of the morning. As the stars faded out in the gathering light of a cold Pune morning, Rajani's attention started drifting, and she began sketching the scene before us on some paper she found in her purse, focusing on select members of the audience. The miracle was that despite being made to sit through this six-hour ordeal, she did not call our wedding off!

∞

Just before Rajani and I met, I had planned a visit to Paris through an Indo-French exchange programme funded by the governments of the two countries. Such visits had played an important role in the careers of young mathematicians like Narasimhan and Seshadri at TIFR in the 1950s and 1960s: their sojourns in Paris had led to breakthroughs in their work when they returned to TIFR. I was quite excited about the visit as Paris was still a Mecca for number theory, home to many prominent number theorists. The seminar calendar in Paris was the envy of the number theory world. Serre was now retired but still active on the mathematical scene in Paris, and another draw was the prospect of meeting him and also hopefully making good progress towards his conjecture in the city that he had worked in all his life. With memories of how well my sojourn in Sapporo had turned out for me, I hoped that being in Paris for a longish period would enable me to make progress in my research. Specifically I hoped to be able to climb further and produce higher and higher lifts of mod p Galois symmetries, beyond the mod p^2 lifts that I had recently proved to exist in Bombay. Taking place soon after our wedding, which was at the end of 1996, the four-month trip to Paris would also be a honeymoon of sorts for Rajani and myself, albeit a working honeymoon for me.

The Paris we settled into, with a tiny budget, was not the Paris of popular imagination. Our rented apartment in Antony, a suburb of Paris to the south of the main city, was very modest. The bathroom was small and one could hardly move in the shower. There was no fridge, but since it was winter, we got by with keeping perishable items like milk on the kitchen windowsill to keep them cold. The kitchen had a small round table with a yellow veneer at which we ate sitting on two wooden stools. After finishing our meals we tucked the wooden stools under the table.

In contrast to our tiny flat, the florist near it exuded prosperity with its extravagant and ever-changing, kaleidoscopic arrangements of exotic flowers in its shop windows. When we passed by we often stopped to see these fantastical and imaginative arrangements just as one might stop in front of a painting in a museum. We did not initially venture into the shop, intimidated by its opulence. When we finally did, we found ourselves in a warm and humid, almost tropical, environment. The air was soft and fragrant, and one felt, coming in from the cold air outside, that one's face was being gently massaged with a warm towel. We bought some white lilies and pink flowers that had a papery texture. The florist made an exquisite bouquet out of them, adding to it some leaves and sprigs of baby's breath, and we carried it out of the shop feeling that we had bought a work of art. The flowers filled our small flat with their fragrance.

We soon settled into a pattern. While I spent most weekdays going to work to Université Paris 13 in Villetaneuse – a suburb to the north of Paris, quite distant from the centre of the city – Rajani explored areas in the centre of Paris. She had bought the Michelin guide for Paris and used it to visit the many tourist attractions of the city. Sometimes I skipped work and we both played the tourist. That we could not understand much of the French spoken around us also added to the mystery and allure of Paris. Being there for four months made us more than just casual tourists. We felt the tug of life in Paris while still feeling like foreigners.

Writing from India, I had arranged to meet Serre a couple of weeks after I arrived. Serre was giving a series of lectures at the Collège de France and he had suggested that I meet him for lunch after his lecture. I think we had arranged that I would attend part of his lecture. I had known Serre's address for a long time as I had been writing to him ever since I had been a graduate student. Like his work, the address seemed to have a certain elegance and brevity to it.

```
J-P. Serre
Collège de France
3 Rue d'Ulm
Paris Cedex 75005
France
```

In the land of Descartes it made sense that the addresses had a Cartesian rigour to them. However, this was not where I was meeting Serre. He had written to me that the main building of the Collège, dating back to the fifteenth century, was undergoing repairs and the lectures were in another building on Rue d'Ulm close to it. Serre had just retired a couple of years ago from the Collège and he told me that after retirement, emeritus professors were forbidden to offer their own courses at the Collège. Thus, the series of lectures he was giving were under the auspices of a seminar run by a friend and colleague of his at the Collège. The Collège was in the heart of Paris, while Villetaneuse, where the Université Paris 13, which I was visiting was located, was far away from central Paris.

∞

On the day of my rendezvous with Serre I reached the Luxembourg metro station early and had time to wander in the big garden next to the station. It was cold and cloudy and the Jardin du Luxembourg was deserted. There were people wrapped in overcoats hurrying through the garden using it as a shortcut to where they wanted to go. The fountain in the centre of the garden had a forlorn look to it. On sunnier days there would be people sitting on the heavy green metal chairs around it. There would be families and couples and friends and solitaries strolling around, scrunching pebbles underfoot. But just now on this early morning in February all was quiet. The tall horse chestnut and plane trees that I walked amongst were still leafless. The garden was in the classical French tradition and further away I could see the topiaries. Nature was not left alone to its devices in French landscaping, there was always the presence of the guiding human hand.

The cold was bracing and got me into the mood for a mathematical encounter. I associated going to conferences or lectures in mathematics, most of them in the Western world, with cold mornings and mathematicians standing around drinking coffee before the talks started. There was small talk and mathematical discussions; a few people would be working at a blackboard in the lounge. As I walked to our appointment I wondered what mathematics I could tell Serre about. I had written a handful of papers of uncertain importance, while Serre was one of the most celebrated living mathematicians.

I entered the lecture room during a break in his talk. The audience was not very big, a handful of people sat scattered in a small windowless room. Serre had already gone to the blackboard and was about to resume his seminar. He nodded in my direction. The lecture was in French; I could understand some of it. He jotted down some of what he said on the blackboard. He circled a symbol to emphasize its importance. I was in the heart of the French mathematical world. If walls have ears, then the walls of this room had heard and absorbed far more mathematics than I ever would.

Serre was now in his early seventies – several years older than when I had last seen him at the 'Motives' conference in Seattle – but still sprightly. He came from the south of France. People from his region were more talkative, and Serre had said somewhere that for him lecturing was like carrying on a conversation with a chalk in hand. He was lecturing on a topic in group theory. Serre was a renowned expositor, in his articles and in his talks. The lucidity of his lectures made the maths seem natural. After one left the lecture room one still had to struggle with the difficulty of the material and come to terms with it. On this occasion I felt I could have followed more if I had made more of an effort. But I was distracted as part of my mind was thinking ahead to the lunch with Serre. What could I tell him which would interest him?

When the lecture was over, Serre came over to where I was sitting and said: 'Bon, let's go!' I walked along with him to his office which was up a couple of flights of stairs. Serre was fit and beat me to his office door. He was known to be a competitive man!

Serre said that the lecture must have been difficult for me to understand as it was in French. 'How long are you in Paris?' he asked. When I said I was there for four months, he said decisively: 'Then you should learn some French.' He had booked a table for lunch in a brasserie nearby and he suggested that we walk to it right away. We could come back to his office after lunch to discuss some mathematics. The brasserie was a couple of blocks away, near the Panthéon. Fortunately I did not have to do much to keep the conversation up.

Serre asked me if I was following a course of lectures in Paris. When I told him about the ongoing p-adic Hodge theory semester at the Institut Henri Poincaré (IHP), which was close by, he recommended that I attend the lectures by Jean-Marc Fontaine. Fontaine was one of the founders of p-adic Hodge theory and over the last fifteen years had built up with remarkable tenacity and ingenuity a theory that had become central to modern number theory. Fontaine was one of Serre's very few direct students. John Tate, Serre's close friend, did work in the 1960s that laid the foundations of p-adic Hodge theory. Fontaine was the master architect of the great edifice that had been built on those foundations. 'It is amusing to watch him lecture. He paces furiously up and down before the blackboard. Sometimes he is so excited that he falls off the podium! And of course his theory of Galois symmetries is interesting.'

There was a pleasant lightness to the conversation. He made me feel that mathematics was as much part of the French way of life as good food and wine. He talked about the mathematics he had just discussed in his lecture. To better explain a point he pulled out a pen and wrote down on a napkin an expression that was the key to the theorems he had discussed. In the midst of explaining a proof he exclaimed 'uffff', wringing his hands in the air, to indicate how delicate a certain calculation was. I asked him about his conjecture and he explained to me how a certain calculation of Fontaine had been key to its formulation. He advised me that I would be better off taking buses that ran overground than the underground metro trains, as on buses one could see the city. He told me that he had problems with his knees, but that they had good taste: they did not like going down the steps to a metro, but did not mind descending down a ski slope.

I was flattered by Serre's taking interest in my getting to know Paris. This seemed to fit with his generosity in responding with interest to the small ideas that I had sent him from Bombay in our earlier correspondence. Sitting opposite him at the table in the brasserie, I almost forgot that he was the person who had done such glorious research, made breakthroughs, written thousands of pages of mathematics, and written textbooks which were the gold standard for exposition in the subjects they covered. Did he carry all this mathematics within him even as he drank his wine and gave me advice about living in Paris? When the bill arrived, Serre refused my offer to split *l'addition*.

Back in his office, he gave me some of his recent reprints when I asked for them. There was a big filing cabinet in the office in which Serre kept his papers. Amongst the papers he gave me was the published version of a letter Serre had written to his friend Tate which came in handy for me later in making calculations for the paper generalizing my thesis. The correspondence between Serre and Tate, carried out mostly through letters (so snail mail rather than email) had led to many developments in number theory which shaped the course of the subject for several decades from the 1950s onwards. Both liked sports: Tate played basketball, while Serre liked to ski and rock climb. Serre visited Harvard, where Tate worked, once every two years to give a course there. Some of these courses became the material for books. Serre was a major influence on the students at Harvard.

I asked him my question about my restriction problem and he suggested to me names of experts who might have helpful things to say. I caught the RER B line back to Antony. I felt I should have taken the napkin on which Serre had written, as a memory of the lunch. It would have been a bit like having a napkin Picasso had sketched on, transforming it into art and a valuable memento and keepsake. Now it was too late to go back and retrieve it. I had read Serre's books and papers, and knew his mathematical style and voice through them, but meeting him in person gave me a sense of how he was in real life, a man of the world and not just a great mind who had shaped modern number theory. It also made me feel that I had to do much better work so that next time we met I could tell him something new and compelling. I did not see him again during our Paris stay.

∞

Throughout the four months in Paris, I kept thinking about my lifting question. But Rajani's presence ensured that I did not carry the problem with me at all times. During the evenings we went to a garden near our flat. It had a row of tall poplar trees. As spring approached, we noticed leaves returning to the trees. They trembled in the breeze, doing a constant dance on the spot. Someone told us that these trees were called *tremblants* colloquially because of the constant trembling motion of their leaves.

I was, as Serre had advised, attending Jean-Marc Fontaine's course at the IHP and on the days he lectured I did not go to Villetaneuse. After hearing his lecture in the morning, I lined up outside a boulangerie to buy a sandwich, more often than not a baguette with camembert and lettuce, sometimes brie and walnuts. I took it with me to eat in the enormous Jardin du Luxembourg. Sometimes I was with a colleague, most times I was by myself. It was quiet and when in the garden one did not feel one was in the middle of one of the prominent cities of the world. I sat on one of the heavy green metal chairs near the fountain, thinking about the lifting problem. After lunch, twice a week I would take a solo walk around the Latin Quarter, thinking on it about the maths I was working on.

Some of my other interactions with mathematicians in Paris were less heartening than my encounter with Serre. I went to meet someone who was an expert in Ramanujan symmetries and talked to him about my thesis results related to congruences of Ramanujan symmetries. In the midst of my explaining these on the blackboard in his office, he began quizzing me on whether my results had any applications, meaning had they been of use in solving other mathematical problems. I did not have a ready answer to the unexpected question, and he seemed to lose interest in our conversation. It would be another seven years before the efforts in my thesis work led to striking applications when they inspired some of the steps in our proof of Serre's conjecture.

I would return to Antony some weekday evenings before Rajani came back from the city. There was no sofa to sit or lie in, and the stools in the kitchen were not ideal to sit on and muse about mathematics. I used to lie down on the mattress on the floor of our bedroom thinking about liftings. (Most of the furniture in the flat started falling apart. The door of the cupboard in the other room came unhinged in the first few weeks of our arrival in Paris.) The windows of our bedroom had metal shutters which were typical of flats in Paris. We scarcely ever used them even at nights. I had kept the windows open. The days were becoming longer. We had been here now for around three months, and it was almost spring. The sky had streaks of orange and light fluffy clouds. I could hear birds chirping in the distance. Perhaps it was the changing seasons that gave me a flash of inspiration: I realized that if I could lift mod p Galois symmetries I would be able to solve my restriction problem too! Lifts when combined with the technique of Wiles from his proof of FLT would do the job. The argument I found seemed a bit like cheating: it was very short, and was more like a trick than a theoretical insight. It felt like serendipitously finding a tunnel that could be used to get to the other side of a terrain that seemed impossible to pass overground. It felt less heroic using the tunnel than moving overtly across the field dodging enemy fire. Again, the mere fact that I had been carrying these two seemingly unrelated problems, of lifting Galois symmetries and my restriction problem, for more than two years in my mind – and getting nowhere with them after my initial success in producing a mod p^2 lifting – had resulted in them getting tied together like Siamese twins.

The restriction problem had suggested a line of attack that had led me to the proof of mod p^2 liftings in Bombay. Now a year after that development, the inspiration flowed in the other direction: lifts of mod p Galois symmetries together with Wiles's results solved my other restriction problem. I had worked so hard and failed at proving such a result by more organic methods over the past year when working in Bombay. Now the problem had fallen to a synthetic method that combined two different techniques and results. One of the results, namely lifts of mod p Galois symmetries, was still not available. But the observation seemed in the right spirit and was a surprising mélange of two ideas. It was further motivation to try and construct p-adic (not just mod p^2) lifts of mod p Galois symmetries.

∞

The upbeat feeling did not last. Soon after returning to Bombay at the end of the four months in Paris, I learnt that Ravi Ramakrishna, a young mathematician of around my age working at Cornell University, had solved the lifting problem. I had fallen short in my attempt to get lifts of mod p Galois symmetries, and now someone else had done it. This was like a sucker punch.

But in a few days I recovered and felt all was not lost, and became intent on understanding how he had proved the result that had eluded my best efforts for the past two years. When I saw his paper I realized that what I had been trying was not sufficient to solve the problem. But having tried and failed in solving the lifting problem, I was ripe to appreciate the solution. It was very beautiful and clever and I spent many weeks trying to understand the ideas. There was also the consolation prize of having a solution to the restriction problem in my bag now: this was because of the insight I had gained in Paris that its solution was a corollary to lifting mod p Galois symmetries. Maths problems were like dominos, the falling of one led to the falling of many others.

Ramakrishna had worked on the problem for several years. He was the colleague who had said about the consequence of Serre's conjecture for liftings: 'If it were Bob's conjecture, I wouldn't have believed it!' Now he had gone and proved it, inventing a method that was miraculously simple and perfect. Perhaps he had imbibed his tenacity from his adviser – no other than Andrew Wiles.

Results like Ramakrishna's bore the stamp of individual creativity rather than coming from a system, or assembly line, with different workers working out complicated implications or extensions of known methods.

I tried to rationalize to myself the two years I had spent in my unsuccessful attempt to get liftings. The experience of tussling with a problem unsuccessfully could itself form the basis of future successes as it gave one a point of view. To succeed was ideal, but to have tried and failed could also confer some advantages. It led to an enthusiastic appreciation of the difficulties that the person who had succeeded had overcome, which could help one understand more deeply the method that had worked.

To be overwhelmed by a piece of mathematics or music seemed to me to be an essential part of my personality. This may not mean I understood the piece of mathematics fully, but it had become a part of me nevertheless.

A few months after returning from Paris, I made another mathematical contribution that had some impact. I saw a paper by the French mathematician Marie-France Vignéras – one of the few women I had encountered in my field – in which she proved important results towards the mod p 'local Langlands correspondence'. She had worked on this problem for many years and had written a foundational book on the subject. It was a 'local analogue' of Serre's conjecture. The paper I saw was the final step which achieved her goal. It was not the ideal result as it had some unnecessary conditions. Her proof was also long and technical. I realized on looking at it that if one used a more *global* argument and used Carayol's lemma, which I was very fond of, one could give a much simpler argument which proved a complete result. I wrote to her about my idea in an email message. I also sketched the proof to her. She wrote it up nicely and published her paper in *Inventiones*. The main theorem of the paper was very useful and her paper was widely quoted. This marked a new phase of my work. I had begun in my research to respond to the work of other people and not just pursue an autonomous line of inquiry.

∞

We settled back into the rhythms of life in Bombay. We continued to stay for a couple of years after our marriage in my parents' flat, before moving into the flat I had been assigned in the TIFR housing colony. Buildings in the colony built after Bhabha's time were shoddy, government-issued constructions; gone was the sense of aesthetics which Bhabha had brought to the buildings on campus.

In spite of this move from Worli to our assigned flat being a downgrade in the quality of our abodes, we enjoyed setting it up, hunting for ethnic furniture, going for late night movies, eating at restaurants. TIFR was close to the lively area of Colaba. From the west-facing windows of our flat one could see only water, which made us feel that we were passengers on a ship that had stalled mid-ocean. Rajani had the fuller day, working at a hospital in a less salubrious part of Bombay. She was doing her postgraduate residency at a municipal hospital in Lower Parel. It was a low-lying area that got flooded every year during the monsoons. She drove there in our olive green Wagon R, which was a mutt of a car, a hybrid between a station wagon and a small sedan, every weekday and on Saturday when she worked for half the day.

In my job there were no attendance requirements, no muster to sign, while Rajani had to report to work at 9 a.m. sharp. Her commute sometimes took over an hour each way. She was pursuing her MD in clinical physiology, a residency which she took in her stride and enjoyed – that is her temperament, to make the most of what there is – even if she missed assisting in surgeries and doing some on her own, as she had done in her internship after her MBBS.

This was a compromise that Rajani had made to solve our 'two-body problem', a term used in academic departments when hiring someone who had a spouse who also needed a job in the same city. There is a famous problem in classical mechanics called the 'three-body problem' where given initial positions and velocities of three bodies – for example, the sun, earth and moon – one has to solve for their future trajectory using Newton's laws of motion and theory of gravitation. There is no general closed-form solution to the three-body problem, while solving for the future motion of two interacting point masses is straightforward. The real world 'two-body problem' of partners finding jobs in the same city on the other hand, while not unsolvable, was still quite difficult, and most times there is no perfect solution, as was the case here.

Rajani told me about her busy day at the hospital. For my part, I lamented that I had not been very productive. There was no exoskeleton to my day, none of the external constraints which could impose a shape on it, limit it; it was free to flow formlessly, the shape had to be willed by me. I joked to her that it would be wonderful if one could turn the clocks back by a few days or weeks or months, and having worked hard and accomplished something definite in the invented time, be able in the present moment to look back upon the fulfilling work of that period.

10

Back to America

When I returned to Bombay at the end of 1994 after the struggles of my PhD years, I felt I had escaped from a house on fire just before its beams had come crashing down. I was determined to never take up a long-term position in the United States. I almost felt like someone with post-traumatic stress disorder (PTSD). Working in the relative isolation of TIFR allowed me to mature as a mathematician. My distance from the renowned centres of learning in my subject in the West worked to my advantage. I was able to pursue my own line of thinking without other distractions and without being overwhelmed by the influence of a dominant leader. I am not sure I would have done well working under direction and being asked to contribute to a programme led by others. Being near family at a time when my mother was sick, and working in a city where I had roots gave me a sense of security and that, too, helped me find my feet in research.

Historically, TIFR has been an island of excellence in the country. It led a renaissance in Indian mathematics starting in the late 1950s that lasted for more than three decades. Important theorems were proved in India, mainly at TIFR. The salaries had never been high, but the gulf between those salaries and what one could make in the outside world had not been immense. When India was a young socialist country, there was also a sense that one's work as a scientist or mathematician was part of the country's growth and progress. All that was now changing. The economic liberalization that started in the late 1980s and picked up in the 1990s brought greater prosperity, greater inequality, and perhaps a feeling of being more marginal as an academic working in an increasingly market-driven India. The sense of identification with a nation-building project had receded somewhat and this perhaps led young researchers to being drawn increasingly to work in the West.

Many of the faculty at TIFR were locally trained. The hiring of its own students was at least partly because the institute struggled to attract back as faculty quality Indian researchers who had finished doctoral or postdoctoral work in the West. It was hard to match the resources available for research abroad, and create a sustaining ecosystem for doing sciences in India that could vie with what was available in countries like the United States. The returns had started diminishing.

I worked in an area in which there was little local expertise. There might have been an expectation that I could make TIFR a centre for the relationship between Ramanujan and Galois symmetries. The subject had entered a phase of explosive growth after Wiles's breakthrough in 1994. (It was a bit like what was said about the Wall Street of the 1990s: you only had to be there to be showered with manna.) A senior colleague at TIFR once told a group of us who had gone out for a drink that as the younger generation, it was on us to prove a landmark mathematical result. This might ignite a revival in mathematical research in TIFR in the fading years of the twentieth century in a way similar to how the Narasimhan–

Seshadri theorem had galvanized the School of Mathematics in the 1960s. My later work on Serre's conjecture could conceivably have played such a trigger role, but that was still a few years away, and personally I was being pulled towards widening my horizons and working in the more challenging and dynamic environment of the United States.

A zestful six-week visit to Boston around the fall of 2000, during which I enjoyed discussing mathematics with colleagues, and travelling across the country to talk about my work, had probably sharpened my desire to try out working in the United States. Now that I had done some mathematics that had attracted notice, it felt different being back in the United States, compared to when I had been a struggling graduate student with no original research under my belt. The PTSD had lifted.

I was invited by Fred Diamond, who worked at Brandeis University, in the Boston area. I had known his work since my graduate student days. Recently, Fred had done exciting work related to extending Wiles's breakthrough ideas. So I was happy to accept his invitation and have the opportunity of discussing mathematics with him and other mathematicians nearby.

∞

Boston, like Paris, was one of the centres for my subject. Staying in a rented room in an apartment in Porter Square, not far from Harvard Square, I used the opportunity to meet Richard Taylor at Harvard, whom I had known since my days at Caltech. He had visited Caltech for a quarter and had given a course there which I had attended, and I had corresponded with him about my thesis. He was an avid mountaineer, and was famously disciplined and organized. He had many students at Harvard whom he met regularly every week, and had by now a formidable track record of having trained many excellent PhD students who had written substantial theses under his direction. I was keen to tell him about my work and see if I could learn something new by talking to him. He had a sharp mind, thinking clearly and quickly on his feet.

I explained to him at the board in his office my idea for solving the restriction problem. When I had started wondering about it a couple of years ago, I had asked Taylor about the problem and he had said that although he had also himself thought about the question and even touted it around to a few experts, he had not been able to make any progress to answering it. As I explained the idea, it was gratifying to see that the solution surprised him: both by the fact that it had been solved and also by the manner of the solution that seemed so simple after the event.

I also surprised him when I told him about my idea which had helped Vignéras in her work. Such one-on-one discussions with colleagues and experts were invaluable: email correspondence was very helpful but there was nothing to replace the magic of being in the same room with someone, which meant sometimes that one's whole self was in the conversation and one learnt not only from what was said but also more subliminally through the vibes of the room.

I spoke to Taylor about a paper that I had submitted more than a year ago to the prestigious journal *Inventiones mathematicae* which deepened the results of my thesis. Taylor was the editor who was handling my submission and it turned out that the referee he had sent the paper to had stopped responding. Taylor took upon himself the task of refereeing the paper. I had written the paper badly, and he made me work hard, pushing me to write it with greater precision and in a way that it could be useful to others. I was grateful for the effort he took in forcing me to improve the results and the exposition.

I spent many hours in the apartment at Porter Square working on revising the paper. I did go sailing one weekend with the apartment's friendly owner, but most of the time I worked on a keyboard that was linked to the TV in the flat. It was slow going, but I wanted to get this done as the paper had languished with the journal for over a year before Taylor had decided to referee it himself. In the course of trying to make my results explicit I used Serre's letter to Tate, the one he had given me in his office on Rue d'Ulm in Paris. Serre's letter helped me make my results in the paper precise. This was a coming together of mathematics I had been thinking about since 1995.

I had found the basic method to go beyond the results of my thesis within the first few months of working at TIFR in Bombay. But to implement the method and spell out the consequences took me several years. During the Paris trip I was confused about the method leading to contradictions in one particular case. Realizing why my method failed to deal with this case resolved this rather tortuous weeks-long period of confusion for me. This was a bit like Serre being relieved at noticing a small counterexample to his conjecture, which allowed him to pin down exactly the divergence between the naive and sophisticated versions of his conjectures. The counterexample to Serre's conjecture was like a small flaw, a beauty spot that almost enhanced its charms. Understanding why something did not work in an extreme case made one better understand and be confident about why the method generally worked.

∞

Within a few months of our conversations, Taylor wrote a paper in which he proved Artin's conjecture in a few more two-dimensional cases. One of the key new ideas in the paper was the one I had found in Paris: to use lifts for solving the restriction problem. This was the new ingredient Taylor added in this paper to his earlier brew of methods to target the two-dimensional Artin's conjecture and get some new cases of it. Taylor acknowledged my idea with the sentence 'We learned this argument from C. Khare' in the paper.

Taylor's paper was mimicked by other mathematicians to get new cases of Serre's conjecture. These results proved cases of Serre's conjecture that went beyond the known cases which Wiles had used as input into his proof of many cases of the elliptic symmetry conjecture. But the methods used by Taylor and those who had followed him could, by their very nature, work only in a limited number of new cases, and the general case of Serre's conjecture still seemed completely out of reach. Yet this was a hint that although Wiles had used known cases of Serre's conjecture as a starting point in his attack on the elliptic symmetry conjecture, his methods might be capable of proving new cases of Serre's conjecture when used in novel ways.

∞

Around the time I visited Brandeis, Diamond along with Christophe Breuil (who worked in Paris), Brian Conrad (who worked at Harvard) and Taylor proved the elliptic symmetry conjecture in full generality after Wiles's breakthrough had proved it in a large class of cases which sufficed to prove FLT. This was a long and highly complex paper and represented a type of mathematics which I could never do. In my work I tried to follow my own intuition and find ideas that were more naive, simple and direct. I felt like an insect, a water strider, which uses the surface tension of water to hover delicately on the surface of a pond and scutter around. Water striders don't have the wherewithal to deal with the water giving way under their legs. I analogously felt my best chance of success in mathematical research was to float on the surface of mathematical theories, and profit from their depth, without getting myself into deeper waters that could drown me, never to surface again. For instance, in the first few years after my PhD, I focused more on using Wiles's theorems to draw consequences towards Serre's conjecture, rather than doing a deep dive into his methods to understand their finer nuances.

Often mathematicians vanished after a few publications; some of these disappearances might have resulted from wandering into difficult and treacherous mathematical terrain. It was important for me to know my weaknesses and be able to manage them, and even turn them into strengths as they could help prevent me from getting into areas which were too technical for my taste, and even a little over-cultivated, and thus had less scope left in them for simple creative ideas. I felt I had never overcome any of my limitations in mathematics, but rather tried to make the subject adapt to my limitations, like pouring something into the mould of one's self. And this was true right from the beginning, even as a way into the subject, not just after having acquired a viewpoint and some expertise in it. My weaknesses stood out clearly in my mind: strengths are in a sense harder to assess for oneself. Strengths typically emerge in the course of working on something; they are more diffuse in their nature than weaknesses, which are apparent from the start.

During the Boston visit I went on a whirlwind tour of the United States, lecturing on my results. I gave talks in Tucson, Los Angeles, Pasadena and Berkeley. This was the first time I was returning to Pasadena and Los Angeles after graduating from there a few years ago.

∞

When I applied for positions in the United States, spurred on by my Boston trip, I was delighted by the response. It was hard to break back into the US system after having left it more than five years ago. I soon embarked on a 'job talk' tour of North America, interviewing at the University of Georgia, University of Utah and University of Toronto. This was my chance to make a strong case to be hired. Ravi Ramakrishna, who happened to be visiting India before I left, gave me a valuable tip. He said giving a good talk could make a huge difference in enthusing people to hire you, and a bad talk could sabotage your chances. The talk, he emphasized, should be directed at the faculty working outside one's area, as they were the ones who needed to be convinced. The ones working in the same area were already interested in you, at least enough to invite you for an interview.

By this time, my paper in *Inventiones mathematicae*, which deepened my thesis results, had been published. This strengthened my CV. Publications in prestigious journals count for a lot. Especially for people outside one's area, this is perhaps the chief marker of excellence as they cannot independently judge the quality of the work. In all three places, I gave a colloquium talk, summarizing the highlights of my work since my thesis.

Returning to Bombay after the job tour, I felt as I had done in the summers after my annual exams in Cambridge. I had waited nervously for the letter from my tutor telling me about the results of exams that I felt I had neither bombed nor aced. Somewhat in the same vein, I felt my job interviews had gone okay, but it was hard to tell if I had made a good enough impression to get hired. I was able to guess who the competition might be by looking at the departmental websites for announcements of 'Special Colloquia' (another name for a job talk) in the hiring season. Some of the competition was flashier, and some had just genuinely done better work. I was a bit of a lone ranger in my research and career. I did not have the patronage of influential mathematicians, so I figured I would be at a disadvantage vis-à-vis some of the competition. But on the whole I felt I stood a good chance.

I first heard from Georgia and they offered me a tenure-track position as an assistant professor. Utah was slower in making me an offer. My visit there had been in the middle of a snowstorm. Salt Lake City had looked very pretty and exotic to me, nestling in the lap of the Wasatch range of snow-clad mountains. My footsteps in freshly fallen snow left marks as they might do on wet sand at a beach. I felt upbeat when the person on the hiring committee at Utah told me that I had, through my talk, overcome scepticism about hiring someone from outside the United States, and with little teaching experience. The University of Toronto, which was in a cosmopolitan big city, besides having a good department, did not offer me a job.

I was leaning towards Utah. It was Mormon country, which made it seem culturally alien. I had never imagined working there. But then the department had a good reputation and had done remarkably well in the field of algebraic geometry. Perhaps the mountains and the snow were an inspiring environment to do mathematics. (Later, after I had my breakthrough when working there, a colleague quipped that there must be something in the water there which made people prove great theorems.) For a department to do well, it just took someone on the faculty with vision to hire good people, and a handful of such people could transform a place, forming a nucleus around which the department could grow. Weil had once cheekily said, and with some accuracy, that first-rate people hire first-rate people, and second-rate people hire third-rate people. Of course, there was subjectivity involved in deciding who was first-rate. One could not rule out biases towards certain areas in the subject, or towards certain kinds of mathematicians. In the end Lady Luck might have the last say on how a place shaped up.

The offers were a gratifying vindication of the progress in my research, but I had to make a tough decision: did I really want to move to the US? The reasons for not going stacked up easily. Bombay was home, I had done reasonably well at TIFR, and had started making a mark in the subject. Neither Rajani nor I had family in the country. My mother's health was declining, and it was anyone's guess how much longer she had. It could be months or years. Even in her enfeebled state, after twelve years of cirrhosis, she was still the bedrock of our family, the person we vied to take care of, the emotional centre of our world. TIFR had done its best to keep me by giving me an accelerated promotion. In the US, I would just be one reasonably good mathematician amongst many, not as good as the best. I would be merely adding to the surfeit of talent in the country. Staying in India and working at TIFR, I could make more of a difference, given the small numbers of mathematicians active in research working in India.

But now that the offers had come in, it was hard to turn away from the United States. Not going would be like not taking the next logical step in my career, almost like shying away from the challenge of proving my worth in the States. I would begin as an outsider to the system, which would push me in ways that could benefit my work. It would be a new life, and perhaps, I thought to myself, the disruption too would be good in the long run. It was quipped sometimes that mathematicians came cheap as they did not need big labs – just pen and paper, some exposure to the right training and opportunities for interacting with good mathematicians. Yet, the greater resources it offered had made the US a magnet, attracting mathematicians from all over the world. I wanted the experience of working in the United States, being part of its vibrant mathematical community. Making a new life in America seemed both scary and alluring.

∞

After much debate at home, my wife and I decided that I should take up the Utah offer. Some of my colleagues at TIFR regarded this as a betrayal of the cause of lifting the quality of mathematics in the country. I was not staying back to fight the good fight! I felt torn myself. But the wide world was calling, and overcoming our worries, my wife and I decided to give Utah a shot. I was not burning my bridges just as yet: we could come back if things did not work out as I would be on leave from TIFR for a little while. I deferred taking the position at Utah by a semester and started in the spring semester of 2002, which would begin in January.

My mother's health was deteriorating. The illness had hollowed her body, she limped because a stroke had weakened her right side. She had weathered many storms, lying with eyes closed as her body trembled like a leaf. Yet whenever she had respite from these storms, she braved (with help) the steep stairs of the building and went out. She once said casually that the body was doing its thing, but this did not change who she was inside as a person. One could almost think of her as a saint who had overcome her physical strife by some inner abiding grace more than an act of will.

We all struggled to see her waste away. For my father and sister it was even harder as they had lived with her in the same Worli flat throughout her long decline. As I wavered about leaving Bombay for Utah, she urged me to take the Utah job if it was good for my career. I will be back in a few weeks to see you, I told her. The

Winter Olympics were going to be held in Salt Lake City around a month after the spring semester classes started and there was going to be a month-long break for the university. I would come back to Bombay for that month.

∞

I landed by myself in Salt Lake City in the winter holidays, a few days before the start of classes. Rajani had stayed back to finish the final exams for her MD degree. When I looked out at night from the windows of the rented, furnished apartment on the eleventh floor of Sunset Towers, I saw lights burning like fireflies, extending all the way to the snow-covered mountains which ringed Salt Lake. The city was laid out on a grid. I had a temporary office in the basement of the maths department, and when I sat there I felt I had come a long way. Not just the distance of 8,000 miles from Bombay, which actually seemed light years away, but also a long way away from my graduate student days at Caltech. This was going to be a very different campus experience. At the same time, I had left my comfort zone and was in a sense starting afresh. I would have to prove my credentials as part of the mathematical community here.

I already had an inkling that this wasn't going to be smooth sailing while applying for a National Science Foundation (NSF) grant from India after I accepted the Utah job. This was for funding my further research: the grant supported PhD students and visitors, and travel to conferences. My position at Utah was not yet permanent and getting an NSF grant was something universities looked for before promoting faculty to a tenured (permanent) position. The application to the NSF was done through the university. The grant manager in Utah had been slow to respond and had botched up the application, misspelling my name horribly even after I had corrected her several times. I would not get the grant the first two years I applied for it.

In the reports that came along with the rejection, one of the experts said that the principal investigator (PI), that is me, specialized in simple original ideas but had not hit the jackpot. The expert's low rating of my proposal sank it. The next year I submitted a proposal, it was again rejected. An expert's comment was: 'The PI specializes in new ideas, rather than technical work, and one cannot anticipate in advance what new idea one will have.' The reviewer went on to say that the proposed projects either did not seem interesting, or not plausibly something that I could do. The reviewers criticized the organization and style of my proposal. I could console myself by arguing that these were subjective assessments but I longed to do work that would soar above judgement calls, subjective or otherwise.

∞

Most days in Salt Lake were sunny with blue skies, and in the morning the snow dazzled one's eyes. The vivid fiery bands of orange and crimson stretched across darkening skies, forming a dramatic backdrop to the snow-covered peaks of the Wasatch range, were thrilling to watch as I walked back home from the department on wintry evenings. In the quiet days before the semester started, when I had little occasion to speak to anyone, and with the beauty of the snow-covered mountains all around me, I felt I was on a retreat in a Shangri-La or in the mountainous region invoked in Thomas Mann's *The Magic Mountain*.

I was assigned to teach a course in Real Analysis in a building a few minutes walk from the department. A good proportion of the undergraduates in Utah, mainly local, came from Mormon families. I had learnt from others in the department that quite a few were a little older than average. They had spent two years or so on 'mission' doing service or spreading the word of the faith. The Mormon Church had gone from strength to strength and perhaps was one of the fastest-growing religions. There were large Mormon communities in places as far away from Utah as the Pacific Islands. I had previously encountered young Mormon missionaries, clean cut in white shirts and wearing badges with names like Johansson or Mortensen or Jorgensen that had a Scandinavian ring to them. They would carry the Book of Mormon and ask very politely if you had a minute to spare (a minute that could lead to nothing less than saving of your soul!). The church maintained extensive genealogical records as even the dead could be baptized. All religions have their oddities, but as a friend of mine put it, older religions have the advantage of having been around for centuries, with glorious music like Bach's to bolster them, leading one to overlook their bizarre aspects.

Many of the students in my class resembled the missionaries I had encountered. Since a fair fraction of them were married, it was not unusual to be asked for an extension on a homework because a child had fallen sick. Mathematics kept me grounded in this unfamiliar terrain. Some of the students were very good: many local students stayed on at Utah, even if they could have gone to fancier universities, because of the draw of living within their community. It was not hard to settle into the rhythm of teaching thrice a week in the early morning, hurrying to get to class in snow flurries, attending an occasional faculty meeting, listening to seminars in the afternoons, and going back late in the evenings to my flat in Sunset Towers.

After a few weeks I was able to move from my makeshift office to a nice office on the ground floor of a building that had been recently gutted and then renovated. The office was on President's Circle right in the heart of campus and through my window I saw students rushing past it to their classes. Later in the spring the circle would be festooned with the blossoms of the cherry trees which stood all round its circumference. The Winter Olympics were going to be held in Salt Lake City in just a few weeks. Many of the sporting events took place in and around Park City up in the Wasatch mountains. There was a new tram line which had been laid in Salt Lake City because of the Winter Olympics. One of my new friends in the department remarked that he liked the finality of the announcement on the public address system of the final stop at the university: 'You have reached the end of the line.'

∞

I went back to Bombay in February, as planned, to be with my mother. She was even frailer than when I had left. Her kidneys had started failing and we took her every few days to Jaslok Hospital for dialysis, bringing her back after a few hours. At home, we brought her out into the balcony so that she could look out at the sea. My mother was not communicating any more, and so what she felt within, or how sentient she was, could only be guessed. My father was in a state of collapse.

I had heard that my grandfather had a breakdown when a close friend of his passed away. For months he had scarcely got out of his bed. My father's breakdown had traces of my grandfather's. My father lamented that he had neglected his wife. Taking to poetry later, he wrote that a Ganges had flowed in his backyard, while he had remained dry. We tried to reassure him that our mother had loved him with all her heart, admired his many qualities and enjoyed his success. But he was inconsolable. A new specialist my sister had contacted eventually told us that nothing more could be done for my mother. We decided as a family that we would not artificially prolong her life by putting her on a ventilator. She passed away on 12 March 2002 at Hinduja Hospital. She was not yet sixty-five.

The days seemed to turn slack after the tightness they had been pulled into by all the tension and uncertainty over her health, and the frantic efforts to reverse her steep decline. I shaved my head as per the custom. I waited for the extended rituals and ceremonies to be over so that I could grieve for her more privately. The grieving never really stops, especially when someone has died too young. Anything of beauty, goodness or excellence now brings tears to my eyes, and I sense these tears are for my mother. Sometimes, when dealing with a crisis, I close my eyes and think of the time when she lay dying in the Hinduja Hospital, and that gives me perspective.

∞

In my research in the new surroundings in Salt Lake City I continued with the themes that had been prominent in my work during my years at TIFR after my PhD. I kept Serre's conjecture in my mind as a goal. There was no direct way to attack it. When Serre had first made the conjecture in 1973, many important mathematicians such as Deligne had been sceptical. It seemed almost too good to be true. But once stated, various things happened around it: verifying it in special cases, the connection with FLT that made Serre refine the conjecture to make it very precise and quantitative, the wonderful work done to show that a qualitative form of the conjecture implied its more precise form.

For number theorists, the guiding conjectures in the subject, like the one of Serre, inspired them to excesses of efforts. Their role as stimuli could be likened to the irresistible pull of the silver medallion of the moon, hanging tantalizingly in the dark night sky, on the imagination and ambitions of myriads of earthbound adventurers. The desire to set foot on the moon could not be achieved for many centuries. But much before it became possible to land on the moon, lunar ambitions had shaped many technological innovations which ultimately led to developing rockets that could overcome the earth's gravitational pull and soar into space to reach the moon.

Similarly it might be that the conjecture was completely out of reach and could take decades more to prove. But fortunately it was not an all-or-nothing problem: one could immerse oneself in thinking about it, following leads and questions suggested by it even if the solution itself seemed unreachable. Without being fully conscious of it, proving Serre's conjecture had become my moonshot since the time I began working on questions suggested by it as a young researcher in Bombay.

∞

Rajani and I decided to try and have a baby in Salt Lake and it turned out to be a somewhat hazardous enterprise. Our daughter was born in a major snowstorm. We had to be careful driving back from the hospital as the car sometimes slipped, not getting enough traction. If it slipped, one had to resist one's instinct to turn too quickly in the other direction to counteract the slipping. Our daughter's name, Arushi, means the first ray of sunlight.

When she was born her eyes seemed light blue. They are a light brown colour now. In my mother's final days, I had experienced death as something that brought to a screeching halt all that one did to care for someone, leaving a void behind. A birth was the very opposite: suddenly, we needed a myriad things – crib, car seat, soft blankets, sheets to swaddle her in, a rocking chair to rock her to sleep. One was struck by how much we bought to take care of such a small creature, and still, all this was not enough to placate her. In the first few weeks after she was born, it seemed to me in my sleep-deprived, harried state that she cried almost all through the night. I wondered if the transition from the womb to the world outside it affected her like jet lag and the crying was because of the pain of adjusting to the circadian rhythms of the new world.

Through those long nights when I slept lightly to keep watch and give Rajani a break from feeding and taking care of Arushi, I tried to think about the maths in a paper that I was writing with a few colleagues in France and in the United States. The mathematics offered distraction and an escape into another world that was calmer.

∞

Thinking of lifting mod *p* Galois symmetries became a leitmotif of my research, something I kept coming back to, in different contexts and from different directions. It was a statement implied by Serre's conjecture, Ramakrishna had found a beautiful method to show lifts existed, and I felt excited to see if one could do more. The fact that I myself had tried to get lifts over two years of thinking, and failed, had helped me put down roots in this domain of inquiry! Gebhard Boeckle from Germany visited me for a few weeks in Salt Lake City. He had visited me in TIFR and we had started working on a project about an analogue of Serre's conjecture over 'function fields'. Function fields were interesting in themselves, but they were also like a laboratory in which one could develop methods and experiment with ideas that could come in useful in the case of questions about rational numbers (Serre's conjecture being an example) which were more central to number theory.

Gebhard asked if one could think of lifting questions in the function fields setting and generalize the liftings methods of Ramakrishna and Wiles to that case. (Ramakrishna lifted mod p Galois symmetries to p-adic Galois symmetries, while Wiles lifted the Ramanujan property of a mod p Galois symmetry to many of its p-adic lifts.) I became excited about working on this proposal of Gebhard when I noticed that generalizing Ramakrishna's method would allow one to deduce as a corollary an analogue of Serre's conjecture for function fields in great generality.

I have mentioned in the introduction André Weil's letter to his sister Simone Weil in which he compared analogies in mathematics to the Rosetta Stone with the same text written in different scripts. In the letter Weil had a particular analogy between questions about rational numbers and function fields in mind, and how phenomena in the function field case could shed light on the harder case of phenomena related to the rational numbers.

It turned out that my work with Gebhard on an analogue of Serre's conjecture acted like a Rosetta Stone for me in my later work on Serre's conjecture: my experience of thinking of its analogue led to crucial insights into the original form of the conjecture. Around the same time I worked out a new application with Ramakrishna of his lifting method. I also wrote up a new proof of Wiles's results using Ramakrishna's results, thus connecting their two different lifting techniques. Both papers were submitted to *Inventiones mathematicae*.

I slowly discovered that one of my main strengths as a mathematician was that I could obsess about something for long periods of time. I remembered a funny story of obsession a friend and fellow student, James, once told me in Cambridge. Sitting tall and awkward in my room in Wolfson Court, the sun glinting off his oversized glasses, James narrated how he had once become obsessed with counting the grains of sugar in a bag. Deep into the night he picked one grain and put it into a second bag, then added another, then another. The number he reached has perhaps stayed forever in his mind.

I was going to be put up for tenure at Utah soon and I was worried about not having gotten an NSF grant so far. I had also been rejected for a Sloan Fellowship which was another standard milestone for someone doing well in their early career research. I fretted about these failures, little realizing that bigger things were coming my way, the pattern conforming to something my mother used to say to me as a child: that I struggled with what others found easy, and did things that were difficult for others. It also echoed my father's bravado-filled grand statement 'I do only the impossible!'

∞

Rajani and I came back to Bombay with Arushi when she was a little less than six months old. I had got the NSF grant on my third try just before I left for India on what would be a semester-long sabbatical. By this time I had a couple of more papers accepted at *Inventiones mathematicae*. These, and having been in the US academic system for two years now, may have helped along with the alleged lucky properties of the number three.

The Worli flat, still the one place in the world that felt most like home, was full of photos of my mother. We had arrived in time for a celebration. My sister was getting married, several years after me. As my mother's main caregiver, she had put her own life on hold for years. My father would now be by himself in the Worli flat, surrounded by photos of my mother, and my grandfather, both gurus in his private pantheon. Amid the joy of the celebration, indecision haunted me: Should I come back to Bombay to be with my father and rejoin TIFR from which I was still on leave? It seemed to be my destiny to be never living fully anywhere, caught between East and West. I got a temporary office at TIFR to use during my Bombay visit. The maths faculty told me that I would have to decide soon whether I wanted to stay on at TIFR. I was allowed a few more months to make up my mind. In the end, I would resign from TIFR and we would go back to Salt Lake. My father seemed to be okay being on his own.

∞

There was a trip, meanwhile, that I was preparing for, without a clear sense of what it was about. This was to Strasbourg in the Alsace region in France, more specifically the mathematics department of the Université Louis Pasteur de Strasbourg. I would be there at the invitation of Jean-Pierre Wintenberger, who worked there. I was curious to know why he had invited me, as our work and mathematical interests did not overlap all that much. Wintenberger and I were both number theorists, but of different kinds. He was part of the French school of p-adic Hodge theory, while I was a product of the American–Japanese school that studied congruences between Ramanujan symmetries. While there were overlaps, the fields were quite different. The school I belonged to was mainly a consumer of the results generated by his school.

Serre likens mathematicians travelling around the world, visiting colleagues and giving lectures at mathematics departments across the globe, to the Brownian motion of particles suspended in a liquid or gas. Such visits can indeed sometimes seem random and purposeless. But on a rare such visit, a meeting in person may lead to a throwaway remark or a casual comment or to being asked a speculative question, that might lead to the discovery of an important new idea. I did not expect much to come from my Strasbourg visit, thinking that it would be like the generic mathematical visit of this sort: I couldn't have been more wrong.

Around a week before I left for Strasbourg I went to see a cricket match at the Brabourne Stadium in Bombay, carrying with me a recent preprint of his that Wintenberger had sent me. I felt this might have clues to why he was interested in talking to me. Wintenberger's paper was written in French and was titled '*Sur les représentations p-adiques géométriques de conducteur 1 et de dimension 2 de* $G_{\mathbb{Q}}$'. G.H. Hardy has written in his *A Mathematician's Apology* about spending days watching cricket at Fenner's, the cricket ground in Cambridge. He would sit in a circle of admirers, reading mathematical papers and grading exam papers as he watched the game. He divided mathematicians into classes: the Bradman class was the highest, Don Bradman being a legendary Australian batsman who was contemporaneous with Hardy.

As it happened I was watching the current Australian cricket team, which was touring India. The opening match of the tour that I had come for, against the local Bombay team, was not consequential, a practice game for the touring team. It being a working weekday, there were few spectators around. In a country where cricket was said to be almost like a religion, this game was like a small private celebration with very few devotees in attendance. I carried a cap, a water bottle and Wintenberger's paper in my rucksack. Like Hardy I aimed to do some mathematics while watching the cricket and pulled out the paper. Most of the time nothing happens in a cricket match, and the atmosphere in this game was particularly soporific and suitable for browsing and musing about the paper between seeing snatches of the game.

∞

Wintenberger's paper used a recent work of Richard Taylor in which he had proved an attenuated version of Serre's conjecture, called a 'potential version' of Serre's conjecture. In spite of the potential version being a very diluted version of Serre's conjecture, Taylor's work showed that it still had surprisingly strong consequences. This again relied on the technique of Wiles that was the main engine of his proof of FLT. Hida had once mentioned to me the possibility of proving a potential version of Serre's conjecture when he visited TIFR soon after my thesis. I did not pay as much attention to this as I should have. Research was full of near-misses. Especially in a crowded competitive field one was bound to bump into people and tread on the toes of other researchers as one went about one's business. One of the consequences of Taylor's result was that in many interesting cases p-adic Galois symmetries could be made part of compatible systems of Galois symmetries. This was to play a fundamental role in the proof of Serre's conjecture.

The seating arrangements in my part of the Brabourne Stadium were basic, with the spectators sitting on concrete slabs. The Australians batted first. Matthew Hayden, their big burly opener, seemed to be gaining the upper hand against the Bombay spinner Sairaj Bahutule, disrupting the bowler's line and length by his powerful and audacious, inelegant yet effective, sweeping. With his powerful frame, strong shoulders and long reach Matthew Hayden was almost bullying the bowler and bossing him around. Hayden swept his way to a quickfire 60.

Even as I watched the cricket my mind kept returning to Wintenberger's main observation in his paper. He used the bridges provided by compatible systems of Galois symmetries to travel from an arbitrarily large prime p to a very small prime number like 3. Using this he deduced that certain p-adic symmetries with small levels did not exist.[43] Wiles had referred to the role the magic of small primes played in his marvellous proof of FLT, and Wintenberger's proof was another instance of the magic of small primes.

All told, Wintenberger's paper did not seem, initially, very exciting to me. The idea of propagating a single p-adic Galois symmetry to a compatible system was already there in other papers and Wintenberger's result seemed to be a simple corollary. Besides the main result, there was a scattering of remarks about alternative ways of proving it. There were throwaway comments that suggested the author felt more could be done along these lines, but this was tentatively suggested. It was as if a person was not able to articulate something on their mind.

∞

Weeks later, I would have a thrilling conversation with Wintenberger about this very paper. I would realize then that what had really bothered me about this paper was the feeling that what was left unsaid might be far more consequential than what was said. Reading Wintenberger's paper at the Brabourne Stadium was like being at a magic show in which the magician performed a few tricks that did not seem that exciting. Sitting in the audience, a little bored and restive, one somehow got the sense that the magician was holding something interesting up their sleeve which they had not yet mastered enough to perform in public, or perhaps had not even figured out fully as yet.

The match straggled on. The shape of the roof of the stadium was elliptical. The waxing shadow it cast on the ground – as the sun made its way across the sky, morning to midday to late afternoon – held the light of the rest of the field that was still in the sun, like a vessel holding water. Periodically, the ball made a sweet thudding sound when it hit the middle of the bat. This made me look up from my browsing of the French paper and peer into the middle distance at the pitch in the middle of the ground.

∞

I came back to the stadium the next day with a friend from TIFR. This time I was more engaged in the proceedings: we chatted, talking shop about maths, but also commented upon the cricket. The Australians had declared the innings and were now fielding. Their big fast bowlers charged to the wicket and delivered their accurate thunderbolts. Glenn McGrath looked as mean as the miserliness of his bowling analysis suggested: it was hard to score off him because of his accuracy which never made for ease at the crease till he was bowling. To survive at the crease and score runs against McGrath, one had to learn to become comfortable with the discomfort his bowling caused. If one did this, one might eventually profit from small errors in length McGrath committed, lapses in his metronomic accuracy growing out of his frustration at being thwarted over a period of time and denied a wicket.

This seemed analogous to doing mathematics where one might benefit from getting used to, and possibly even comfortable with, being uncomfortable, by working in contexts in which one did not feel totally at ease and secure about one's background and knowledge, but despite this being able to contribute new ideas by hanging in and slowly developing the right intuitions. If one stuck only to what one was comfortable with, it was perhaps a sign that one was not trying a hard enough problem. A good problem made demands on you and made you grow, taking you over the limits you had set in your own mind to what you could hope to learn, or use, or accomplish.

11

Breaking Through in Strasbourg

The first thing I noticed from the shuttle bus was the lone spire of the Strasbourg's cathedral, rising from the flat plains. I remembered the old, magnificent reddish-brown stone building from my previous visit in 1997. Henri Carayol was my host during those few days in 1997, when I visited to give a talk in the department. He was a gracious host, receiving Rajani and me at the station. After my talk, we went to an Italian restaurant on the other side of the Ill river, which runs through the town. We drank a glass of Gewürztraminer, one of the speciality wines of the Alsace region, and liked its sweet floral bouquet. This left us with a lasting predilection for the wine, which goes well with the strong flavours of Indian food.

This time, it was Jean-Pierre Wintenberger who met me at the bus stop, and drove me to the place he had helped me to rent, about a half-hour walk away from the mathematics department. The flat was a bit odd, with rooms all in one line, like bogeys of a train. The visit had come about because mathematics departments in France were able to invite researchers every year as *professeur invité* (invited professor) typically for month-long visits. The invitees were persons of interest to someone on the faculty and there would probably be one or two names every year that were selected after a faculty vote. Wintenberger had nominated me for the position. I did not have high hopes of the visit and expected to give a lecture or two, go for a few hours every day to the department and be on my own for much of the time. I did not know Wintenberger very well. I had met him when he had visited TIFR a few years ago but we had not talked much then. I recall that when I saw him from a distance in the corridor of the third floor of TIFR, he had looked to me like a blind mendicant; this impression may have been because he had narrow eyes with a faraway, lost look at times. He was quite lean and I learnt when I got to know him well later that he was sporty and enjoyed physical activity like swimming and skiing.

Over the next few days, Wintenberger helped me settle in. He took me to the department library and introduced me to the librarian. I would be allowed to borrow books from the library, which was a pleasant set of rooms with large windows that looked out into a green indoor space. One of the more cumbersome formalities I had to complete was opening a bank account. Opening the account necessitated many trips down a small path lined with tall poplar trees, their leaves trembling in the slight breeze. These were the same trees Rajani and I had liked in Paris, with their leaves shimmering high up, reflecting the light almost like little mirrors. These walks around the campus and along the tree-lined path to the bank helped break the ice with Wintenberger. He had just returned from a trip to Oberwolfach, a centre for mathematics in Germany. (Alsace bordered Germany and the region had changed hands between Germany and France many times.) His car had broken down on the way back and was in the garage. He talked about his teaching assignments which he seemed to take rather seriously.

∞

Unexpectedly, one day in the first week of my visit, on our way back to the department from the bank, Wintenberger asked me a question that he said he had thought about without any success: Did I know how to get lifts of mod p Galois symmetries of level N and weight k to p-adic Galois symmetries of the *same* level and weight? These were predicted by the precise form of Serre's conjectures that he had made in his paper in 1987, refining his more qualitative conjectures from the 1970s. The key lay in the level and weight of the lift being the same as of its mod p shadow. We will call such lifts *minimal lifts*. The existence of minimal lifts for mod p Galois symmetries would be the analogue of Ribet's celebrated work I had studied obsessively that proved the existence of minimal lifts in the world of Ramanujan symmetries.

In Ramakrishna's lifting theorem the p-adic lifts he produced of a mod p Galois symmetry of level N typically had a level much larger than N . His method did not seem capable of producing minimal lifts. In my work with Boeckle I had inter alia probably subconsciously realized that potential modularity allowed one to carry over to the setting of Serre's conjecture an argument for the existence of minimal lifts that had been used for the analogue of Serre's conjecture. This was an instance of the use of the number theoretic analogue of the Rosetta Stone, helping to crack a more challenging lifting problem by analogy with the more tractable 'function field' world. Thus, without having been fully conscious of it, I had probably known the answer to Wintenberger's question since the time I worked on the project with Boeckle on an analogue of Serre's conjecture. A throwaway remark in the paper written with Ramakrishna around the same time (as my work with Boeckle) points to this realization. This implicit knowledge was catalysed to a full-fledged awareness of it by Wintenberger's question.

It was as if someone asked me directions to an address that I did not know off the top of my head, but which by a strange happenstance I knew I had noted on a piece of paper somewhere. On searching on my person, I quickly found the note in my pocket and I could help the person who had asked with directions to their destination; a destination that, when it was first mentioned, I didn't even know existed in the fully conscious part of my mind.

Wintenberger was a bit taken aback by my confident assertion, and even slightly incredulous, that I knew how to produce minimal lifts. I sketched to him the basic idea, the details of which I had never worked out. I did not give him a watertight argument as I myself had not pondered the details, but I could convince him that this argument should work in principle, and it at least seemed very promising. Wintenberger told me, perhaps right then or a little later, that he had tried to prove the existence of minimal lifts for the last several months, but had gotten nowhere with it.

I think it was key that I discovered the idea for minimal lifts in passing, in a 'relaxed' frame of mind, when I was not looking for them and did not have an application in mind. When one looks for something too specifically and urgently, it becomes harder to find. Wintenberger had asked various experts in Paris (and perhaps elsewhere), and they had been very pessimistic that one could prove the existence of minimal lifts without first proving Serre's conjecture. To his interlocutors, this implication of Serre's conjecture seemed as hard to prove as the conjecture itself. As it turned out, such lifts became the key step in our proof of the conjecture. The argument came out of my history of working on the conjecture, and using my Rosetta Stone. One had to have the right point of view, otherwise one could sink in the quicksand pursuing plausible but misleading approaches. Our method for lifting is now called the

'Khare–Wintenberger (KW) method': it has become a versatile tool for getting the most general results towards producing lifts of mod p Galois symmetries with prescribed properties. (In the mathematical literature, the alphabetical order is followed when naming concepts or in authorship of papers which are an outcome of joint work. This is quite different from the practice in many other scientific disciplines.)

∞

We were standing near the maths department, underneath a tree, discussing Wintenberger's question. The sun was out. Wintenberger had not yet told me why he was interested in minimal lifts, whether it was for a further application or just for its own sake. Perhaps he hesitated for a few minutes before telling me his reasons for being interested in minimal lifts. I had surprised Wintenberger with my thunderbolt and now he surprised me with not one but two of his own. He explained to me that minimal lifts could be used to show, following the strategy of the paper that I had read and found unsurprising at the cricket match, to prove some initial cases of Serre's conjecture for mod p Galois symmetries of weight 2 and level 1 for all primes p! These were non-existence results that were predicted by the Serre's conjecture conjecture, as there are no Ramanujan symmetries of weight 2 and level 1.

The proof relied on minimal lifts, combined with the results of Wiles, and Tate's result proving Serre's conjecture for mod 2 Galois symmetries in level 1. When Serre had written to Tate in 1973 formulating the level 1 version of his conjecture, Tate immediately, almost by return post, sent Serre a beautiful proof of his conjecture for mod 2 Galois symmetries. Serre extended the argument to $p = 3$. These results showed that in fact there were no mod 2 and mod 3 Galois symmetries in level 1. Tate's argument used classical methods in a surprising way proving a result that one would not have expected to be proved in this manner. Tate also explained why his methods would not work for mod p Galois symmetries of level 1 for primes p larger than 3, and thus as astonishing as his proof was, it could not yield a proof of the level 1 conjecture. Nevertheless these results of Tate and Serre turned out to be vital for our work; they provided the ignition to deduce from them more cases of Serre's conjecture for mod p Galois symmetries of small weights and levels for *all* primes p rather than just the primes $p = 2$ or 3.

Wintenberger's first thunderbolt explained why I had found his paper, scattered and ineffectual. The result he proved in the preprint did not surprise me, but combined with the existence of minimal lifts (that he was seeking, and that I knew implicitly how to get) one got spectacular consequences, namely proof of some new initial cases of Serre's conjecture.

It was indeed like a magician being distracted by figuring out a trick that, if it worked, would trump all the tricks performed during the show. And I had been blind, not able to read his mind, and connect the existence of minimal lifts to getting consequences for Serre's conjecture using the argument in his preprint, which after the event seemed like a connection that was almost obvious and one I should have made. He needed to spell out what was implicit in his paper for me to see it: this was an instance of the alchemy of meeting in person leading to a breakthrough which may have eluded us otherwise.

Thus we had the first decisive results towards Serre's conjecture (at least with proofs sketched in conversation which would have to be filled in later) that afternoon. These results seemed astonishing to me as just before that conversation I would not have even dreamed of proving them. They made serious inroads into the conjecture in a way that earlier work had failed to make. Wintenberger then further explained that if one assumed extensions of known lifting results of the type pioneered by Wiles, this would even yield all of Serre's conjecture in the level 1 case (i.e. $N = 1$ and all weights k).

∞

The second thunderbolt he struck me with was a beautiful idea of 'killing ramification' that, assuming extensions of Wiles's lifting results that were not yet known then, would reduce the general case of Serre's conjecture as formulated in his Duke paper in 1987 to the level 1 case he formulated in his letter to Tate in 1973.

'Killing ramification' is a technique that reduces proving Serre's conjecture for Galois symmetries of level N at least 2 to proving the conjecture for mod p Galois symmetries of smaller level than N.[44]

The key insight of our work was like a clue written on a piece of paper that had been torn into two halves. One half was with Wintenberger in France and the other with me in India. I didn't even know I had that torn half-note in my possession till it surfaced upon Wintenberger asking me his question.

That afternoon, standing on the lawn on the campus, we pieced together the note that had been torn into two by joining the halves, one in each of our possession, along their jagged edges! In school when learning Euclidean geometry, the task is to figure out the degree of an angle, or length of a side, given the data of degrees of other angles and side-lengths. Often the key is to make an auxiliary construction, such as drawing an auxiliary line through a given point, which cracks open a problem. My conversation with Wintenberger that day in October, as we stood on the campus of the Université Louis Pasteur de Strasbourg, was like drawing a line in a diagram which reveals the picture hidden in it. Till the line was drawn, the diagram had seemed indecipherable. We now had some initial cases of Serre's conjecture and even a path to prove all of it.

That evening I went back to my rented flat and just lay on the bed for several hours trying to think through the ideas that we had discussed and told each other about. I tried to stress test the ideas to see if they were right, and they seemed to be solid. There were details to be worked out to prove the existence of minimal lifts, but I was convinced the argument was good. The applications to the weight $k = 2$ and level $N = 1$ case of Serre's conjecture, which followed from minimal lifts and Wintenberger's original paper, seemed as astonishing and correct to me as when we had spoken earlier that afternoon. I could not get over my amazement, verging on incredulity, at these arguments which seemed so simple, but still convincing and striking at the heart of the conjecture. I got confused thinking about Wintenberger's idea of 'killing ramification', as it seemed to give something for nothing: but it checked out as well. His idea relied heavily on the existence of minimal lifts. The existence of minimal lifts and compatible systems played the role of pulleys and levers for us to transfer the Ramanujan property between mod p Galois symmetries which for each prime p lived in different worlds.

∞

We had a new strategy to prove Serre's conjecture that overcame the main obstacle to using Wiles's method effectively for this purpose. Wiles's method deduced the Ramanujan property for a p-adic Galois symmetry from knowing the property for a small fragment of it, namely its 'mod p reduction'. As Serre's conjecture was about the Ramanujan property of mod p Galois symmetries, attempting to apply Wiles's method to prove the conjecture directly led to a catch-22 situation: one would have to assume the conjecture to prove it. Our strategy turned the picture around and showed that if one could generalize Wiles's method sufficiently one had a path to prove all of Serre's conjecture.

What made our approach overcome the catch-22 was that it used a novel way to measure the difficulty of proving the conjecture for a given mod p Galois symmetry. Our measure was based on the weight k and level N of the Galois symmetry while earlier methods had measured the difficulty in terms of the 'shape' of the Galois symmetry. It was like changing a hold in a wrestling match that floors an opponent who until then had seemed invincible. Now the challenge was to make Wiles's method more versatile which was still a technically daunting problem, but it at least did not seem impossible.

My argument for the existence of minimal lifts was a synthesis of results and themes in the literature. It had a feature common in my work of seeming simple after it had been discovered. It would not have occurred to me without a long-term engagement with the mathematics involved. Perhaps the same was true of Wintenberger's idea of 'killing ramification', a skilful surgical intervention that excised a diseased tissue or organ, or in this case got rid of primes in the level of the Galois symmetry. The French term *longue durée*, used in historical studies that emphasized long-term historical structures over short-term studies of cause and effect, seemed relevant and key to understanding the development of mathematical ideas. To trace the arc of an idea needed longitudinal studies. For example, Wiles's marvellous revelation, which led to his paper with Taylor that overcame brilliantly the last obstacle in his path to FLT, was related to arguments that he had developed many years before in his papers on the proof of a result on quite a different topic. My former adviser Haruzo Hida's work had also influenced Wiles over a period of years. Most good ideas in mathematics emerged from years of thinking and fiddling around with certain themes and *idées fixes*.

The entire scheme of our attack on Serre's conjecture needed results of the type pioneered by Wiles. The arguments in some cases invoked known versions of these results in which case we got unconditional results like the proof of Serre's conjecture for weight 2 and level 1. In general they reduced Serre's conjecture to as yet unknown extensions of Wiles's method that one could hope were provable eventually by experts in the method.

∞

The next morning I tried to find Wintenberger in his office. He was busy with a student. I was a visitor with no formal duties here, while he had things to take care of like teaching, faculty meetings and hiring committee meetings. Often when I sought him out he could not talk, but came later to see me in my office. We discussed some more, and decided that we should start writing our arguments down. The reduction of Serre's conjecture to proving very difficult and unknown lifting theorems in the spirit of Wiles's method was amazing, but it was still a conditional result. In our write-up we planned to prove the existence of minimal lifts, and deduce unconditional results for Serre's conjecture, and then present the strategy that used minimal lifts to reduce Serre's conjecture to what seemed like technical but very hard extensions of Wiles's technique. They didn't seem like problems that could be resolved any time soon, but still the argument showed that what had seemed completely out of reach was within striking range.

I often walked through the Place de la Cathédrale, thinking about how to get more unconditional cases of Serre's conjecture using our strategy. The area was crowded during the day, with tourists ambling around. The gaunt and imposing cathedral made for a forbidding counterpoint to the shops and restaurants around it, as well as to the tourists who flocked from all over Europe to tour Alsace, the cathedral being a key attraction. The shops sold postcards, and keychains and other tourist keepsakes. The restaurants around the cathedral were mainly traditional winstubs in which one could have specialities of Alsacienne cuisine. The cuisine was heavy on pork and so I avoided eating there.

Sometimes on these walks, I stepped inside the cathedral for a few minutes. The quiet, solemn atmosphere seemed like a rebuke to the commercial activities centred on tourists just outside its massive doors. In the Middle Ages, instead of the modern-day tourists getting out of buses who took in the Cathédrale as one of the points of interest on a holiday in this region, there would have been pilgrims – tourists of another kind, more religious – coming to visit the famous cathedral, to attend a mass or a funeral service, or a baptism, get communion, to offer prayers and receive benediction.

The Strasbourg cathedral was, for many years in the thirteenth and fourteenth centuries, the tallest structure in the world. The hushed air in its vast interior was like that of a library. The footsteps of the tourists, who otherwise were trying to be quiet and respectful of the religious space, echoed in the vaulted space. I liked visiting churches. Without being religious per se, I was drawn to the atmospherics of religion. I remember lighting a candle in the cathedral during our Strasbourg visit in the late spring of 1997, putting some coins into the box meant for collections for the cathedral, hoping that it would bring us good luck. I thought I should do the same this time, but never got round to it. I had experienced a singular stroke of good fortune already and perhaps deemed it unnecessary, or felt greedy, to try and get luckier.

One evening I went to a concert at the Opéra National du Rhin. It was a performance of Handel's oratorio, Theodora. Handel's eighteenth-century opera was about a Christian martyr Theodora and her Roman lover. The entire story in this modern, almost crazed, staging of it had been transposed to twentieth-century America. Handel's music was sung by nurses dressed in white uniforms and workmen or firemen dressed in orange mackintoshes. The crucifixion scene took place in a prison in Texas, with Theodora and her lover lying on a gurney, waiting to be taken to be electrocuted. There were beautiful arias and powerful recitatives throughout the performance. The staging was by the controversial American theatre director Peter Sellars. I found the music and the staging quite bracing and emotional. Handel's music survived being wrenched – retaining its power to move and beauty to delight – into the sphere of twentieth-century American politics and controversies around the death penalty.

∞

I felt too distracted to start writing down what we knew how to prove. I wanted to see if we could prove more cases of Serre's conjecture. Just to have a strategy to prove all of it was nice, but did not seem satisfying. I did not think at all about how one could start proving the Wiles-type results needed for our strategy. This seemed beyond my ken and was in any case not something we could try and do in the little time of around three weeks Wintenberger and I had left together in Strasbourg. It seemed more profitable to see if one could find tricks to use our basic strategy combined with other more ad hoc means to get more cases of Serre's conjecture.

The limited applicability of our strategy to get unconditional results forced us to find artful ways to implement it.

A novel aspect of our results, compared to earlier results on Serre's conjecture for mod p Galois symmetries, was that they did not impose any limitation on the prime p. We proved uniform results for mod p Galois symmetries of low levels and low weights that were valid for all primes p. This accorded with Serre's conjecture, which predicted that for all primes p, mod p Galois symmetries of specified level and weight arose from a collection of Ramanujan symmetries that was independent of p. I had used a version of this feature of Serre's conjecture a few years ago in my result that Serre's conjecture implied Artin's conjecture.

The case of the conjecture for mod p Galois symmetries of weight $k = 2$ and level $N = 1$ had been singled out for special attention in a small subsection of Serre's 1987 Duke paper; it was the mod p analogue of what Wintenberger had done in his preprint, and was far more striking. Sitting at my desk in the large shared office, one floor up from Wintenberger's office, in a liminal attic-like space, I tried to see if one could get more cases of Serre's conjecture. Serre's conjecture predicted that, for all primes p, there are *no* mod p Galois symmetries of weight 2 and levels at most 10 for all primes p since there are no Ramanujan symmetries of those small weights and levels. While we could not see how to get results in weights k bigger than 2 so far, our methods yielded directly some more cases of Serre's conjecture, for mod p Galois symmetries in weight $k = 2$ and levels $N = 1, 2, 3, 5, 7, 13$ for all primes p, deducing this from the known results for small primes p. Wintenberger was not very excited by these results for slightly larger levels N than 1 as they followed easily from the method that we had used to get the case of weight 2 and level 1.

Ramanujan symmetries are 'continuous' (like waves in the sea), while Galois symmetries are 'discrete' (like a skiff bobbing on the waves). Converting a Galois symmetry to a Ramanujan symmetry is a powerful act of prestidigitation that has astonishing consequences like implying FLT. In fact, en passant, as a consequence of our ideas, we got a new proof of FLT as well. More precisely our non-existence results for mod p Galois symmetries of weight 2 and level 2 implied the theorem. This new proof used crucially Wiles's lifting method. But it was in a way more direct. It bypassed several difficult ingredients in Wiles's proof. This application captures the key features of our work of creating minimal lifts and making them part of compatible systems. It also illustrates the greater generality of our results. Wiles's work could rule out mod p Galois symmetries of weight 2 and level 2 that came from elliptic curves, which sufficed for the Fermat application, while our work ruled out far more possible sources (unrelated to elliptic curves at the outset).

We now had a sniff of the solution of Serre's conjecture, and like a hound following its nose, we could not help pursuing the scent over the next few weeks, months, and years. I sometimes excitedly went down one floor to knock on Wintenberger's office. If he was not busy we would discuss our work. I told him about a new case we could get. René Schoof was a Dutch mathematician working in Rome. A result of Schoof gave cases of Serre's conjecture for small primes p in weight 2 and level 11. Combining this with our method we could prove that mod p Galois symmetries of weight 2 and level 11 for all primes p were Ramanujan. There is a (unique) Ramanujan symmetry of weight 2 and level 11. Thus in this case we were proving Serre's conjecture in a case when there was a symmetry of that weight and level.

We were simultaneously trying to fill in all the details needed to write down the existence of minimal lifts and its implications that we already knew how to get. Perhaps I was more intent on pressing on and seeing what more we could prove, while Wintenberger was engaged in tightening up our proofs. We had not started writing anything formally, but knew that we would have to do this soon. Our arguments seemed so transparent once we had found them that we wondered how they had not been discovered earlier.

∞

Wintenberger invited me to his place for dinner one evening. He lived by himself. Wintenberger had a quietness about him, and I think he preferred to be low-key in his affect. But there was still an intensity to him. He was in a sense an insider to the French school of arithmetic geometry, Jean-Marc Fontaine's first student. Fontaine was then at the beginning of his remarkable work on *p*-adic Hodge theory. Fontaine and Wintenberger proved a theorem that became foundational to the field of *p*-adic Hodge theory. Wintenberger had proved further deep and subtle theorems in the field after that. His publications were few in number, but important.

Wintenberger and I had arrived at working on Serre's conjecture by completely disjointed paths. Wintenberger got to it because of his work on another conjecture in number theory. I came to it more directly; I had been interested in Serre's conjecture since my PhD thesis in 1995. I studied congruences between Ramanujan symmetries in my thesis, and then got interested in questions of lifting Galois symmetries. Thus we came from different mathematical backgrounds to Serre's conjecture and I think our collaboration benefited from this diversity of interest and training we brought to it.

In different ways, both Wintenberger and I were outsiders. While belonging to the mainstream of French mathematics, with his understated personality, Wintenberger seemed an outsider by temperament. Perhaps this had led him to the surprising turn in his work towards Serre's conjecture. I was an outsider to the mathematical establishment, especially in the United States. I did not mind this. From the outside one got a fresher, uncluttered perspective on things, like viewing the tall buildings in Manhattan from a point in New Jersey across the Hudson river. It liberated me from following closely the mainstream of the subject, allowing my work to be like a small stream that ran in its course parallel to the mainstream at times, sometimes coming closer, even crossing it, and then skipping or meandering away.

I missed Rajani and Arushi that evening, particularly because at dinner we talked about Wintenberger's children from a previous marriage. I called Rajani after getting back to my flat and told her that the Strasbourg visit was proving surprisingly productive. Rajani was familiar with some of the mathematical terms that would pop up in my gossipy conversations with my mathematician friends. She had known of my interest in Serre's conjecture right from when we first met and got married. I told her, in my latest conversation from Strasbourg, that we had made some remarkable progress towards it. Of course it was complicated to tell her what we had done, or its importance, but I am sure she heard the excitement in my voice.

∞

I wandered around the university campus, continually thinking about ways to winkle out more cases of Serre's conjecture using our strategy. It was frustrating that so far we had only a very limited number of cases in our bag. These followed without much effort from our overall scheme of proof. I was searching for another idea to go further and get more cases. I walked in the tree-lined passage which went from the department to the branch of the bank where I had an account. My feet scuffled through the leaves on the ground. We were deeper into autumn now. I went to the library in the department to sit and think or look at references.

In the late afternoons when the lights came on, it looked serene. Libraries were like Noah's Ark containing within them important parts of the collective wisdom of human effort and thought. Like the Reading Room in TIFR, which with its lights on when seen from the path along the Arabian Sea beckoned one to it, I was drawn to the library at Strasbourg in the late afternoons. It was getting darker earlier than when I had arrived just a few weeks ago. I sat thinking at one of the desks, with a book open before me, staring out through the windows. The library was quiet, there were mainly graduate students studying at the other desks. During periods of concentration on something specific, the mind becomes ductile and gets drawn into a thin filament, which seems infinitely long as one cannot see its ends, with no breadth and only length, probing its way to the core of a problem, threading the eye of its needle.

∞

I was tantalized by our result for mod *p* Galois symmetries in weight 2 and level 11.[45] Our work was a dynamic process analogous to creating new particles of different charges and spins by smashing particles together in accelerators. One evening, walking back home from the mathematics department, I realized that the 'KW' method allowed one to 'spin-off' an 11-adic Galois symmetry of weight 12 and level 1, lifting a mod 11 symmetry of weight 12 and level 1, into another 11-adic lift of weight 2 and level 11. This mimicked in the world purely of Galois symmetries the congruence discovered in the 1970s by Serre and Swinnerton-Dyer between Ramanujan symmetries. In a flash it came to me that if we created these two types of lifts of a mod 11 Galois symmetry of level $N = 1$ and weight $k = 12$ ('colliding' as it were at this mod 11 Galois symmetry), we could leverage our earlier result proving Serre's conjecture conjecture for mod p Galois symmetries of weight $k = 2$ and level $N = 11$ to get that any mod 11 Galois symmetry of weight $k = 12$ and level $N = 1$ had to come from the Ramanujan Δ-function. And then by our method we could instantly parley this to show that for *any* prime p, a mod p Galois symmetry of weight $k = 12$ and level $N = 1$ had to come from the Ramanujan Δ-function.

When I told Wintenberger about the result, he actually looked excited. We had discussed getting unconditional results in higher weight but had not been able to come up with an argument. Ramanujan's 1916 paper in which he had made conjectures about the Δ-function had led to Serre's work on Galois symmetries associated to Δ, described in his paper in the Séminaire Delange-Pisot-Poitou in 1967, and thereon to the formulation of his conjecture. Thus it was particularly satisfying to prove the case of Serre's conjecture that related to the Δ-function. Using the same method we quickly proved that Serre's conjecture in level $N = 1$ is true in weights 2, 4, 6, 8, 12, 14. Only even weights k are relevant in level $N = 1$ because the symmetries considered in Serre's conjecture rule out odd weights immediately. We could not handle the weight 10 case. Within a fixed level, say $N = 1$, the difficulty of proving the conjecture increased with the weight k. To prove Serre's conjecture in higher and higher weights was an uphill battle as we had to fight against the greater difficulties that our strategy ran into: as the weight increased, the difficulty of the generalizations Wiles's method we needed also increased.

From our results we could deduce Serre's conjecture in level 1 for the primes 5 and 7. This went beyond the Tate-Serre proof of Serre's conjecture $N = 1$ for the primes 2 and 3. We showed that, in fact, there were no mod p Galois symmetries in level 1 and with p at most 7.[46] These results went beyond the scope of Tate's beautiful method: this was exciting progress!

∞

Wintenberger thoughtfully suggested that we go one evening to an Indian restaurant called Le Punjab which was close to the Place de la Cathédrale. He knew I was vegetarian and that it would be easier for me to find something to eat there. He came with a friend of his, Pascale, who worked as an accountant in an office nearby. She was not shy of saying the stereotypical thing that was often said to me as an Indian: she loved Indian food! But she said it with such openness and good cheer that coming from her it was not annoying at all. She was vivacious and talked much more than Wintenberger, perhaps five times as much. Her English was much better as well. She had lived in England for a while and also had some English ancestry. The evening was a lot of fun, and we all contributed to finishing a bottle of a nice Riesling from the region, which elevated our spirits further. I conjectured that Pascale was Wintenberger's girlfriend, and this was later confirmed by Wintenberger. They had just recently met.

I had started writing down our ideas even as I tried to push our methods as far as they could go. I would come to the department and go to my desk in the shared office. I wanted to tell people about our breakthrough, but felt that we needed to first pin down all details by writing them out and also try to get further cases that would use our strategy. I wrote to some friends about the recent progress, but I did not spell out any details, so perhaps they did not get a sense of the magnitude of what we had done. It was as if we were under a vow of silence till we had written our arguments down and made sure we had picked up all the unconditional cases of Serre's conjecture that our general strategy led to. The general case still seemed inaccessible. We were working towards releasing our work presenting our strategy and proving special cases of the conjecture. We believed this would excite the community and stimulate experts to try and prove the Wiles-type results needed to push our strategy further.

Wintenberger invited me to attend a violin concert that Pascale and he were going to on a weekend. The concert hall was further away past the cathedral than I had ever been. As an encore the violinist played Bach's Chaconne from his Partita Number Two for the solo violin. I had a recording of it by Arthur Grumiaux of it that I had heard a few times. Hearing it played live had a tremendous emotional impact on me. It was fierce and obsessive music. 'Chaconne' means dance music, but the tone of Bach's piece was somber and lyrical. In some parts it sounded anguished. As we walked out of the concert hall, Wintenberger remarked that this eighteenth-century piece of music sounded as if it had just been composed, that it felt modern and contemporary, abstract and uncompromising in its rigour. Pascale and Wintenberger took the tram back. I wanted to walk back and absorb the emotions the music had aroused. It was a foggy, cold, late October night with fall verging on winter. The spire of the Cathédrale was partly obscured by the fog, vanishing from view when I entered the warren of streets in the old parts of the city around it.

I remembered a verse from the Gita that André Weil had liked and quoted in his autobiography which had stayed in my mind:

patraṁ puṣhpaṁ phalaṁ toyaṁ yo me bhaktyā prayachchhati
tadahaṁ bhaktyupahṛitam aśhnāmi prayatātmanaḥ

The words are uttered by Krishna who says that if he is offered, with true love, a leaf, a flower, a fruit, some water, he will accept it. Everything, the verse seemed to be saying, was grist to the mill of the workings of the universe, a bit like mathematics, I thought, which accepts good ideas regardless of their provenance. My mood that evening, which conflated the intensity of Bach's Chaconne with the experience of thinking about Serre's conjecture over the last few days, was one of surrender. I wanted to offer up all that we had done to a beneficent force, one that had surely been behind us in the last few weeks.

∞

I shared the large office on the top floor of the department with a floating population of visitors who came and left. One of my companions in the office was a visiting mathematician from Senegal. He stayed in Strasbourg all through my time there and was there on a longer visit than mine. His name was Baba Dikhtar and over the course of the month I spent sharing the office with him we became friends. I liked his easygoing manner. His English, even if not as good as his French, was still quite good and I could chit-chat with him more easily than with Wintenberger.

Perhaps the fact that both India and Senegal had been colonies, of the English and French respectively, made us feel an unspoken bond with each other. Inequalities between the rich and poorer countries persist into the present day, often reflecting a history of colonization or alternate contemporary versions of it. Even in a subject like pure mathematics there was an aspect of this. Many a time, ideas discovered by someone working away from the main centres were systematized and generalized by experts who were more prominent and working in the developed world, with greater resources available to them and higher visibility. Their work was often quoted as the reference and the contribution of the person who had made the initial breakthrough was all but forgotten.

Baba was visiting through a cooperation programme between France and Senegal. He was not working closely with anyone at Strasbourg during his visit. In my earlier visits to France I too had been more or less adrift, making them more of a holiday than a working visit. This time it was different for me. I had intense contact with Wintenberger.

Sometimes Baba Dikhtar and I went out for lunch together for an espresso. There was a stylish place on campus with a lively atmosphere where students and faculty went for coffee, with a lively atmosphere. One day we crossed the river to the other side of town and strolled across the massive Place Kléber. I wanted to buy a dress for my daughter who would be ten months old by the time I went back to Bombay. Baba kindly agreed to come with me and help me select a dress. He had no insecurities about being available in this way. I would have found it hard to ask this of a colleague from the United States, for example. Rajani and I had liked the Jacadi label from our trips to France the previous times, and I bought a pretty frock for Arushi with polka dots and a pair of tights. Baba Dikhtar and I exchanged numbers, but I have not seen him since that time in Strasbourg. His kindness and ease of being has stayed with me, though.

∞

Our colleagues in the number theory group had no idea about the exciting developments that were happening in Strasbourg under their noses! The time was not ripe. I gave a talk at the university – the obligatory seminar by a visiting researcher – about some earlier work and not about our freshly done work on Serre's conjecture.

There had been impressive progress extending the scope of the methods introduced in the work of Wiles in 1994, but there were still many limitations that we had to fight against when implementing our new strategy to prove Serre's conjecture. There was one particularly sticky point: our method became slippery when the mod p shadow or reduction of the p-adic Galois symmetry was 'degenerate'. In this case, the only known results were due to Chris Skinner and Andrew Wiles. Skinner had been a graduate student of Wiles at Princeton. Their method was very intricate and poorly understood by the community, and it had a serious technical restriction that it imposed on the lifts. Their theorem was vital for us to deduce the cases that we had proved. To overcome the knottier difficulties that our method ran up against when deployed in the general case, one would have to get a more versatile version of the Skinner–Wiles theorem. This seemed like a very hard problem that could take years to be resolved. It seemed not in my wheelhouse and I instead tried to see if our strategy could be tweaked so that it became more efficient and more widely applicable.

One day, when trying to find variations of our strategy I stumbled across something that seemed very pretty even if not directly usable at this point. In our strategy for the level 1 case, via minimal lifts and compatible systems, we could in principle reduce the conjecture to proving extremely difficult 3-adic theorems which went well beyond what the Skinner–Wiles method gave. Instead I discovered one could implement our strategy for proving the conjecture in level $N = 1$ for mod p Galois symmetries more gradually, breaking one giant step into many smaller steps, by using an induction on the prime number p. The ignition result for the induction to get started was the Tate–Serre result proving Serre's conjecture in level 1 for the primes $p = 2$ and 3.[47]

Modifying our tactics, rather than our overall strategy, in this way still did not immediately yield any new case of the conjecture. But it did make the unknown Wiles-type results that would be needed look a little less intimidating. This modification took into account an old theorem about prime numbers called Bertrand's postulate which says that between any number and twice it there is always a prime number.[48] While at the moment the gain of the inductive strategy was mainly psychological, the idea of induction on primes p was to play a key role in our later work on Serre's conjecture.

There is almost no successful argument in mathematics which uses an induction on primes p. This is partly because prime numbers are sporadic, much too individualistic and unruly, with maverick and eccentric personalities, to be able to cooperate with each other and act in concert. It was the magic of minimal lifts and compatible systems that made prime numbers toe the line enough to make possible, in principle, an inductive argument on primes in our strategy to prove Serre's conjecture.

∞

I was looking forward to a rendezvous in Paris I had set up with Serre. Soon after I fixed this, however, I overheard Wintenberger telling a colleague at lunch that Serre's wife had just died. My lunch appointment would be within days of her passing. I wrote at once to Serre that I just heard of his bereavement and offered to cancel the lunch. Serre wrote back saying that he would like to keep our appointment. Wintenberger suggested that Pascale and he drive me to Nancy, en route to Paris, for a concert by Hilary Hahn, a brilliant young violinist. I could stay the night there and take the train the next day to Paris, while they would drive back to Strasbourg.

We travelled from Strasbourg to Nancy in Wintenberger's car. It was a weekend and we arrived early. We spent the day walking around and had lunch. At the concert, the violinist Hilary Hahn had an intense, yet pleasing, presence on stage and her playing was precise and virtuosic. She played a lot of Bach's music. The full length concert did not make the same impact on me as the fragment of the Chaconne which lasted just a few minutes. In Paris, I stayed a night with friends who were mathematicians. I did not tell them about the recent exciting work with Wintenberger. But the next morning, when I met another French mathematician, Gäetan Chenevier, with whom I had recently written a paper, I could not contain myself and spilled the beans to him about our results towards Serre's conjecture. The effect on him was what I had hoped for: he was astonished. I told him to keep my news to himself till we wrote up and circulated our preprint about the work we had done.

Serre was already waiting for me at a table covered with a white tablecloth. After I expressed my condolences to him, we started discussing some mathematics. I tried to tell him about our recent work and in particular that we could prove the case of his conjecture related to the Ramanujan Δ-function. This did not seem to have registered with him: he certainly did not do a double take. Serre knew I was going to give an afternoon seminar at the IHP and decided to attend. As we walked up the sloping streets to the IHP from the restaurant, the effects of the wine we had drunk began to tell on me and by the time I started my talk, I was quite buzzed. I do not remember what I spoke about, except that it was certainly not about my recent work with Wintenberger. Serre later told me that he understood little of what I said in the lecture, but as I wrote a lot on the blackboard he managed to get the gist. Perhaps my strong Indian accent, and that I spoke quite fast, had made my earlier revelation at lunch incomprehensible to him as well.

When I returned to Strasbourg, Wintenberger and I summarized for ourselves what we had done over the month. We could show that there were no mod p Galois symmetries of certain low weights and levels as predicted by Serre, and even more satisfyingly that the only mod p Galois symmetry level 1 and weight 12 was the one that arose from Ramanujan's Δ-function. We also had a strategy to prove all of Serre's conjecture assuming broad generalizations of the results pioneered by Wiles. We still had to complete writing up our theorems and proofs and announce our strategy to prove Serre's conjecture conditional on new Wiles-type results.

Finally, just before I left, we celebrated our wholly unexpected achievement with the number theorists at Strasbourg at an elegant restaurant called La Casserole near the Cathédrale. We sat at a long table in an inner, smaller room served by waiters dressed formally in suits, looking like lawyers. Expensive restaurants sometimes looked to me like the fancy chambers of a firm of lawyers. The cutlery on the table was striking and modern. The flat forks and spoons were laid diagonally which enhanced the feeling that the restaurant was at the cutting edge. The pastel colours of the wall and the lights enveloped the restaurant in a gentle glow. The food was delicately prepared. We left in good spirits having drunk several glasses of excellent wine each.

Wintenberger came to drop me at the Lufthansa bus stop near the train station in the Place Gutenberg. I told him that in a couple of weeks I would send him a version of the manuscript that we had both written parts of and after that he would have the lock on the manuscript. Wintenberger did not say much. In our interactions I was always the more voluble person. I got on to the bus and waved goodbye to him at the end of what had been the most exciting few weeks of my entire working life.

12

The Level 1 Case

I was like a man possessed after my return to Bombay. I worked on the draft of our paper, sending the file to Wintenberger and waiting for his comments, and then pressed ahead after taking them into account. The work glided forward frictionlessly like a skater moving smoothly across an ice rink. Our paper seemed to almost achieve the heady ideal of being purely about the ideas and very little technical work was needed to make them work. The grunge of the hard technical work might come later if we could make progress in our general strategy to get all of Serre's conjecture.

The Test series between Australia and India had progressed while I was away in Strasbourg. (Just before leaving for Strasbourg, I had been to a tour match at the Brabourne Stadium right at the beginning of the Australian tour.) The Australians had come determined to avenge their defeat in the previous Test series played in India in 2001. The team led by Steve Waugh had dubbed this tour their final frontier, as they had beaten all other teams at home and abroad. They had accomplished their goal in the three Tests played in October, and I had followed the score from Strasbourg on the internet. They led the series by 2-0 and the last inconsequential

Test was going to be played at the Wankhede Stadium in Bombay. This was a newer stadium just a few hundred yards away from the Brabourne Stadium. I went for some of the sessions with a friend from TIFR. Dipping in and out of the Test match gave a good rhythm to the work of writing up our results, providing hours-long relief in which I could be away from the intense work of writing out our proofs. The game was played on a treacherous wicket that assisted spin outrageously. It was a very low-scoring game. On the last day the crowds lustily supported the Indian team as their left arm spinner Murali Kartik spun Australia out for a very low score, making India win by the skin of their teeth. The Test ended well before the scheduled five days. The win felt rigged. The pitch had been too biased in favour of spin for the win to have the sweet aftertaste of a game won fair and square.

I was trying to keep away from thinking about ways to get more cases of Serre's conjecture till Wintenberger and I finished writing the paper with the results we had so far. Our plan was to make our paper available on the web, while simultaneously submitting it to what was generally regarded as the most prestigious mathematics journal: *Annals of Mathematics*. Making the paper available on the web would make it public, while submitting it to a journal would ensure that the proof would be vetted before it was published. Publication after a thorough checking in prestigious journals counted for a lot in the subject. The refereeing of maths papers was an important safeguard to ensure that wrong arguments did not become currency in the subject. The error in Wiles's initial proof of FLT had been discovered in the refereeing of his manuscript.

∞

The first missing case of our results in the level 1 case was the weight 10 case. My mind kept getting pulled into thinking about this case, but I had to be disciplined and to postpone thinking about it seriously until we finished our paper. I also did not have any good ideas about how to get that case unconditionally. The weights we had got so far – 2, 4, 6, 8, 12, 14 – had the property that they were all one more than a prime (except for the smallest weight 2!). The weight 10 was smaller than the weights 12 and 14 that we already had in the bag, but we could not get it using our approach to the other small weights.

In the first week of December we let the cat out of the bag. We made our paper public. The proof of the general case of the conjecture using our proposed strategy, which we laid out, was now fair game for anyone wanting to have a crack at it. It still seemed unlikely that there would be a quick resolution. The generalizations we needed of the results of Wiles seemed very hard to get. During the last few days in Strasbourg, Wintenberger and I had discussed the possibility of trying to make progress towards these needed results. But neither of us was an expert in the methods of Wiles. The hardest case to generalize seemed to be the case of the Skinner–Wiles result. I postponed thinking seriously about this. I felt unprepared to do this and didn't know how to even start. Perhaps I would spend the next weeks and months trying to absorb the techniques that had been developed so far. Wiles's method was a principle that had proved flexible and versatile and through concerted efforts of the community of mathematicians working in this area it had been extended to cover many new cases. This required a lot of technical skill, hard work, and new insights. So it felt inevitable that the results we needed would become available sooner or later, through the efforts of other experts. But it might take a couple of years, or maybe a decade, or even more. We were not confident that we could contribute much more to the solution of the conjecture.

∞

Meanwhile, Rajani and I were busy preparing, though with a heavy heart, for our move back to Salt Lake City. We were returning after more than six months. Salt Lake City was pretty in winter, but sometimes it felt like a moonscape to us, very far away from home and unnerving. We had family in Bombay, and felt an ease in Bombay that we did not have as immigrants in Utah. Spending Christmas in a Courtyard Marriott, while we looked for an apartment, felt like a quintessentially immigrant experience. It was slightly depressing to eat breakfast in the cafeteria with strangers in the festive season. There had not been much of a reaction to our paper going public. But then there came a response from Richard Taylor, while I was still at the Marriott, which meant a lot. Wintenberger and I had sent a few people our paper by email, including Taylor, in addition to putting it up on the web. Taylor wrote back to say that he was on holiday with his family, and wished that he had looked at the paper earlier. He complimented us on our results, and strategy, and said that our proof of the conjecture for Galois symmetries related to the Δ-function was beautiful.

The Wasatch mountains were covered in snow. Salt Lake City was cold, but everyone told us that it was still not as bitterly cold as other places could get. There were long spells of days that were bright and sunny. Such days were somewhat counterintuitively colder than when it snowed and the skies were low and heavy. When it snowed, with brooding skies and a gloom in the air, snow adrift in the air like blown cotton, the mood was quiet and intense. In the monsoons in

Bombay there was a similar intensity when it rained heavily. The snow fell more quietly than the Bombay rains. In Salt Lake City one could be surprised looking out of the window in the morning to see the earth turned white, blanketed with snow, and the air shaken with a charged brightness.

Within a couple of weeks of having arrived, Rajani and Arushi had to leave for India to attend a wedding in the family that had come up unexpectedly. I drove them under overcast skies to the airport. They would stay in India till March, when I planned to go back for a week for the celebration of 50 years of my father's accounting firm. I drove back from the airport on the I-80 freeway, deserted on an early Sunday morning. It was snowing lightly and I felt desolate. Rather than go back to an empty apartment, I drove to my office on President's Circle on the University of Utah campus. The building was eerily empty.

It was not clear what Wintenberger and I could do next. To walk on the path we had charted to the general case of the conjecture seemed daunting, and it was hard to get oneself to take even the initial steps. I sat for a couple of hours in my office, musing about what I could think about in the next several days and weeks. I was teaching a course, but that would not take up too much of my time, perhaps just a few hours a week. With my family away, that would leave plenty of time for myself. I felt more at ease thinking of the particular rather than the general, and this made me want to find tricks to get some more cases of Serre's conjecture using our strategy. But it seemed almost impossible to get any more cases than we already had without proving the Wiles-type generalizations our strategy needed. I was stuck.

I took a walk around the President's Circle and also went further up the campus to the Student Union building. I went off campus to the residential area near it. This was called Federal Heights and had big mansions and few pedestrians. I walked a few blocks up from the university trying to fiddle around with the missing weight 10 case. There seemed to be nothing much I could do about it, but it was something to focus on and distract myself from the melancholy that had seized me after I dropped Rajani and Arushi off at the airport. In the coming days it was like an itch I could not stop scratching.

The first week of classes started with a flurry of activity. I also had a couple of students working with me towards their thesis. One of them, Tommaso Centeleghe, was from Bologna in Italy, and we had started talking about mathematics after he attended my graduate course on number theory. He was talented, and had an enthusiasm about him that energized me. Hanging out with him became one of my chief ways of socializing that semester. He had a winning smile, was friendly and easygoing and had a certain ease when talking with faculty. He had studied at Bologna with a Bulgarian friend Jorro and they had both come to Utah in the same year for their PhD. There was an algebraic geometer on the faculty at the university in Bologna who had ties to the mathematics department at Utah. Jorro worked for his thesis in algebraic geometry, while my conversations with Tommaso converted him into a number theorist.

Within the first couple of weeks of classes starting, I got an email from Schoof. We had used a result of his for our proof of the case of Serre's conjecture (the weight 12, level 1 case) related to the Δ-function. He wrote to me asking if there was any further news about Serre's conjecture. He asked if we had been able to fill the missing weight 10 case. He also told me that he had extended his results classifying mod p Galois symmetries of weight 2 and level $N = 11$ for small primes p now to levels $N = 17$ and 19. From this we could immediately deduce Serre's conjecture for mod p Galois symmetries of level 1, and weights 18 and 20, for all primes p using our methods. It was something to have more cases of the conjecture than we had proved in our paper. But if we needed more and more results of the kind Schoof was proving, pinning down mod p Galois symmetries of small weights and levels for small primes p, we would be stuck as such results could be available for only a limited number of small weights and levels and primes given the methods Schoof was using. To prove the general level 1 case of the conjecture, we would have to wean ourselves off such results. Also the results of Schoof did not allow us to fill in the hole at weight 10, and now the new hole at weight 16: we had weights 2, 4, 6, 8, 12, 14, 18, 20.

I could not stop thinking about the weight 10 case. I thought about it on the bus rides to work, on walks around campus, and in Federal Heights and other neighbourhoods. I did my best thinking on the move. Like in my long walks along the river in Sapporo, to and from the mathematics department, it was the journey that mattered more than the destination. I had to be careful as I walked on slippery pavements in between banks of hardened dirty snow, which was in muddied contrast to freshly fallen snow that would carpet the ground like velvety soft fallen petals after a snowstorm.

The department was deserted on weekends although occasionally I saw a light under someone's door. On reaching the department, I would often come back after less than an hour spent in my office, checking email, surfing the web, staring out from the big windows in my ground floor office on to the President's Circle. All my efforts seemed to go nowhere. There was not much I could do to dislodge the weight 10 case. Sometimes I feigned giving up on it, hoping to shift it to the periphery of my attention and see something move at the edge of my field of vision that had escaped me when fully focused on it. Nothing seemed to work.

But within a week, something did. On a walk in the Sugarhouse area around my apartment I found a way to get the weight 10 case using Schoof's new result that he had emailed me about. This was progress, but again merely proved one more case of the conjecture, by a novel twist of the earlier strategy. This would not yield further cases. It was more exciting than getting the weights 18 and 20 cases from Schoof's result which were immediate corollaries to it given our methods. This weight 10 deduction used a new move. It seemed restricted in its scope, but it gave us an extra case in level 1: now we had the level 1 cases in weights 2, 4, 6, 8, 10, 12, 14, 18, 20. There was a glaring gap at weight 16 like a missing tooth in a set of pearly white teeth!

Thinking about the weight 10 case made me more adept at using the KW method: as I began to flex its power I saw that using it one could manipulate Galois symmetries with almost the same ease as Ramanujan symmetries and this could be used to get our strategy for Serre's conjecture to work in more cases. This was to lead in the next few days to the breakthrough in the level 1 proof.

One weekday morning, within a few days of the email exchange with Schoof, I noticed something about the weight 16 case on the bus to the university. Tweaking our basic method by using the KW lifting method to produce more congruences between Galois symmetries I could get this case as well. It used a new type of prime switching. I got off the bus early; I felt the need to walk and not be stuck on a bus. The argument was novel. It was again suggested by my experience with manipulating Ramanujan symmetries in my thesis, and mimicked in the Galois world relations between Ramanujan symmetries that one got by using Carayol's lemma. I had interpolated an extra prime switch to get the weight 16 case.

The argument for the weight 16 case seemed more exciting to me than the weight 10 case, and also offered more traction when

I thought of trying to push it further to get more cases of the level 1 case of the conjecture. The method resembled a sitar player creating a new melody by moving his left hand between the frets of the sitar – like moving between primes – while at the same time bending the strings with the other hand – like the congruences the argument used.

∞

Meanwhile, back in the real world, the washing machine in the apartment had broken down. Our landlord was dragging his feet in getting it fixed. After he fixed it once, it broke down again. I felt acutely the loneliness of life in Utah. After worldly Strasbourg with its plazas full of people, Salt Lake City with its big wide roads and sidewalks almost bereft of pedestrians felt lacking in charm. Salt Lake City was too much about snow and mountains and Mormonism and the rugged individualism of American life. The United States was in many senses the easiest country in the world to be an immigrant in and blend into the heterogeneity of the salad bowl mix of life here. Yet to me the vibe of life as an immigrant had the slight chill of a laboratory in which everything had been optimized so that one could work and use one's time and abilities to the fullest.

There was the compensatory excitement of these new tricks and the new cases I had gotten of Serre's conjecture in my lonely weeks in Salt Lake City. Mathematics needs long-term engagement and most of the times, it is hard to make progress in the problem one is stuck on within a few days, or even weeks or months sometimes. This means that in the everyday, practical things almost always take precedence as they come typically with short deadlines and demand immediate action. The solutions, however painful, do not need breakthroughs. Yet one had to find a way to keep thinking about mathematics through all the flux of practical matters, with their associated tedium and gratification, and make progress in long-term projects. In the end these could count much more than matters that had overridden their importance in the short term. The Wordsworthian spots of time that glowed in memory and bulked in the mind in their significance were mainly about these immersive, even if sometimes very restless, periods that could always have been deferred and given way to the everyday.

These few weeks in the winter of 2005 seemed exceptional: I had smelt blood and felt that a breakthrough could happen any moment! There was a faculty meeting later that day. These meetings took place in the big lecture amphitheatre where I had given my job talk in 2000 when I had interviewed here. I normally had very little to say at these meetings and sat in the last few rows. I had taken a yellow pad along and doodled on the paper as I tried to figure out if there were some more cases I could get with this latest trick. I wrote to Wintenberger about the recent developments when I got to my office. In those days there were no smartphones and I needed to be at my computer to compose email messages.

Wintenberger had been quiet in the last few days. I had made definite progress beyond what we had done in Strasbourg, but it was still not good enough to be able to have a crack at the level $N = 1$ case of Serre's conjecture in all weights k. I was focusing exclusively on the level 1 case, which was the form in which Serre had originally made his conjecture in 1973. If one could get the entire level 1 case, one would be hopeful that one could get all of Serre's conjecture because of Wintenberger's beautiful idea of 'killing ramification', which reduced in principle the general conjecture to the level 1 case. To get these cases of weight 10 and 16, I was still using Schoof's results classifying mod p Galois symmetries of small levels and weights for small primes p, and those results had more or less run dry.

To become truly effective and general, our methods needed to kick their addiction to using such results for small weights, levels and primes that were remarkable and almost accidental but, or maybe hence, also limited. It was a bit like a country living too much off its oil resources instead of using its lucky start to build an economy that slowly weaned itself off this dwindling resource and found more sustainable ways to prosper. We had to find a general argument that would use results like the ones Schoof had communicated to me as a starting point, and then take over and be self-sufficient, rather than needing every time the rush of a new such result as a 'base case' to advance a few more steps.

I was still excited by this progress and thought the idea that had worked in the weight 16 case, of constructing weight 2 lifts, and moving between mod p Galois symmetries in a compatible system for varying p, might help take us further. Our strategy had caught a new wind, and I was hopeful that it could go further with this extra wind in its sails.

The next few days there was no progress. But I was now obsessed with the problem in a way I had not been since the trip to Strasbourg. Around this time of the year the Sundance Film Festival spilled over into the Salt Lake City area. It was a festival founded by the actor Robert Redford, who had a home in Utah, and most of it took place up in the mountains in Park City. Some of the films were shown at theatres in Salt Lake City. Rajani and I had driven up to Park City in the past. But this time I was content to watch a couple of films at a theatre near the university.

One night soon thereafter I could not sleep and lay twisting and turning in my bed in the apartment on Elizabeth Street. I had just spent the entire evening in front of the TV. I could not have said what I had watched: my mind was churning, trying to find an idea that would use the different kinds of lifts the KW method created and prime switching, to implement the inductive strategy we had reported in our paper, so that it would not need any new Wiles-type results.

As evening became night, I kept trying to modify the argument that had worked in the weight 16 case so that it would become more general. I never drew my curtains in bedrooms I slept in if I could help it. I did not like to sleep in the pitch dark; it made me feel cut off from the world. On the desk opposite the bed there was a digital clock that told the time in red numerals. I wanted the absolution of sleep that would give me a break from constantly tinkering with lifts, compatible systems, and trying to string them together to see if I could get more cases of the conjecture. But I was not able to stop considering one more variation before giving up for the night. My eyes went to the red numerals on the clock as I turned from one side to the other. The red numbers and the flashing dots that separated hours from minutes glowed like the embers of a fire dying out in a fireplace.

When it was just past 1 a.m. I thought of an argument that looked promising: use weight 2 lifts at a prime p, switch to a prime factor q of $p-1$, and lift that mod q Galois symmetry to another compatible system (a move between Galois symmetries that mimicked what Carayol's lemma accomplished for Ramanujan symmetries), and come back to the prime p one had started with. I feared that after doing these elaborate moves one may not have gained anything. But thinking of the idea more, and analysing where one would be by the time one returned via this circular motion to p, I saw that perhaps I had won!

The idea of induction on primes when carried out in this circuitous way might work without needing the input of unknown, difficult Wiles-type results. Going back and forth in this manner, using weight 2 liftings, ensured that if one ran into a difficulty then it was a case covered by the work of Skinner-Wiles. This improved on the inductive step as conceived in the earlier work, and generalized the idea I had found to do the weight 16 case. To check that this new idea really worked, I needed to know the weight of the mod p symmetry when one arrived back via this procedure. A heuristic calculation suggested that one should have reduced the weight (so one can induct on primes p!) if one had been calculated enough when making these moves. The weight could be one of two possibilities and one had to exercise care so that both possibilities were less than the weight one had started with. I thought it very likely I could ensure this. But this relied on knowing a result that I would have to look up in references that I did not have access to until I went to the library the next morning. I could also ask an expert by email, or do both.

The next morning I went early to the library in the department. I waited impatiently in my office till the library opened. Unable to sit still in my office, I went and waited outside the library for the doors to open. I entered as soon as the librarian opened the doors a few agonizing minutes later than the official time. I found the paper I was looking for which confirmed my heuristic calculation of the night before about the weight of the Galois symmetry when one returned to the prime p. This was the most exciting moment in my career, topping even the thrilling few weeks in Strasbourg. I felt I had the entire level 1 case of the conjecture, the form in which

Serre first made the conjecture in 1973, in my bag. This would need to be confirmed by writing up all the details, but in my euphoria, I felt this was a formality.

A minor point in this argument was to avoid primes q for which $q - 1$ is a power of 2: these are called Fermat primes. These had showed up in the work of Gauss on straightedge (no markings) and compass constructions of regular N-gons. He found an exact criterion when a regular N-gon can be so constructed, the answer being that N has to be divisible only by powers of 2, and the very rare Fermat primes, that too only to their first power. Fermat primes are prime numbers of the form $F_n = 2^{2^n} + 1$. Fermat had casually asserted that the F_n's were prime for all non-negative integers n. The Fermat numbers F_n are prime for $n = 0, 1, 2, 3, 4$, where F_n is 3, 5, 17, 257 and 65537; F_5 is not prime, being divisible by 641. Fermat in this case was too rash, rushing to conclusions on the basis of the first five Fermat numbers being prime: there is no other known Fermat prime beyond F_4! Unlike FLT, the question of whether or not there are infinitely many Fermat primes, while being hard, feels like a minor question and has not led to interesting new mathematics. So not all questions or conjectures of great mathematicians are true or important. The reason I had to avoid Fermat primes in my argument for the level 1 case was that 2-adic Wiles-type results were harder to come by. For the proof of the general case Wintenberger and I would have to prove such new 2-adic results, as in that case they were unavoidable. But this work was still a few months away in the future.

The entire proof was a piece of reverse engineering. Serre's conjecture was about a relationship between mod p Galois symmetries and mod p Ramanujan symmetries. The world of mod p Ramanujan symmetries was highly structured and developed. The conjecture predicted that all mod p Galois symmetries were mod p Ramanujan symmetries. Mod p Ramanujan symmetries have p-adic Ramanujan lifts with prescribed properties that had been constructed in works of Ribet, Carayol, Diamond–Taylor and in my thesis. The proof of the level 1 case depended on using the KW lifting method to recreate features of Ramanujan symmetries on the side of Galois symmetries as predicted by Serre's conjecture. Once one created the theory of congruences on the Galois side, and combined it with the existence of compatible systems, mod p Galois symmetries became surprisingly malleable. This was a key input into the proof of the level 1 conjecture.

I had worked on Ramanujan symmetries since my thesis, and spent years thinking about lifting Galois symmetries. The work on Serre's conjecture was drawing on the experience I had built up throughout my mathematical life. Almost everything that I learnt or engaged with seriously in mathematics got used in the proof of Serre's conjecture. I muse sometimes that I would like to die as someone whose every scrap of knowledge and expertise has been used up in his lifetime. In Hindu funeral rites, there is a custom of making rice balls and leaving them out in the open for birds to peck at. If a crow comes and pecks at them quickly it is taken as a sign that the deceased has passed on with no desires unfulfilled. If there is a similar custom that symbolizes having used all that one has learnt in the course of a mathematical career, I would want a murder of crows to come and consume the rice balls right away!

∞

Now, the pressure was on to write these arguments up and see that they survived this process. I wanted to announce the proof of the level 1 case, but I first wanted to at least have a rough written version of it. I was still not completely sure of one or two points. The new argument used some finer but still classical results about distributions of primes, slightly refining Bertrand's postulate that we had already quoted for our strategy in the paper we had written a couple of months ago. I had to make sure that the numerical calculations worked out. I felt confident that it would all work out in spite of the slight anxiety about some technical points. The argument had a clear new idea that overcame the difficulties we had faced when implementing our strategy to do the level 1 case.

I wrote to Wintenberger about the new idea. I had not heard from him for the last several days and was puzzled that he was not responding to my excited and frequent messages. Perhaps I had not been coherent enough in my hastily drafted email messages for him to be able to understand the new ideas. I figured he might also be busy with some other matters, or perhaps might be thinking hard about how to start on proving the Wiles-type results that a direct use of our strategy required. I had spent the last few weeks trying to find tricks that would avoid needing these, and if I was not deluding myself and had not overlooked something, these avoidant tendencies had helped me make the breakthrough in the level 1 case.

Ever since we had released our preprint in early December of 2004, just a little over two months ago, there had been the possibility that someone would scoop us by coming up with arguments to make our strategy work unconditionally. We had also somewhat contradictorily not been optimistic about any progress in the short term as the technical results needed for our strategy to go further seemed formidably hard to prove. After the month in Strasbourg, we seemed to be deadlocked. But in just about two months the ground had shifted and we had made dramatic progress. The idea of using weight 2 lifts, and going back and forth between primes resolved the deadlock in a very unexpected way.

The method of the level 1 proof reminded me of spaghetti junctions at which one switches between freeways. At critical points of the level 1 proof one had to jump from one compatible system to the other. The new move I discovered past midnight resembled manoeuvres required for parallel parking, going into and out of a narrow space at different angles, with the turning of the wheels constantly calibrated during the back and forth, till the car slotted in almost perfectly with its bumpers almost touching the car in front and behind.

Writing a first draft of this paper turned out to be easier than other papers I had written. The new idea almost generated the whole paper. This was like the earlier paper, which was mainly about our new ideas and did not require any elaborate technical footwork. After a few weeks of work I had a version of the manuscript written. I sent it to Wintenberger and waited for his reply. In a few days he wrote back telling me that his father had fallen ill and passed away and he had been busy with that. We decided that I would write the level 1 paper on my own and that we would recombine forces to tackle Serre's conjecture for general levels N.

I circulated the paper by email to a few colleagues in March 2005. This time there were many enthusiastic responses. Many people sent their congratulations, among them Serre. We had not heard back from *Annals of Mathematics* about the first paper. I decided to submit the level 1 paper to *Duke Mathematical Journal*, as Taylor was an editor there and he suggested it. It seemed likely that Taylor would get the papers refereed efficiently. That Serre had also published his conjectures in the same journal was another argument in favour of submitting there.

Ribet explained in lectures he later gave on our work that the key to the proof in the level 1 case was that the Ramanujan property of Galois symmetries is 'contagious'. Once one had a starting point provided by the Tate–Serre result that proved the level 1 conjecture for small primes *p*, the other mod *p* symmetries in level 1 got rapidly infected with the Ramanujan property. The contagion spread from one prime to the next via the inductive argument, using minimal lifts that were made part of compatible systems, which linked them.

∞

I had obsessed over several years about lifts of Galois symmetries that were implied by Serre's conjecture. It was one of the main strands of my work. Although I could not make decisive progress for a long time, the small results I proved made me feel that if I tried a little more, and risked a little more of my capital of time on the conjecture, I might succeed in proving something significant related to it. The proof of the level 1 case proved the conjecture in the form Serre had originally formulated it in 1975. It felt like finally hitting the jackpot!

The implications of the conjecture acted like a guide to those who sought to prove it. Judging which implications might be key was a matter of taste and most crucially luck. It seemed like a lucky break that the implication about various types of lifts – minimal lifts and others – that I had obsessed over for years turned out to be key to our proof of cases of Serre's conjecture and in our strategy to prove all of it. It was crucial to the proof of the level 1 case. It could well have been that the proof needed other methods which I had never thought about.

The topography of the path to the level 1 case was reminiscent of the winding, intersecting paths surrounding the Cathédrale in

Strasbourg which led to different views of its lone Gothic spire. Serre's conjecture had oriented my mathematical work throughout my career, like the recurring motif of the spire of the Strasbourg cathedral might have guided pilgrims in their journey to it. There was still the general case of Serre's conjecture for all levels N to do but I postponed thinking about it till Wintenberger and I could discuss it again. Modifying our strategy taking into account the new ideas in the level 1 case promised to get us quite a way towards proving the general conjecture. How far we could go would have to be worked out in the coming months.

∞

Later, at the beginning of July 2005, I was back in Strasbourg for a conference organized by Wintenberger and his colleagues. He had invited me to speak at it before I had the proof of the level 1 case.

The hotel in Strasbourg was more like a gaol. The rooms were musty and small and hot. It was on a big square that was always noisy. Using the cramped lift with its sliding grille doors felt like being in a cage. My lecture was scheduled in the middle of the conference. A conference is experienced in two parts, one before one's talk and one after. In the before phase, one is restless, listening to other talks but thinking of one's own impending talk. Rehearsing the opening and jumping to its end. It was hard to go through it all in my mind. I felt that I should write it down to take it out of my mind. But I would keep worrying about the talk without writing notes for it, procrastinating till the night before. After my talk I either felt relieved and even happy if the talk had gone well, able to engage with others and listen attentively to talks that interested me, or crestfallen if it had not, carrying out a post-mortem on the talk and wishing to have another go at it.

I was returning to the scene of our breakthrough work on the conjecture within less than a year. I was nervous about my talk, and thought about it as I walked the familiar streets of the city around the cathedral. In the previous visit I had walked on foggy nights in these very streets, searching for ideas to do more cases of the level 1 conjecture. Now I walked past the cathedral, and strolled in the botanical garden near the university, thinking through the ideas of the proof of the entire level 1 case which had come much sooner than expected.

Serre had come for the conference, as had some of the other leading French number theorists. Some of them had probably especially come to hear about the latest developments towards the proof of Serre's conjecture. I started nervously but warmed up as I got to the proof of the level 1 case. After my talk, a listener commented that during my lecture I had seemed like a Tarzan jumping from vine to vine, prime to prime, and it was a lot of fun. Jean-Marc Fontaine came up to me after my lecture and asked if I would like to join a small group for lunch. Fontaine, Serre and I, along with a few others, went for lunch to an Indian restaurant on a quay near the river. My former adviser Haruzo Hida had also come for the conference. We went to a bar full of students in the evening after a day of lectures. He said that listening to the proof made him happy, it brought a smile to his face.

At the conference banquet, held at a seafood restaurant in the centre of Strasbourg, I got asked one question several times that evening. How far were we from the general case of the conjecture, for all levels *N*? Wintenberger and I said that we were optimistic that now we had the ideas needed to get almost all of Serre's conjecture using extensions of known Wiles-type theorems. These extensions seemed doable but we had yet to figure out the details. Our initial strategy had used as input hard and unknown extensions of Wiles' work, but now after the level 1 case had fallen we felt we could get away with extensions that seemed far more accessible. But this work still had to be done, so for the moment we were not claiming anything beyond the level 1 case. In mathematics both the beauty and the devil lay partly in the details.

Just before the conference in Strasbourg, I had spent a few weeks in Paris visiting the Université Paris 13 in Villetaneuse, the same university in the north of Paris I had visited almost a decade ago, in 1997. After I gave a lecture there, I went with a group of mathematicians for lunch. As we crossed a road, a French motorist whizzed past us. One of the mathematicians in the group was Mark Kisin, a leading number theorist who has made important contributions to Wiles-type lifting methods. He joked that they should ensure that I survived until at least I had proved all of Serre's conjecture. It was our duty now to finish its proof!

∞

Later that year, I gave a colloquium in the department at Utah on my proof of the level 1 case. I spent most of my time narrating the arc of the conjecture from Ramanujan's 1916 paper to Serre's first official formulation of his conjecture in 1975. At that time the conjecture was almost a fantasy as it seemed so out of reach of the methods available then. A few days later my tenure case was discussed and voted on in the department. My work on Serre's conjecture had made it a slam dunk. I still could not quite believe it though, that after working on Serre's conjecture since my TIFR days, here I was, at the cusp of proving all of it.

13

The Oddest Prime of Them All

The general rule is that one goes to the prime 2 only as a last resort. It is the odd one out amongst the primes, being the only prime which is even. The prime 2 is very tricky to work with: one has to contend with issues that are peculiar to the prime 2 as it does not behave like the generic prime.[49] But it was indeed the prime 2 that Wintenberger and I were having to contend with as we entered the final phase of our marathon.

Wintenberger had visited me in Utah soon after I had the idea which settled the level 1 case. We now had our sights set on the general case of the conjecture, and felt that the visit would help move things along. We went on a small hike in the mountains around Salt Lake. The snow had melted and the mountains were dry and brown. We began discussing what we could do to overcome the hurdles on the path to a proof of Serre's conjecture for all levels N.

Wintenberger's idea of 'killing ramification' that had stunned me in Strasbourg in principle reduced the general case to the level 1 case. The main difficulty we faced was that a direct application of it led us smack into needing Wiles-type results in the most difficult case. To get past this impasse, we would need very tricky generalizations of the delicate results of Skinner–Wiles that did not seem accessible at all.

On the walk, we hit upon the idea of using an auxiliary prime to avoid the pitfalls on our path from level $N = 1$ to the general level N case of Serre's conjecture; this was yet another application of the KW lifting method. Wintenberger dubbed this saviour auxiliary prime q our 'angel prime'. It would act like Virgil to our Dante, guiding us through the twists and turns of our strategy till it brought us to the safe haven of the level 1 case which we could navigate without its help.

The difficulty in implementing our basic strategy to proving Serre's conjecture was that it needed unknown Wiles-type results. 'Killing ramification' inducted on the level N, while the level 1 proof inducted on the weight k, a proxy for the prime p, and when used in tandem we could see a path to the proof of the general conjecture. Induction was the driving logic of the strategy. The essence of induction is a way to reduce the unknown to the known – deduce Serre's conjecture for mod p Galois symmetries from its truth for symmetries of either smaller weight, level or primes p – and Wiles-type results were what allowed one to carry out the induction. The introduction of an angelic prime was the final tweak in the process of softening up the ingredients needed for the strategy. The winding path we were devising was like a path that snaked up a mountain-side gaining steadily on its peak.

In the introduction to Wiles's paper on FLT, he writes that he had first tried to work with the prime 2. One of the important turns in his progress was that after a few months of grappling with 2, he realized that he could instead work with the next prime 3 because of known cases of Serre's conjecture for mod 3 symmetries. The prime 2 was key to our strategy as it allowed us to carry out the 'induction on level N' via lifts whose Ramanujan property was guaranteed by difficult and important results of Kisin. The fact that 2 is the smallest prime was partly why it was now important to us. Our basic strategy to attack the conjecture, that we had found in Strasbourg, needed 2-adic results in an essential way to get it for mod p Galois symmetries for odd primes p of even level. Thus, 2-adic ingredients were unavoidable, and the latest turn in our work just wove them in more integrally into the fabric of the entire proof. When we started thinking in more detail about some of the ingredients needed in the argument of Wiles which we had to adapt to the 2-adic case, we saw that there was a potential problem, till we realized that our angelic prime saved us here again.

∞

By this time Wintenberger and I were confident of getting more or less all of Serre's conjecture. However, there was still a lot of writing to be done. Besides having to prove the 2-adic results that we would need, we had to generalize many existing results in the literature. We were not going to be done any time soon.

To be honest, the work that remained did not seem exciting. The result would be complete and satisfying, but the details of the proof would be tedious and hard work to write down. The earlier work had been a breeze once we had the ideas; to get the full conjecture we would have to struggle. The law of conservation of effort seemed to have caught up with us. This was only to be expected, but it still got me down. It was like a hangover after the heady intoxication of the Strasbourg breakthrough and the proof of the level 1 case. Feeling low after creating a work of art or proving a long-sought-for theorem is not uncommon. Wiles had spoken of a certain wistfulness he felt after proving FLT, about the world being deprived of a beautiful problem. Personally, for Wiles it had meant that his private seven-year odyssey was over.

∞

To have some sense of moving forward, even while we struggled with the maverick prime 2 and the nitty-gritty of proving the 2-adic theorems, we decided to write down an account of our proof of the general case of Serre's conjecture, conditional on proving the 2-adic results. This would ensure that once we had the 2-adic ingredients, we would be done with the proof in full generality of Serre's conjecture. This turned out to be a relatively short paper of around 20 pages, essentially synthesizing the various ideas we had till date. It was just a promissory note for now, as we still had to come up with the proofs of the 2-adic modularity lifting results.

The promissory paper was called 'Serre's Modularity Conjecture I'. Part II would contain the heavy technical 2-adic work. In Part I we deduced the two-dimensional Artin's conjecture that I had observed earlier was a consequence of Serre's conjecture. Our work gave the first general results proving the Ramanujan property of 'non-solvable' Galois symmetries. These had seemed out of reach even after Wiles's work due to its reliance on certain known 'solvable' cases of Serre's conjecture. We did not release Part I, as we felt morally obliged to wait to release the more technical (and still to be worked out!) Part II, on which it leaned heavily.

Wintenberger and I corresponded by email and wrote different parts of the Part II manuscript, which kept getting longer and longer. We had worked out a division of labour: he worked more on the side of Galois symmetries, while I worked more on the Ramanujan symmetries terrain. Serre's conjecture built a bridge between these two worlds, and Wiles's method drew on methods from both fields in his marvellous method. None of the obstacles we kept running into turned out to be insurmountable. Wintenberger was more patient through the process than I was. Serre sent me a couple of emails during this period of slow progress towards the general case, asking if we had more cases beyond the level 1 result. Each time I had to respond with a placeholder: there were no new cases to announce just as yet, but we were confident of getting the whole shebang soon.

During this listless period of hard grind I was buoyed by a comment of Serre that was relayed to me. He had reportedly said that the proof of the level 1 case of his conjecture, and a proof of the celebrated Poincaré conjecture by the Russian mathematician Grigori Perelman, were the two most exciting results in mathematics of the last several years.

Perelman had announced his pathbreaking work by quietly making his papers available on the web. Subsequently he lectured on his work in some places in the United States, and then disappeared from the public eye, going back to leading his life as a private citizen in St. Petersburg. The problem had a 1million-dollar bounty attached to it, which Perelman did not accept. Nor did he show up to receive a Fields Medal that was later awarded to him. Topologists in different parts of the world worked out the details of his strategy and found that Perelman had provided all the ideas, and they just needed to be unfolded in more detail to produce a totally rigorous proof. There was an article in the *New Yorker* about Perelman's work in which he was portrayed as a brilliant recluse, living with his mother and buying cheap nosebleed tickets to the St. Petersburg opera house. The drama and mystery of the events, the magnitude of Perelman's achievement, and the mystique and intrigue about the personalities involved made for a good story. To have my work mentioned along with Perelman's work by Serre was very flattering.

∞

Wintenberger and I met again in Paris in the summer of 2006. This time I was invited for a month-long visit as professor invité to Université Paris 11 in Orsay, a suburb of Paris which lay to the south of the city. I gave a series of lectures on our work on Serre's conjecture. Serre came for one of the lectures. Afterwards we went for lunch as a group where someone mentioned a mathematician, known to be rather disconnected from the real world, who was being interviewed by a journal after winning a prize. People at the table wondered if the interviewer might ask questions about the prizewinner's personal life, at which someone quipped that the first question might be whether he had a personal life! As we came out of the restaurant, Serre spotted a small bird on the grass and exclaimed: *'C'est magnifique!'*

We submitted our two papers to *Inventiones mathematicae* in early 2007, almost two years after the level 1 breakthrough. We coordinated with Kisin to write up extensions of his results to the prime 2, so that we could deduce all of Serre's conjecture rather than just the case when the level of the mod p Galois symmetry is odd. He submitted his paper to *Inventiones* at the same time as our Parts I and II.

∞

I gave a talk on the progress towards the proof of Serre's conjecture at the Institute for Advanced Study in Princeton, focusing on my proof of the level 1 case. I walked back for the tea after the seminar with the prominent Princeton number theorist Peter Sarnak. He was excited by the talk and told me that proofs in mathematics that used induction on prime numbers were exceedingly rare. The one case we could think of was Gauss's first proof of quadratic reciprocity which had used such an induction. Serre's conjecture was in the lineage of quadratic reciprocity and thus it was a nice coincidence that Gauss's first proof of it and our proof both relied on induction on primes.

In France, our proof was met with great enthusiasm. Many of the leading figures of the succeeding generation of French number theorists, like Jean-Marc Fontaine, were close to Serre. This may have been an added reason for their enthusiasm for our proof of his conjecture. There was a two-week-long summer school in 2007 dedicated to giving a full account of our proof of Serre's conjecture. It was held in Luminy, not far from Marseille. Almost everyone who had played a role in the subject came for it. It was supposed to unofficially be a conference for Serre's 80th birthday. Serre had always refused to have a conference for any of his milestone birthdays. I had been part of the planning of the lecture schedule, consisting of talks by experts giving a detailed summary of the steps of the proof of the conjecture. Fontaine was the main organizer of the conference. At the conference, there were lectures in the mornings and afternoons. There was enough free time for people to go on hikes, and to go down to the Calanques and swim in the sea. In the evenings mathematicians young and old, as well as graduate students, hung out, drinking, chatting, playing ping-pong. I gave the last two talks of the conference, presenting the proof, building on the lectures before me.

My level 1 paper at Duke was accepted quickly. It was refereed by three experts and it was a relief to have the proof ratified. Our first paper which we had submitted to the *Annals* took almost three years to be accepted, even though it was short and not technical. Although this is a somewhat extreme case, the refereeing process can tax the patience of researchers who are usually dying to get their ideas out into the world. Refereeing should ideally be a forensic examination of the proof to see if it checks out, but it is also not so rare that delays in the refereeing come down just to a paper languishing on a referee's desk. Galois' case is an extreme example of this, his papers were simply lost by the establishment French mathematicians he had sent them to.

∞

While we were wrestling with the general case, there came a development that was beyond anything I would have thought possible when I was a struggling graduate student in Pasadena, or a young researcher making incremental progress in Bombay. In late October 2007, Michel Ledoux, the chair of the prize committee for the Fermat Prize, wrote to me to say that the committee had awarded me the 2007 Fermat Prize 'for the proof in collaboration with Jean-Pierre Wintenberger of Serre's modularity conjecture in number theory'. (Wintenberger was past age 45 and ineligible for the prize.)

This prestigious prize is awarded by the university in Toulouse to someone who has made decisive contributions to the fields Fermat had worked in, rotating between the three areas of calculus of variations, probability and number theory. Amongst the previous winners in number theory were Ken Ribet, Andrew Wiles and Richard Taylor. Ledoux added to my delight at receiving this news by telling me that Jean-Marc Fontaine and Gérard Laumon had nominated me for the prize. Fontaine was a hugely important figure in modern number theory and the leader of the French school of *p*-adic Hodge theory that had played a crucial role in our work on Serre's conjecture. Laumon was a leading figure in the important French school of 'automorphic forms' based in Paris. It seemed fitting that the first appreciation of our work came from France, and that too from Toulouse. France was the land of Pierre de Fermat and Jean-Pierre Serre, and Fermat was from Toulouse.

We were still waiting to hear from *Inventiones mathematicae* about our papers. We got a report on the shorter of the two submissions in December of 2007. It was a positive report but we would still have to wait for the vetting of Part II. Meanwhile, the date of the ceremony in Toulouse was fixed as 18 March 2008. Michel Ledoux told me that Serre would attend. But the path to mathematical achievement is rarely smooth, as the case of Wiles and Fermat illustrated in the most public of ways. On 6 March 2008, we got a nasty surprise in an email from the secretary at *Inventiones mathematicae*. Crestfallen, I wrote immediately to Jean Marc-Fontaine, and also Serre, identical letters.

Thurs, Mar 6, 2008, 11:28 AM.

Dear Jean-Marc,

I have been looking forward to going to Toulouse on the 18th, and was in a happy frame of mind till yesterday!

Our final papers on the proof of the S-conjecture

Serre's modularity conjecture: Parts I and II are in the process of being refereed for Inventiones. They were submitted last February: we got a report on Part I in December, and modulo a few minor points that we addressed, this was OK.

Yesterday we received one comment from the referee (the only one we have received on part II) pointing out that our proof of Lemma 4.8 in part II is incorrect!

This is indeed the case, and we have made a mistake about this. Lemma 4.8 is crucial for the modularity lifting theorems we prove later as it gives us the existence of the auxiliary primes that are used.

In the proof of lemma 4.8 we made an elementary (and so all the more egregious) mistake of working with ad^0 coefficients rather than its dual (which is the same when working in all residue characteristics except 2!).

Thus at the moment the work in Part II is incomplete for proving 2-adic modularity lifting results that are crucially quoted in Part I. This probably also affects (hopefully only temporarily) Kisin's 2-adic modularity lifting results that finished the proof of the conjecture.

To clarify (probably needlessly!), this error does not affect the earlier paper with Wintenberger (to appear in Annals), and the Duke paper where the level one case of the conjecture is proved.

While we are cautiously hopeful that we can fix this error that was pointed out to us yesterday, it's unlikely we will be able to be convinced about this by the 18th of this month (the day of the Fermat ceremony).

This puts me in a bind to say the least. I will also write to the convener of the Fermat prize (M. Ledoux) about this, as also Serre who is coming for it.

Best wishes,

Shekhar

If mathematical proofs are like huge machines, lemmas are like the nuts and bolts which hold the machine together. A faulty lemma can make the machine inoperative, and without Lemma 4.8, our proof of 2-adic lifting theorems simply did not work.

Fontaine replied within a day, with a generous and reassuring reply. (Fontaine's email has been lightly edited for grammar and spelling.)

Fri, Mar 7, 2008 at 10:59 AM:

Dear Shekhar,

Of course, I understand that this is rather unpleasant for you. I would like to try to convince you that this is not really serious.

1. All the organizers of Luminy's summer school should feel as uncomfortable as you because we have not seen the mistake.

2. There is no doubt at all that the proof of Serre's conjecture for level 1 is already an incredible breakthrough. If you had proven only that, Fermat's prize would have been given to you as well.

I am also absolutely convinced that this gap will be fixed soon. The situation is quite different from Wiles's gap: there is an important part of the result which is still proved and you probably won't need a big new idea to fill the gap.

Therefore the only unpleasant thing is that this was discovered just now. I agree that it is not likely that you'll get rid of it before getting the prize (the pressure is too big, anyway!).

I have already discussed this problem with Serre and Laumon. They agree with me. I wrote to Ledoux to tell him what we think about that.

I expect they will give you the prize for having proved a very important special case of Serre's conjecture and they will wish you good luck for completing the proof soon.

```
   I hope you'll be able to enjoy coming to Toulouse
anyway. Do not forget to ask to see Fermat's statue
in Toulouse's hotel de ville.  I suggest you go there
with Serre. By the way, you'll be coming to Toulouse
just after the local elections in France which are
expected to be particularly interesting in Toulouse.
   Best wishes,
   Jean-Marc
```

This letter remains something precious for me: full of grace, empathy, also because it captures the man, from his charming franglais to his range of interests, which included politics.

My meetings with Fontaine over the years had made a strong impression on me. He had a force of personality that must have helped him develop with exemplary single-mindedness the magnificent theory closely linked to his name. He brought passion to any topic he would discuss, be it mathematics or politics. His appreciation of our work and his very supportive message was extremely helpful in getting us through this difficult period. We hoped that fixing our mistake would not need a breathtakingly new idea such as the one Wiles had come up with to fix his initially faulty proof of FLT. The prime 2 has many peculiarities, but it still seemed very unlikely that results which were known for all odd primes p would not carry over to the 2-adic case after modifications. Even if one could be optimistic on these general grounds, we were still naturally very anxious to find a way to prove what we needed in the 2-adic case. The 2-adic results were essential to the consequences in Part I.

Through the journal, the referee of our two papers submitted to *Inventiones* communicated that he would not mind making his name known to the authors. Our referee turned out to be Fred Diamond, whom I had known since my graduate student days, and who I had visited in Brandeis for a crucial six-week-long period a few years ago. He is a very careful mathematician, and one of the world experts on Galois and Ramanujan symmetries. We felt very grateful to Fred for having gone through our paper with a fine-toothed comb and in the process uncovered our error.

Like in a whodunit with an insignificant character everyone has overlooked turning out to be the murderer, in a mathematical proof a detail that seems trivial can kill a proof, and is often the culprit hiding in plain sight. Our faulty Lemma 4.8 was a case in point. In the weeks after our mistake was pointed out, Wintenberger and I worked feverishly to try and fix the argument, also consulting with Kisin by email. Wintenberger was more stoic than me when the problem with our proof was pointed out; he was instrumental in finding the arguments that actually worked in the 2-adic case. These became far more elaborate and interesting, and turned out to be the deepest and most compelling part of Part II of our work. We had recovered from the scare and, importantly, Wintenberger and I had a viable route to the 2-adic results before I left for Toulouse.

Our papers were finally accepted at *Inventiones* on 28 May 2009. We asked Serre if he would allow us to dedicate the papers to him, and suggested that we could write: *to Jean-Pierre Serre, with admiration*. Serre accepted, but, typical of the man, said he would prefer something simpler: *to Jean-Pierre Serre*. The primary feeling was of relief that we had swum to the safety of the shore. The proof had survived albeit with more work, demanding an emergency injection of new and delicate ideas to deal with 2-adic results. Our faltering in the final ascent in our attack on the proof of the conjecture added an element of drama to the climax. Rajani was a steadying presence through the travails of trying to fix our mistake, and Arushi provided welcome distraction. Our mistake at the end was like the cramps a runner might experience when near the end of a race: weary legs make the last few metres seem like an eternity.

∞

Rajani, Arushi and I flew into Toulouse around the middle of March of 2008, just a couple of days before the prize ceremony. Toulouse is called La Ville Rose (the Pink City) as many of the buildings, especially in its historic centre, are made of pinkish terracotta bricks.

Mathematics seemed less marginal to the general culture in France compared to the United States. Roads in France were named after writers and thinkers and musicians and mathematicians. Toulouse had one of the oldest universities in the world, dating back to the thirteenth century. Fermat had worked in Toulouse in the seventeenth century, not at the university but as a judge; there were no mathematics departments then, and universities were devoted to classical and theological studies. I had first heard of the Fermat Prize as a graduate student. A survey paper by Ken Ribet, 'From the Shimura–Taniyama conjecture to Fermat's Last Theorem', that I read as a graduate student was published in the *Annales de la Faculté des Sciences de Toulouse*. It had been written in the context of his getting the inaugural Prix Fermat in 1989. He gave an exposition of his work which showed that the elliptic symmetry conjecture implied FLT. Now, as a winner, I would also have to submit an article to the same journal.

There was a dreamlike feeling to the day of the prize ceremony in Toulouse. Serre, flying down from Paris, came directly from the airport for the first event of the day, a lunch with some colleagues from the maths department at the university in Toulouse. I do not remember if we discussed the 2-adic troubles. We probably did not, as the memories I have from the lunch are that I was in good spirits, no longer roiled by our flawed Lemma 4.8.

After lunch I gave my mathematical presentation in a room with rows of long wooden benches. My father and Serre sat next to each other in one of the front rows. My father, true to his personality, was not inhibited by being next to a great mathematician. He started telling Serre, much to my embarrassment, about the prize-winning essay I had written in junior college about zero! He proudly recalled my witticism at the end of the essay, which he was very fond of, that zero denotes the 'presence of an absence'. Serre had been reading a newspaper and kept it aside while my father went on about me. I thought I saw a tremor of irritation pass over Serre's face as he asked my father what did this mean exactly, presence of an absence. My father was of course unfazed and explained some more. I wished I could just disappear from the scene. However, Serre many years later told me he fondly remembered meeting my father at the ceremony in Toulouse: they had connected as men of the same generation. Indeed, they were born within a year of each other. They were both in their early eighties when they met for the first and only time.

I do not remember much of my lecture: it was a variation of my standard colloquium talk about Galois symmetries and Ramanujan symmetries, and a lot of the maths in it I had learnt either directly from Serre's papers, or had been influenced by his writings to discover. Serre's lucid writings have been a major influence on at least two generations of number theorists, forming an essential part of their training. He had formed my tastes in number theory. I do not think that Serre learnt anything new from my lecture and for my family it was of course incomprehensible. In other words, I think it all went as planned. Later, we all stood talking and took photos of Serre with me and my family, including my sister Padmini who had flown down with my father. Arnaud Ponsin, a French friend whom I had met when I worked at TIFR – he worked in the pharmaceutical industry and was deputed to work for a few years in Bombay – also came for the ceremony.

The prize ceremony was held in the Hôtel de Région. The brochure announcing the ceremony was in a bold red.

Ceremonie de remise du Prix Fermat 2007
à Chandrashekhar KHARE
«pour sa démonstration, avec Jean-Pierre Wintenberger, de la conjecture de modularité de Serre en théorie des nombres»[50]

I went on the stage and received the prize which came with a cash award of 20,000 euros and a scroll rolled up in a leather case that had a rich red colour. I was also given a gold-plated coin. Serre sat in the audience and his presence at the ceremony lent it weight and for me increased its value manifold. The one person singularly unimpressed by the ceremony was my daughter Arushi. She was bored throughout, and seemed to be living in a parallel universe playing with her doll as a succession of people came on stage and gave orations in French.

∞

Part of the excitement of getting the Fermat Prize was to be recognized for my work in a country in which I was a foreigner. I had neither grown up here nor studied or worked here. My fascination for France had its origin in being an admirer of French mathematics and being in awe of the mathematical culture in Paris. For me, France was the land of historical figures of mathematics like Descartes,

Fermat, Galois, and mathematicians of the modern era like André Weil and Jean-Pierre Serre. Thus, it was an intellectual relationship that turned into a fondness for the country – I discovered France through its mathematics. My wife and I both developed an affinity to the country through our four-month stay there in 1997 and my subsequent mathematical visits. I recall in particular the beautiful countryside we travelled through on a road trip to Normandy we made in a very small car with one of Rajani's friends. On that trip we saw cows that were significantly larger than the ones in India. They seemed almost bourgeois in comparison, like rich fat burghers compared to farmhands.

The varieties of cheese we discovered in 1997 as an olfactory and gustatory revelation, the wine and food, the fabulous Rue du Faubourg Saint-Honoré with its artistic and excessive shop window displays, were all part of our attraction to France. Although I was vegetarian and my wife ate only a very limited variety of meats, we liked going to restaurants in France: it was like a person with impaired vision enjoying their visits to the cinema! We loved the theatrics of French dining, even if we could not eat many items on the menu, enjoying what we could eat, including the wine and cheese and dessert.

Fermat had influenced my life as a mathematician at several turns of my career. I had never cared per se about Fermat's Last Theorem, yet it had tugged at my mathematical interests many times. Fermat is one of the founders of modern number theory; even if he lived in the seventeenth century, his methods and viewpoint are relevant in the present day. FLT was a bright shiny object in the sky for number theorists to aim at ever since Fermat jotted it down in the margin of his copy of Diophantus's *Arithmetica* in 1637. It sparked a series of developments in the nineteenth century, leading to the creation of the field of algebraic number theory. The theoretical developments inspired by it led to crucial concepts that now pervade pure mathematics. In the latter part of the twentieth century the approach to FLT via symmetries was consummated in its stunning proof by Andrew Wiles. It has thus twice changed the course of number theory, in episodes separated by more than a century.

On a more personal level, I was led as a graduate student in Pasadena to obsessively study a paper of Ribet partly because of the fame it had acquired through its relevance to FLT. Serre's formulation of the refined version of his conjecture was motivated by trying to make precise Frey's connection between the elliptic symmetry conjecture and FLT. Our proof of Serre's conjecture led to a more direct proof of FLT. All these developments had Fermat and Fermat's Last Theorem running through them like a connecting thread.

There is a photo from that day taken outside the Hôtel de Région in Toulouse where the prize ceremony took place. My father is in the distance, suited and booted. Arushi is in a pink dress in the foreground, full of mischief, making faces. Serre is in the middle distance, in a beige jacket, standing between my daughter and father, looking fondly at Arushi. This photo was taken either just before or after the ceremony.

A friend has a theory based on his personal observations that mathematicians (and perhaps his empirical data is all male) often do their best work after their first child is born. This could be related to something shifting within one, perhaps caring less about work in comparison with the feelings for the child, spending less time on work (there is just less time to spread around), being forced to become more efficient and do more in less time, bringing to work an intensity greater than before, all of this improving the work's quality. (In a related vein, authors sometimes thank their children for the disruptions that made the book possible.) My friend's theory was borne out, at least in my case. Our first breakthrough on Serre's conjecture happened within a year of Arushi's birth. The proof of the level 1 case was when she was just a little over a year old. At the ceremony for the Prix Fermat, she was a little over four years old. This is around the time it took us to prove and publish our proof of Serre's conjecture after the initial breakthrough in October 2004 standing beneath a tree on a lawn in the campus of the Université Louis Pasteur in Strasbourg.

Notes

1. Wiles finally justified Fermat's hunch by proving that *for no power n bigger than 2 are there natural numbers a, b, c which are in the relation* $a^n + b^n = c^n$. The mathematician Carl Friedrich Gauss, who along with Archimedes and Newton is widely regarded as the greatest of all mathematicians, said of Fermat's Last Theorem: 'I confess that Fermat's Theorem as an isolated proposition has very little interest for me, because I could easily lay down a multitude of such propositions, which one could neither prove nor dispose of.'

2. A cautionary tale of something expected to be true turning out to be false even after checking out in many cases is the one about a variant of Fermat's Last Theorem considered by the eighteenth-century Swiss mathematician Leonhard Euler. He conjectured that the sum of three fourth powers cannot be a fourth power. This was disproved almost 200 years after Euler made his guess when Noam Elkies found the counterexample: $2682440^4 + 15365639^4 + 18796760^4 = 20615673^4$.

3. To jog the memory of readers who have left behind quadratic equations after their encounters with them in their classrooms years ago, $X^2 - X - 1 = 0$ is an example of a quadratic equation. One of the solutions of $X^2 - X - 1 = 0$ is the number $\frac{1+\sqrt{5}}{2}$, the other being $\frac{1-\sqrt{5}}{2}$, which is called the golden ratio: the golden ratio has been singled out as an attribute of aesthetically pleasing configurations in many arts ranging from music to architecture.

4. $X^3 - X - 1 = 0$ and $X^4 - X - 1 = 0$ are examples of degree 3 and degree 4 polynomial equations.
5. The symmetries are rearrangements of the solutions which preserve all (algebraic) relations between them.
6. Using his work on symmetries, Galois gave a precise criterion for the solvability of a polynomial equation by radicals. As a consequence he deduced that for polynomial equations of degree 5 and higher, the symmetries of their solutions are usually too complicated to be consistent with solving them by using radicals. Galois' ideas on symmetry deepened the work of his predecessors Neils Abel and Paolo Ruffini on the impossibility of solving quintic (degree 5) equations in general by radicals. To give a concrete example, Galois' theory shows that the quintic equation $X^5 - X - 1 = 0$ cannot be solved by radicals.
7. Ramanujan symmetry is the term used in the book for what is called a modular form in the mathematical literature. There is ample historical motivation to use this term which also means that both the types of symmetries in the book are labelled by names of the people, namely Galois and Ramanujan, who were closely associated with them. This is in keeping with simpler, colloquial names we have coined for some other mathematical concepts. The elliptic symmetry conjecture is called the 'modularity conjecture for elliptic curves over the rationals' in the mathematical literature; Galois symmetries are called 'Galois representations'; Ramanujan symmetries combine what are called modular forms in the literature, with the Galois representations that arise from them.
8. It is so named as it was found in the city of Rosetta by French soldiers during Napoleon's invasion of Egypt at the end of the eighteenth century.
9. In fact when Wiles first announced his results he said that his methods were 'orthogonal' (at right angles) to Serre's conjecture as they seemingly made little impact on it.
10. The list of primes numbers goes

2, 3, 5, 7, 11, 13, 17, 19, 23, 29, 31, 37, 41, 43, 47, 53, 59, 61, 67, 71, 73, ...

A number like 60 that is not prime, and hence not on our list, is called a composite number. Euclid's result on infinitude of primes implies that the dots trail off to infinity, stretching all the way to the horizon and beyond. Here is a proof of Euclid's theorem. Let $p_1, \dots, p_r$ be a list of primes, and consider the number $N = p_1 \times p_2 \times \dots p_r + 1$; N has a prime factor p which can't be any of the ones in our list as N leaves remainder 1 when divided by each of $p_1, \dots, p_r$. This shows that no finite list of primes exhausts all the primes.

The composite number 60 can be factored as

$$60 = 2 \times 2 \times 3 \times 5$$

into prime numbers. Besides rearranging the order of the primes, for instance

$$60 = 2 \times 3 \times 5 \times 2,$$

this decomposition into a product of primes is unique. I am spelling out the Fundamental Theorem of Arithmetic in a particular case. To prove the Fundamental Theorem of Arithmetic one establishes the crucial (and characterizing) property that primes p have: if p is a factor of a product ab of numbers a and b, then p has to be a factor of at least one of a or b. As its name suggests, the Fundamental Theorem of Arithmetic is very important. The depth of a mathematical theorem may not just depend on how difficult it is to prove; it might be more about how it underpins other crucial facts, and holds the subject together.

11. As an example of mod N arithmetic, take $N = 13$. The numbers to contend with in mod 13 arithmetic are 0, 1, 2, 3, ... , 12. In this world $8 + 5 \equiv 0 \pmod{13}$, since $8 + 5 = 13$ leaves the remainder 0 when divided by 13. Similarly 7^{-1}, the reciprocal of 7 mod 13, is 2; said differently, $7 \times 2 \equiv 1 \pmod{13}$, because 14 leaves a remainder of 1 when divided by 13.

12. In general for distinct odd primes p and q, quadratic reciprocity says that p being a square mod q is entangled with q being a square mod

p. This is extremely surprising, as the numbers mod p and mod q are independent in the Chinese Remainder Theorem: we can find numbers with arbitrarily prescribed remainders mod p and mod q.

13. The notion of a group was formalized in the nineteenth century, and has ever since been central to mathematics. The formal definition of a group may not be so enlightening at first, but it might be worth seeing it at least once.

    Definition. A group is a set G equipped with an operation of composition denoted by $\circ$ so that given g, h elements of G, $g \circ h$ (pronounced g composed with h) is also an element in G. The composition $\circ$ satisfies the following axioms:

    - (existence of identity) there is an element e of G, called its identity, such that $e \circ g = g \circ e = g$ for all elements g of G;
    - (associativity) For elements g, h, k of G, $(g \circ h)\ k = g \circ (h \circ k)$;
    - (inverses) for all elements g of G, there is an element h of G, such that $g \circ h = h \circ g = e$; such a h is unique and is denoted by g^{-1}, the inverse of g.

14. In the plane, there are regular n-sided polygons for each number n, and their symmetries form a family of *dihedral* groups. In three dimensions there are only the five regular polyhedra and we had proven this in the homework for our group theory class. These are called Platonic solids: Plato in his dialogue *Timaeus* assigned them to the elements fire (tetrahedron), earth (cube), air (icosahedron) and water (octahedron). The dodecahedron Plato assigned to Heaven! There was something beautiful and compelling and perfect about these regular polyhedra, and also their exiguity, which perhaps prompted the Greeks to make them the basis of their natural philosophy. The icosahedron is also found in nature: certain viruses have icosahedral shapes with 20 triangular faces and 12 edges. (The fact that some biological viruses have 'icosahedral symmetries' adds verisimilitude to the analogy I made in the introduction between mathematical ideas and viruses!)

15. The Galois symmetries associated to solutions of the polynomial equation $X^4 - X - 1 = 0$ are simply all the rearrangements ('permutations') of its four solutions. There are, in all, 24 ways to permute these solutions. Sometimes such Galois symmetries might first present themselves geometrically: for instance, these 24 symmetries are also identified with the symmetries of the cube, which one can think of as permuting the four main diagonals of a cube. The symmetries of the solutions of $X^5 - X - 1 = 0$ are called icosahedral as they can also be identified with symmetries of the icosahedron. Galois symmetries related to symmetries of a cube were to play a decisive role in Wiles's proof of FLT.

16. The numbers $N = 3, 5, 17, 257$ and 65537 are the only known prime numbers for which regular polygons with N sides are constructible using only straightedge and compass. We will come back to these numbers later in our account of the proof of Serre's conjecture.

17. Table 1 lists the first thirty values of $\tau(n)$, and one can can find it in Ramanujan's paper.

n	$\tau(n)$	n	$\tau(n)$
1	1	16	987136
2	-24	17	-6905934
3	252	18	2727432
4	-1472	19	10661420
5	4830	20	-7109760
6	-6048	21	-4219488
7	-16744	22	-12830688
8	84480	23	18643272
9	-113643	24	21288960
10	-115920	25	-25499225
11	534612	26	13865712
12	-370944	27	-73279080
13	-577738	28	24647168
14	401856	29	128406630
15	1217160	30	-29211840

Table 1. Values of τ function

18. Like the prime 7758337633, the largest of the seven known primes for which p divides $\tau(p)$.

19. We give a proof of the irrationality of $\sqrt{2}$ to give a sense of the 'theorem and proof' style of argumentation that fills research papers in mathematics. The proof uses the gambit of an argument by contradiction: you assume what you are aiming to prove is false and show that this leads to an absurdity. The proof we give below is just a few lines. Later on in the book, I will talk about theorems which require much longer proofs, consisting of hundreds of pages of close reasoning, like Wiles's proof of the elliptic symmetry conjecture, or the proof of Serre's conjecture in my work with Wintenberger.

Theorem. $\sqrt{2}$ is an irrational number.

Proof. We want to show $\sqrt{2}$ is not rational. Suppose to the contrary that it is, so we can write

$$\sqrt{2} = \frac{a}{b}$$

as a fraction in reduced form: the numbers a, b do not have any factor in common.

Squaring both sides and cross-multiplying we get $a^2 = 2b^2$. Thus a^2 is even, but the square of an odd number is odd, so we deduce that a itself is even, say, $a = 2m$.

Substituting this back into the equation $2b^2 = a^2$, we get that

$$2b^2 = 4m^2$$

so

$$b^2 = 2m^2$$

This means that b^2 is even, so b also is even.

But a, b can't both be even as a/b is in reduced form, which gives us the desired contradiction.

□

Hardy wrote a paean to this style of argument: The argument by contradiction 'which Euclid loved so much, is one of a mathematician's finest weapons. It is a far finer gambit than any chess play: a chess player may offer the sacrifice of a pawn or even a piece, but a mathematician offers the game.'

20. The reason why higher and higher positive powers of p – like p, p^2, p^3 – are regarded as getting smaller and smaller in the p-adic world is that p^n 'reduces' to 0 modulo p^n.

21. These Galois symmetries for each prime p are very different, but are tied together in a subtle manner encoded by the numbers τ (q) for primes q (that are independent of p). The collection of p-adic Galois symmetries arising from the Δ-function for varying primes p form what is called a 'compatible system of Galois symmetries'.

22. Serre writes in his 1967 paper that André Weil, whose work was a big influence on modern number theory, had asked Serre for a theoretical explanation of the Ramanujan congruences in 1960. After seven years Serre realized that congruence properties of $\tau(n)$ could be understood using Galois symmetries.

23. Thus

    All mod p Galois symmetries are mod p Ramanujan symmetries

    Here by the phrase 'mod p Ramanujan symmetries' I mean Galois symmetries that arise from reduction mod p of p-adic Ramanujan symmetries.

24. The example to keep in mind is the mod p Ramanujan symmetry arising from the Δ-function that arises as the shadow of the p-adic Ramanujan symmetry arising from Δ.

25. For instance, the mod p Galois symmetry arising from Δ has level N = 1 and weight k = 12. The p-adic Ramanujan symmetries also have their own notion of level and weight: the p-adic Ramanujan

symmetries arising from the Ramanujan Δ-function have weight k = 12 and level N = 1. It is no coincidence that the modular symmetry Δ also is of weight 12 and level 1.

26. Serre's definition of the (Serre) weight of a mod p Galois symmetry is one of the key technical contributions of his 1987 paper, and is motivated by several years of experience of working with mod p Ramanujan symmetries in his work with Tate in the 1970s.
27. Here we are specifying the weight and level of a mod p Ramanujan symmetry to be the smallest of the weights and levels of the p-adic Ramanujan symmetries that 'lift' it.
28. It is much easier to describe Ramanujan symmetries of weight k and level N compared to all Galois symmetries of weight k and level N. For instance, it is an easy fact that there are finitely many Ramanujan symmetries of fixed weight and level, which is far from clear for all such Galois symmetries.
29. Mazur's idea was to compare the collection of p-adic Ramanujan symmetries of weight k and level N to the collection of p-adic Galois symmetries of weight k and level N restricting attention to those symmetries whose shadow or reduction verified Serre's conjecture, and therefore was a mod p Ramanujan symmetry. It is good to keep in mind that Ramanujan symmetries are instances of Galois symmetries.
30. The 'deformation theory' perspective threw a bridge across the void that separated modular symmetries (equivalently, their proxy Ramanujan symmetries) on one side, from Galois symmetries on the other side. The deformation theory perspective of proving collections, or families, of p-adic Galois symmetries are of Ramanujan-type, rather than proving this one Galois symmetry at a time, was crucial in Wiles's later proof of the elliptic symmetry conjecture.
31. An example of this is the effort of mathematicians over centuries to solve quintic equations in radicals, before this was shown in the nineteenth century to be impossible in general.

32. This is taken from Shimura's article 'Yutaka Taniyama and His Time: Very Personal Recollections', Bulletin of the London Mathematical Society, Volume 21, Issue 2, March 1989, Pages 186–196.

33. The theorem of Carayol's paper 'Sur les représentations l-adiques associées aux formes modulaires de Hilbert' helped me to rule out certain 'wild congruences' growing on a patch that I had no access to during the final stages of my PhD work.

34. This is taken from Shimura's article 'Yutaka Taniyama and His Time: Very Personal Recollections' Bulletin of the London Mathematical Society, Volume 21, Issue 2, March 1989, pp. 186–196.

35. We can visualize all p-adic Galois symmetries of fixed weight and level, with a specified mod p reduction, as akin to points at the top of a 'cone' which has rising layers of mod p^n Galois symmetries for each n. The specified mod p symmetry is at the tip of the cone. Wiles's revolutionary work deduced the Ramanujan property of all p-adic Galois symmetries of the cone from knowing the Ramanujan property for the mod p reduction at its tip: this was an amazing expansion of the Ramanujan property from a fragment of a p-adic Galois symmetry (namely its mod p reduction) to all of it. Wiles's proof of the elliptic symmetry conjecture was via showing that the p-adic Galois symmetry arising from an 'elliptic curve' was of Ramanujan-type. His proof proceeded by working with 'families' of Galois symmetries of a fixed weight and level and thus the 'deformation theory' perspective was crucial for Wiles's approach.

36. Namely, I wanted to understand levels M of the type N, Np, Np^2, Np^3, ..., for some fixed integer N, and weights k for which there are p-adic Ramanujan symmetries of level M and weight k which lifted a *fixed* mod p Ramanujan symmetry.

37. Serre's conjecture is about the Ramanujan property of all mod p Galois symmetries. This seemed impossible to think about productively as one had no place to begin. Instead, in the theory of congruences

between Ramanujan symmetries, one started with a Ramanujan mod p symmetry and tried to analyse all possible levels N and weights k at which there were p-adic Ramanujan symmetries that gave rise to it. This was a more modest project which exploited the fact that once one realized a mod p Galois symmetry as a Ramanujan symmetry, there was a panoply of geometric techniques to analyse all the p-adic Ramanujan symmetries which gave rise to it. I wanted to fill in the missing 'wild case' of this analysis.

A prototype of the congruences I wanted to study is an important congruence which Serre and Swinnerton–Dyer discovered in the early 1970s. Their congruence modulo 11 is between the unique 11-adic Ramanujan symmetry in weight 12 and level 1 (that arises from the Δ-function) and the unique 11-adic Ramanujan symmetry of weight 2 and level 11. These two 11-adic symmetries are completely different but their reductions mod 11 are the same: they both give rise to the same mod 11 Ramanujan symmetry. In the physics analogy we have used before, it is like being able to change the spin and charge of a particle to produce a new one, like changing a boson to a fermion, while preserving a key property of the original particle.

The flexibility of mod p Ramanujan symmetries that allows them to arise by 'reduction' of p-adic symmetries of different weights and levels turned out to play an important role in the proof of Serre's conjecture in my joint work with Wintenberger. One of the main steps of our proof of Serre's conjecture was to show that Galois symmetries could be manipulated with the same ease as Ramanujan symmetries: one could recreate 'congruences' between Ramanujan symmetries in the world of Galois symmetries. This particular mod 11 congruence of Serre and Swinnerton–Dyer typified a move for Ramanujan symmetries that, by mimicking on the side of Galois symmetries, led to an important breakthrough in the proof of Serre's conjecture. But all of this was more than a decade in the future!

38. This is taken from Shimura's article 'Yutaka Taniyama and His Time: Very Personal Recollections' *Bulletin of the London Mathematical Society*, Volume 21, Issue 2, March 1989, pp. 186–196.

39. Poincaré, Henri. *The Foundations of Science: Science and Hypothesis, the Value of Science, Science and Method*. 1913.

40. Mariana Cook, *Mathematicians: An Outer View of the Inner World*, Princeton University Press (2009): p. 144.

41. From Allyn Jackson's article, 'Comme Appelé du Néant – As If Summoned from the Void: The Life of Alexandre Grothendieck' *Notices of the AMS*, Volume 51, Number 4, pp. 1038–1056.

42. The logic of this implication goes as follows: Mod p Ramanujan symmetries lift to p-adic Ramanujan symmetries, and thus also to p-adic Galois symmetries (as Ramanujan symmetries are in particular also Galois symmetries). As the conjecture asserts that mod p Galois symmetries are of Ramanujan-type, it thus implies that all mod p Galois symmetries lift to p-adic Galois symmetries as well.

43. To make this deduction, Wintenberger also invoked results proved by Jean-Marc Fontaine specific to small level N, and small primes p, like $p = 3$. Fontaine's result implied that certain hypothetical geometric objects with good properties at all primes did not exist. It was a mathematical equivalent of the fact that we know to be true from bitter experience, that perfection is hard to find in this world! Compatible systems allowed one to transfer Fontaine's result from the prime 3 to an arbitrarily large prime p.

44. Attached to mod p Galois symmetries are local symmetries at all primes; these are just given by numbers for all primes q which aren't factors of Np. For primes that are a factor of Np the local symmetry is more complicated: this is the phenomenon of ramification, and such primes are called ramified. The ramification at primes away from p is packaged into the level N, and the ramification at p is packaged into the weight k. 'Killing ramification' got rid of ramified primes one at a

time and relied crucially on the existence of minimal lifts and making them part of a compatible system.

45. It led me to think about the work of Serre and Swinnerton–Dyer relating the unique 11-adic Ramanujan symmetry of weight $k = 12$ and level $N = 1$ (arising from the Δ function) and the unique 11-adic Ramanujan symmetry of weight 2 and level 11, an example that had been part of what led to the breakthrough in my thesis. Having spent time thinking about Ramanujan symmetries turned out to be invaluable experience and preparation for my work with Wintenberger.

    In my thesis work and its further extension, I had understood in depth this type of exchange between levels and weights of p-adic Ramanujan symmetries lifting a fixed mod p Ramanujan symmetry. Lifts of a fixed mod p Ramanujan symmetry to p-adic Ramanujan symmetries of different levels and weights gave it a richer meaning: every lift to a p-adic symmetry of a new weight or level made it part of a new simile and the novel terms of comparison the simile invoked gave a novel perspective on it. Our focus was on finding very different p-adic symmetries with the same 'reduction' modulo p. This captures an essential quality of mathematical creativity: to be able to make connections between apparently unrelated concepts lies at the heart of it.

46. For primes $p \leq 7$ we proved that the level 1 case of the conjecture was true *in vacuo*: there are no mod $p \leq 7$ Galois symmetries in level 1, consistent with the known fact that there are no Ramanujan symmetries of level 1 in that range. This was the limit of such non-existence results: indeed for the next prime $p = 11$ there is the mod 11, level $N = 1$, weight $k = 12$ Galois symmetry arising from the Ramanujan Δ-function.

47. An induction argument is a bit like the process of a row of dominoes toppling after the initial one is given a push. For the inductive strategy in the context of Serre's conjecture, the initial push to fell the first

domino is given by the Tate–Serre result, after which the push is sustained from one domino to the next until the last domino has fallen by using minimal lifts, compatible systems and Wiles-type results. The point of the induction argument is that in principle it deduced Serre's conjecture for mod p Galois symmetries from knowing its truth for primes smaller than p. For instance, if we knew the level 1 conjecture for the prime 113, then one deduced it for the next prime 127, by lifting a mod 127 Galois symmetry to a compatible system of level 1. Then if one considered the 113-adic member of that system, one knew the Ramanujan property of its shadow by assumption, hence one would prove the Ramanujan property for all members of the compatible system if one could extend the range of Wiles-type results slightly.

48. This allowed one by induction to only need Wiles-type results in weights in a more moderate range even though still outside the range of the known cases of such theorems.

49. The point is that the congruence $x \equiv -x \pmod{p}$ has 0 as the only solution for odd primes p, but $x = 1$ also works when $p = 2$!

50. In translation this reads:

    Fermat Prize award ceremony 2007

    to Chandrashekhar KHARE

    'for his demonstration, with Jean-Pierre Wintenberger, of Serre's modularity conjecture in number theory'

Acknowledgements

I view this book as the literary memoir of a mathematician who only incidentally happens to be me. What impelled its writing was not the desire to write my own biography, but rather to evoke, using my own experiences, the struggles of someone who wants to be a mathematician, and recreate for the reader the act of mathematical thinking and obsession. The particulars of the biographical details recounted are important to the world created in the book, but I regard it to be of little importance that they are about me in particular. I just happen to have access to my own self; if only I had the power to create a compelling world of a fictional mathematician, and through that creation capture the essence of a mathematical life, I would have liked that better.

I thank Chiki Sarkar, the publisher of Juggernaut Books, for believing that this account of a mathematician's creative journey would resonate with a wider audience. I owe a great deal to my editor at Juggernaut, Anjali Puri, who helped shape the book into an optimal version of itself. She tamed the wildness of the manuscript I sent her and pushed me to write in a way which would help draw the reader into the human story of the mathematical achievement of proving Serre's conjecture. In the editing, the book transformed from being like the script of a dreamy art house movie, into one targeted towards more mainstream commercial cinema.

This brought a tightness to the writing for which I am grateful. Robert Bresson has said about film-making, 'A film is born three times – once when it is written, once when it is shot, and once when it is edited.' The editing of the book has been as crucial to its realization as editing is to a film.

Anjali left the maths alone, only telling me that it has to be as simple and succinct as possible. Brian Conrad helped me simplify the mathematics and eliminate unnecessary technicality. Brian was very generous in sitting down in a cafe in Palo Alto over a long weekend and returning my manuscript with many passages crossed out in red ink, along with many helpful suggestions about how I could rephrase some of the maths. He also made the inspired suggestion that I should call modular forms, or modular symmetries as I first christened them for the book, Ramanujan symmetries. Thus baptized, they acquired a vivid life on the page, bringing them on an equal footing with their mathematical counterparts, the Galois symmetries, as they were now both named after famous mathematicians whose life-work was intertwined with them.

Many colleagues, friends and family members read versions of the book when it was in the making and offered helpful comments and reactions – Aravind Asok, Akeel Bilgrami, Don Blasius, Mario Bonk, George Boxer, Ashay Burungale, Keith Conrad, Fred Diamond, Hélène Esnault, Najmuddin Fakhruddin, Toby Gee, Michael Harris, Srikanth Iyengar, Arushi Khare, Rajiv Krishnan, Michael Larsen, Barry Mazur, Rajanigandha Naik, Anoop Prasad, Dipendra Prasad, Ravi Ramakrishna, Ken Ribet, Dinesh Thakur, Jack Thorne, Sandeep Varma and Jean-Pierre Serre, amongst others. Serre's appreciation of my book in its early stages was very encouraging. My school friend, Anuj Bhagwati, allowed me to use his office in Kala Ghoda when I struggled to get started on this book. Being able to wander around the streets and go to cafes in the area provided welcome distraction from my struggles. My mathematical collaborations, most often with Srikanth, have kept me alive, mathematically, even as I got more and more lost in finishing the book.

The debt that I owe to my parents is present on every page of the book. My sister, Padmini, has always been a source of strength, love and encouragement. I cannot express enough my gratitude to my wife, Rajani, and my children, Arushi and Vinayak, for putting up with me throughout my immersion in this book, which lasted more than three years. I could not have written it without their love and support.